Mapping the Present

A note on translations

Throughout, key works are referenced back to the original language. In some instances this is not merely desirable but essential – crucial texts of both Heidegger and Foucault are unavailable in English. Where translations do exist, they have generally been used, although they have often been modified, to ensure readability, consistency, and particularly to allow emphasis on the spatial language used.

Mapping the Present

Heidegger, Foucault and the Project of a Spatial History

STUART ELDEN

CONTINUUM
London and New York

In memory of Colin Elden (1946–98)

Continuum
The Tower Building, 11 York Road, London SE1 7NX
370 Lexington Avenue, New York, NY 10017-6503

© 2001 Stuart Elden

Stuart Elden has asserted his right under the Copyright, Designs and Patents Act 1988,
to be identified as the author of this work

British Library Cataloguing in Publication Data
A catalogue record for this book is available from the British Library

ISBN 0 8264 5846 7 HB   0 8264 5847 5 PB

Library of Congress Cataloging in Publication Data

Elden, Stuart, 1971–
Mapping the present: Heidegger, Foucault, and the project of a spatial history / Stuart Elden.
   p. cm.
Includes bibliographical references and index.
ISBN 0–8264–5846–7 (hb) ISBN 0–8264–5847–5 (hb) (alk. paper)
1. Heidegger, Martin, 1889–1976. 2. Foucault, Michel. 3. Space and time. I. Title.

B3279.H49 E395 2001
193—dc21
                                                                2001018896

All rights reserved. No part of this publication may be reproduced,
stored in a retrieval system, or transmitted in any form or by any means,
electronic, mechanical, photocopying or otherwise, without prior
permission in writing from the publisher.

Typeset by Centraserve, Saffron Walden
Printed and bound in Great Britain by
MPG Books Ltd, Bodmin, Cornwall

Contents

Acknowledgements	vii
Abbreviations	viii
Introduction	1
Chapter One: Space and History in *Being and Time*	8
Ontology, History and Time	8
The Space of Dasein and Equipment	15
Reading Kant Phenomenologically	21
Towards Hölderlin and Nietzsche	27
Chapter Two: In the Shadow of Nazism: Reading Hölderlin and Nietzsche	29
Einführung: Introduction	29
I: Hölderlin	33
The Germania and Rhine Hymns	34
The Ister Hymn	40
II: Nietzsche	43
Returning to the *Augenblick*	44
Space and the Body	49
Excursus: The *Beiträge*	56
Power and Perspectivism	57
Chapter Three: Art, Technology, Place and the Political	63
The Origin of the Work of Art	63
Re-thinking the Πόλις	67

The Question of Technology	75
Dwelling Poetically at the Place of the Fourfold	82
Platial Descriptions	84
Art and Space	89
Chapter Four: Towards a Spatial History	**93**
I: A History of Limits	93
Archaeology	95
Genealogy	102
II: Mapping the Present	111
Chapter Five: The Spaces of Power	**120**
I: Re-placing *Madness and Civilisation*	120
Leprosy, Water and Madness	121
Confinement and Correction	124
Observing and Classifying	127
The Birth of Moral Imprisonment	130
II: Not Through Bentham's Eyes	133
A Torturous Sediment	136
The Army, Schools, Monasteries, Factories	139
The Spaces of Medicine	141
The Panopticon and Panopticism	145
Conclusion	**151**
Notes	**155**
Bibliography	**197**
Index	**213**

Acknowledgements

This book is based in large part on my PhD thesis, gained at Brunel University in 1999. I owe a huge debt of thanks to Mark Neocleous, who supervised this thesis and has continued to offer advice, criticism and encouragement throughout. David Wootton and Barbara Goodwin supervised early parts of this work, and Maurice Kogan acted as second supervisor. Michael Dillon and Kevin Hetherington examined the thesis and made a number of useful suggestions. Bela Chatterjee read the entire PhD manuscript and made several pertinent comments. Sharon Cowan helped enormously at the proof stage. I thank them all.

In a work that stresses the importance of place, it is worth noting two particular places where large portions of this work were written: Chamonix-Mt Blanc in the French Alps, and the Swainswick valley outside Bath. I thank Pierre, Geneviève, and Isabelle Prépoignot for their hospitality in the first and Pete Coulson and Jane Underdown for their friendship in the second.

I would also like to thank a number of other people who have been of assistance, either academic or otherwise: Allegra Catolfi Salvoni; Elgin Diaz; Hubert Dreyfus; Sarah Elliott; Julia Garrett; Béatrice Han; Michael Hughes; Jeff Jackson; Morris Kaplan; Eleonore Kofman; Reb McCaffry; Lizzi Pickton; Joanne Reeves-Baker; Jon Sprake; and Maja Zehfuss.

Above all, I owe a great deal to my family – especially my mother Rosemary, Ian, Nicky, Rachel and my grandmother – for their support and encouragement throughout, and to Susan Rizor for her love in the time it took to transform the thesis into this book. This work is dedicated to my father, without whose support I would never have reached this far; sadly he was unable to see its completion.

Versions of parts of this work have previously appeared as: Heidegger's Hölderlin and the Importance of Place, *Journal of the British Society for Phenomenology*, Vol. 30 No. 3, October 1999; Rethinking the *Polis*: Implications of Heidegger's Questioning the Political, *Political Geography*, Vol. 19 No. 4, May 2000; and Reading Genealogy as Historical Ontology, in Alan Rosenberg and Alan Milchman (eds), *Foucault and Heidegger: Critical encounters*, Minneapolis: University of Minnesota Press, 2002.

Abbreviations

I Abbreviations to works by Friedrich Nietzsche

KSA   *Sämtliche Werke: Kritische Studienausgabe*, edited by Giorgio Colli and Mazzino Montinari, Berlin and Munich: W. de Gruyter and Deutscher Taschenbuch Verlag, fifteen volumes, 1980 (cited by volume and page).

Individual works are cited by the following code; references are to the part, section and sub-section by number, rather than the page, as these are the same in all editions.

A   *Der Antichrist* (1888), KSA VI. Translated by Walter Kaufmann as *The Antichrist* in *The Portable Nietzsche*, Harmondsworth: Penguin, 1954.

FW   *Die fröhliche Wissenschaft* (1882, Book V 1887), KSA III. Translated by Walter Kaufmann as *The Gay Science*, New York: Vintage, 1974.

GD   *Götzendämmerung* (1888), KSA VI. Translated by Walter Kaufmann as *The Twilight of the Idols* in *The Portable Nietzsche*, Harmondsworth: Penguin, 1954.

GT   *Die Geburt der Tragödie* (1872), KSA I. Translated by Walter Kaufmann as *The Birth of Tragedy*, New York: Vintage, 1967.

JGB   *Jenseits von Gut und Böse* (1886), KSA V. Translated by Walter Kaufmann as *Beyond Good and Evil*, New York: Vintage, 1966.

M   *Morgenröte* (1881), KSA III. Translated by R. J. Hollingdale as *Daybreak*, Cambridge: Cambridge University Press, 1981.

MAM   *Menschliches, Allzumenschliches* (1878), KSA II. Translated by R. J. Hollingdale as *Human, All Too Human*, Cambridge: Cambridge University Press, 1986.

UB   *Unzeitgemäße Betrachtungen* (1873–6), KSA I. Translated by R. J. Hollingdale as *Untimely Meditations*, Cambridge: Cambridge University Press, 1983.

WM   *Der Wille zur Macht* (Notes from 1883–8), in *Nietzsches Werke*, Leipzig, C. G. Naumann Verlag, ten volumes, 1906, Vols 9 and 10.

Translated by Walter Kaufmann and R. J. Hollingdale as *The Will to Power*, New York: Vintage, 1968.

WS *Der Wanderer und Sein Schatten* (1880) KSA II. Translated by R. J. Hollingdale as *The Wanderer and His Shadow* in *Human, All Too Human*, Cambridge: Cambridge University Press, 1986.

Z *Also sprach Zarathustra* (1883–5), KSA IV. Translated by Walter Kaufmann as *Thus Spoke Zarathustra* in *The Portable Nietzsche*, Harmondsworth: Penguin, 1954.

II Abbreviations to works by Martin Heidegger

GA *Gesamtausgabe*, Frankfurt am Main: Vittorio Klostermann, 1975ff.

GA1 *Frühe Schriften*, 1978.

GA2 *Sein und Zeit*, 1977. Translated by Edward Robinson and John Macquarrie as *Being and Time*, Oxford: Blackwell, 1962, and by Joan Stambaugh as *Being and Time: A translation of Sein und Zeit*, Albany: State University of New York Press, 1996. References are to the marginal pagination found in the English *and* German, which refer to the original text: *Sein und Zeit*, Tübingen: Max Niemeyer, Eleventh edition, 1967.

GA3 *Kant und das Problem der Metaphysik*, 1991. Translated by Richard Taft as *Kant and the Problem of Metaphysics*, Bloomington: Indiana University Press, 1997.

GA4 *Erläuterungen zu Hölderlins Dichtung*, 1981.

GA5 *Holzwege*, 1977. Marginal pagination.

GA6 *Nietzsche*, Two Volumes, 1996. Translated by David Farrell Krell, Frank Capuzzi and Joan Stambaugh as *Nietzsche* (N), San Francisco: Harper Collins, Four Volumes, 1991 and as *The End of Philosophy* (EP), London: Souvenir Press, 1975.

GA9 *Wegmarken*, 1976. Marginal pagination. Translated by various as *Pathmarks*, edited by William McNeill, Cambridge: Cambridge University Press, 1998. Page references are to the numbers in square brackets.

GA10 *Der Satz vom Grund*, 1997. Translated by Reginald Lilly as *The*

Principle of Reason (PR), Bloomington: Indiana University Press, 1991.

GA12 *Unterwegs zur Sprache*, 1985. Marginal pagination. Translated by Peter D. Hertz as *On the Way to Language* (WL), San Francisco: Harper Collins, 1971.

GA13 *Aus der Erfahrung des Denkens*, 1983.

GA15 *Seminare*, 1986.

GA19 *Platon: Sophistes*, 1992. Translated by Richard Rojcewicz and André Schuwer as *Plato's Sophist*, Bloomington: Indiana University Press, 1997.

GA20 *Prolegomena zur Geschichte der Zeitbegriffs*, 1979. Translated by Theodore Kisiel as *History of the Concept of Time: Prolegomena*, Bloomington: Indiana University Press, 1985.

GA21 *Logik: Die Frage nach der Wahrheit*, 1976.

GA22 *Die Grundbegriffe der Antiken Philosophie*, 1993.

GA24 *Die Grundprobleme der Phänomenologie*, 1975. Translated by Albert Hofstader as *The Basic Problems of Phenomenology*, Bloomington: Indiana University Press, 1982.

GA25 *Phänomenologische Interpretation von Kants Kritik der reinen Vernunft*, 1977. Translated by Parvis Emad and Kenneth Maly as *Phenomenological Interpretation of Kant's* Critique of Pure Reason, Bloomington: Indiana University Press, 1997.

GA26 *Metaphysische Anfangsgründe der Logik im Ausgang von Leibniz*, 1978. Translated by Michael Heim as *The Metaphysical Foundations of Logic*, Bloomington: Indiana University Press, 1984.

GA29/30 *Die Grundbegriffe der Metaphysik. Welt – Endlichkeit – Einsamkeit*, 1992. Translated by William McNeill and Nicholas Walker as *The Fundamental Concepts of Metaphysics: World, finitude, solitude*, Bloomington: Indiana University Press, 1995.

GA33 *Aristoteles, Metaphysik Θ 1–3: Von Wesen und Wirklichkeit der Kraft*, 1981.

GA34 *Vom Wesen der Wahrheit: Zu Platons Höhlengleichnis und Theätet*, 1988.

GA39 *Hölderlins Hymnen «Germanien» und «Der Rhein»*, 1980.

GA40	*Einführung in die Metaphysik*, 1983. Translated by Ralph Mannheim as *An Introduction to Metaphysics* (IM), New Haven: Yale University Press, 1959.
GA41	*Die Frage nach dem Ding: Zu Kants Lehre von den transzendentalen Grundsätzen*, 1984.
GA43	*Nietzsche: Der Wille zur Macht als Kunst*, 1985.
GA44	*Nietzsches metaphysische Grundstellung im abendländischen Denken: Die ewige Wiederkehr des Gleichen*, 1986.
GA45	*Grundfragen der Philosophie: Ausgewählte «Probleme» der «Logik»*, 1984. Translated by Richard Rojcewicz and André Schuwer as *Basic Problems of Philosophy: Selected 'Problems' of 'Logic'*, Bloomington: Indiana University Press, 1994.
GA47	*Nietzsches Lehre vom Willen zur Macht als Erkenntnis*, 1989.
GA48	*Nietzsche: Der Europäische Nihilismus*, 1986.
GA50	*1. Nietzsches Metaphysik 2. Einleitung in die Philosophie: Denken und Dichten*, 1990.
GA52	*Hölderlins Hymne «Andenken»*, 1982.
GA53	*Hölderlins Hymne «Der Ister»*, 1984. Translated by William McNeill and Julia Davis as *Hölderlin's Hymn 'The Ister'*, Bloomington: Indiana University Press, 1996.
GA54	*Parmenides*, 1982. Translated by André Schuwer and Richard Rojcewicz as *Parmenides*, Bloomington: Indiana University Press, 1992.
GA55	*Heraklit: (1) Der Anfang des abendländischen Denkens; (2) Logik: Heraklits Lehre vom Logos*, 1979.
GA56/57	*Zur Bestimmung der Philosophie*, 1987.
GA63	*Ontologie (Hermeneutik der Faktizität)*, 1988. Translated by John van Buren as *Ontology: The Hermeneutic of Facticity*, Bloomington: Indiana University Press, 1999.
GA65	*Beiträge zur Philosophie (Vom Ereignis)*, 1989. Translated by Parvis Emad and Kenneth Maly as *Contributions to Philosophy: From Enowning*, Bloomington: Indiana University Press, 1999.
GA79	*Bremer und Freiburger Vorträge*, 1994.

CT   *The Concept of Time/Der Begriff der Zeit*, English-German edition, translated by William McNeill, Blackwell: Oxford, 1992.

G   *Gelassenheit*, Pfullingen: Günther Neske, 1959. Translated by John M. Anderson and E. Hans Freund as *Discourse on Thinking* (DT), New York: Harper & Row, 1966.

ID   *Identity and Difference/Identität und Differenz*, English-German edition, translated by Joan Stambaugh, New York: Harper & Row, 1969.

PIA   Phänomenologische Interpretationen zu Aristotles (Anzeige der hermeneutischen Situation), in *Interprétations Phénoménologiques d'Aristote*, French-German edition, Mauvezin: Trans-Europ-Repress, 1992. Reference to manuscript pages.

Q   *Questions*, translated by various and including in the fourth volume the original protocols of the Thor and Zahringen seminars, Paris: Gallimard, four volumes, 1966–76.

SDU   *Die Selbstbehauptung der deutschen Universität; Das Rektorat 1933/34: Tatsachen und Gedanken*, edited by Herman Heidegger, Frankfurt am Main: Vittorio Klostermann, 1983.

VA   *Vorträge und Aufsätze*, Pfullingen: Günther Neske, Vierte Auflage, 1978.

WHD   *Was heißt Denken?* Tübingen: Max Niemeyer, 1954. Translated by J. Glenn Grey as *What Is Called Thinking?* (WCT), New York: Harper & Row, 1968.

WP   *What Is Philosophy?/Was ist das – die Philosophie?* English-German edition, translated by William Kluback and Jean T. Wilde, London: Vision Press, 1963.

ZSD   *Zur Sache des Denkens*, Tübingen: Max Niemeyer, 1969. Translated by Joan Stambaugh as *On Time and Being* (TB), New York: Harper & Row, 1972.

BW   *Basic Writings*, edited by David Farrell Krell, London: Routledge, revised and expanded edition, 1993.

EGT   *Early Greek Thinking*, translated by David Farrell Krell and Frank A. Capuzzi, New York: Harper & Row, 1975.

HC *The Heidegger Controversy: A critical reader*, edited by Richard Wolin, Cambridge MASS: The MIT Press, 1993.

HS Martin Heidegger & Eugen Fink, *Heraclitus Seminar 1966/67*, translated by Charles E. Seibert, Alabama: University of Alabama Press, 1979.

PLT *Poetry, Language, Thought*, translated by Albert Hofstader, New York: Harper & Row, 1971.

QCT *The Question Concerning Technology and Other Essays*, translated by William Lovitt, New York: Harper & Row, 1977.

The majority of texts translated from the *Gesamtausgabe* have the pagination of the German version at the top of the page, allowing a single page reference. Exceptions are noted above.

III Abbreviations to works by Michel Foucault

AS *L'Archéologie du savoir*, Paris: Gallimard, 1969. Translated by Alan Sheridan as *The Archaeology of Knowledge* (AK), New York: Barnes & Noble, 1972.

DE *Dits et écrits 1954–1988*, edited by Daniel Defert & François, Ewald, Paris: Gallimard, Four Volumes, 1994 (cited by volume and page).

FDS *'Il faut défendre la société': Cours au Collège de France (1975–1976)*, Paris: Seuil/Gallimard, 1997.

FE *The Foucault Effect: Studies in governmentality*, edited by Graham Burchell, Colin Gordon and Peter Miller, Chicago: University of Chicago Press, 1991.

FL *Foucault Live: Interviews 1961–1984*, edited by Sylvère Lotringer, New York: Semiotext[e], 1996.

FR *The Foucault Reader*, edited by Paul Rabinow, Harmondsworth: Penguin, 1991.

HF *Histoire de la folie à l'âge classique* (1961), Paris: Gallimard, 1976. Abridged version translated by Richard Howard as *Madness and Civilisation* (MC), London: Routledge, 1967.

LCP *Language, Counter-Memory, Practice*, edited by Donald F. Bouchard, Oxford: Basil Blackwell, 1977.

Abbreviations

M&C   *Les mots et les choses – Une archéologie des sciences humaines*, Paris, Gallimard, 1966. Translated by Alan Sheridan as *The Order of Things – An Archaeology of the Human Sciences* (OT), London: Routledge, 1970.

MPR   *Moi, Pierre Rivière, ayant égorgé ma mère, ma sœur et mon frère: Un cas de parricide au XIXe siècle*, Paris: Gallimard, 1973.

NC   *Naissance de la clinique: Une archéologie du regard médical*, Paris: PUF, 1963. Translated by Alan Sheridan as *The Birth of the Clinic: An Archaeology of Medical Perception* (BC), London: Routledge, 1973.

OD   *L'Ordre du discours*, Paris: Gallimard, 1970.

P/K   *Power/Knowledge: Selected interviews and other writings 1972–77*, edited by Colin Gordon, Brighton: Harvester, 1980.

PPC   *Politics, Philosophy, Culture: Interviews and other writings 1977–84*, edited by Lawrence D. Kritzman, London: Routledge, 1990.

RC   *Résumé des cours 1970–1982*, Paris: Julliard, 1989.

RR   *Raymond Roussel* (1963), Paris: Gallimard, 1992. Translated by Charles Ruas as *Death and the Labyrinth: The World of Raymond Roussel* (DL), Berkeley: University of California Press, 1986.

SP   *Surveiller et punir – Naissance de la prison*, Paris: Gallimard, 1975. Translated by Alan Sheridan as *Discipline and Punish – The Birth of the Prison* (DP), Harmondsworth: Penguin, 1976.

SS   *Histoire de la sexualité III: Le souci de soi*, Paris: Gallimard, 1984. Translated by Robert Hurley as *The History of Sexuality Volume III: The Care of the Self* (CS), Harmondsworth: Penguin, 1986.

TNP   *This is Not a Pipe*, translated by James Harkess, Berkeley: University of California Press, 1983.

UP   *Histoire de la sexualité II: L'usage des plaisirs*, Paris: Gallimard, 1984. Translated by Robert Hurley as *The History of Sexuality Volume II: The Use of Pleasure* (UsP), Harmondsworth: Penguin, 1985.

VS   *Histoire de la sexualité: La volonté de savoir*, Paris: Gallimard, 1976. Translated by Robert Hurley as *The History of Sexuality Volume I: The Will to Knowledge* (WK), Harmondsworth: Penguin, 1978.

Introduction

The affinities between two of the most influential European thinkers of the twentieth century – Martin Heidegger and Michel Foucault – have been left relatively unexplored. Despite the enormous amount of critical attention that has been given to them separately, there are only a small number of texts that discuss the relation between them. However in an interview given just before his death Foucault made an important comment:

> Heidegger has always been for me the essential philosopher. I began by reading Hegel, then Marx, and I set out to read Heidegger in 1951 or 1952; then in 1952 or 1953 ... I read Nietzsche ... My entire philosophical development was determined by my reading of Heidegger. I nevertheless recognise that Nietzsche outweighed him [*l'a emporté*] ... It is probable that if I had not read Heidegger, I would not have read Nietzsche. I had tried to read Nietzsche in the fifties but Nietzsche alone said nothing to me – whereas Nietzsche and Heidegger: that was a philosophical shock! (DE IV, 703; PPC 250)

Foucault's other references to Heidegger are very brief, and hardly amount to anything. Yet he suggests that his entire philosophical development was determined by Heidegger, and that reading him was central to his understanding of Nietzsche. The reason why Foucault hardly ever mentions Heidegger is, he suggests, that one 'should have a small number of authors with whom one thinks, with whom one works, but about whom one does not write' (DE IV, 703; PPC 250).[1]

It is perhaps understandable that Foucault's lack of reference to Heidegger should be paralleled in the secondary literature, but a detailed reading of both authors shows how deep the influence runs. When Foucault's influences are examined the standard procedure is to make reference to his rejection of parts of Marxism, debate the charge of structuralism, and to acknowledge the debt to Nietzsche – especially on the points of the historical approach and the understanding of power. Sometimes a passing gesture is made to the influence of Bachelard and Canguilhem.[2] My contention in this book is that it is very difficult to properly understand Foucault's work – or, at least, major parts of it – without understanding the influence of Heidegger. Hubert Dreyfus and Paul Rabinow – in a book endorsed by Foucault – trace the influence of Heidegger on the early Foucault, but see a distance between them in Foucault's later work;[3] other commentators make remarks such as these:

> Nietzsche, not Heidegger, defines the horizon from which Foucault most often takes his departure. Heidegger's influence is apparent throughout Foucault's writing, but it is found in a more Nietzschean context.[4]

> Heidegger's influence on Foucault is immense and crucial to an understanding of his work, but the Heideggerian influence on Foucault is mediated by Foucault's understanding of Nietzsche.[5]

This book makes the claim that the reverse of this is actually the case – that Nietzsche's influence on Foucault is indeed immense, but it is continually mediated by Heidegger, and Heidegger's reading of Nietzsche. This is, of course, closer to what Foucault – in the remarks above – actually said.[6]

Foucault read Heidegger in the original German,[7] and we can therefore be sure that in the early 1950s he had access to a range of Heidegger's most important texts – *Being and Time*, the *Letter on Humanism, Holzwege, Erläuterungen zu Hölderlins Dichtung, Vorträge und Aufsätze* – and though the *Nietzsche* volumes were not published until 1961, important essays that anticipated their contents were found in earlier collections.[8] A number of parallels between Heidegger and Foucault immediately present themselves – most of which will not be treated in detail here. As Miller has noted, Heidegger's *Kant and the Problem of Metaphysics* implicitly informs Foucault's second thesis on Kant's *Anthropology*; *The Order of Things* relies on Heidegger's critique of humanism; and *The Archaeology of Knowledge* looks at the anonymous domain where 'one' – Heidegger's *das Man* – speaks.[9] Similarly, Derrida notes the association between the analysis of death in *The Birth of the Clinic* and in Heidegger's work.[10] It would also be interesting to see how important Heidegger's understanding of care [*Sorge*] and concern [*besorgen*] is for Foucault's later work on the care/concern [*souci*] of the self, to examine the related understanding of freedom, and to see how Heidegger's reading of Greek thought relates to Foucault's readings of antiquity.[11]

However, this book is concerned with the relation between these two thinkers on the question of their historical and spatial approaches, and indeed with the general question of the relation between space and history. Questions of spatiality have often been thought to be the preserve of geographers and urbanists, and there have recently been a number of attempts in these fields to critically theorize space.[12] There are, for me, two principal problems with these attempts. One of these is that any theorist who talks of space is unproblematically appropriated as 'one of them', which conflates the work of thinkers whose understandings of space or place are quite different.[13] The specific philosophical, historical, political and geographical situation of the works used is often ignored. However practically valuable, useful and interesting these recent studies may have been, they are often worryingly conceptually weak.

Second, although there has undoubtedly been a heavy bias in favour of history and time in the past, to swing too far the other way through a privileging of geography and space is no solution. Yet much of this recent work does precisely that.[14] Instead, we need to think of the two together: we need to both historicize space and spatialize history. In other words, rather than solely providing an analysis of how the meaning and use of the word 'space' has changed over time – a useful analysis to be sure – we need to recognize how space, place and location are crucial determining factors in any historical study. This is the project of a spatial history.

Michel Foucault has been one of the major thinkers whose work has been seized upon by those who want to argue for the importance of space, and yet relatively little is known about his own use of space in his works. This is due to a number of reasons. First, Foucault wrote only a small number of pieces that *directly* addressed the question of space, and these have been the principal focus of analysis in the works cited above. Other than the incessant emphasis on the Panopticon, the most oft-cited work of Foucault's on space is a lecture given to architects in 1967, but only published just before his death. This lecture is entitled 'Of Other Spaces', and introduces the notion of heterotopias. This work is of undoubted interest, but it offers a history of the concept of space and then proceeds to discuss and analyse many spaces of our modern world. It is important to note that this piece is the exception rather than the rule. The norm for Foucault is to use space not merely as another area to be analysed, but as a central part of the approach itself. From the madhouses of *Histoire de la folie*, the hospitals of *The Birth of the Clinic* and the Rio lectures on the history of medicine, to the plague town, army camp and prisons of *Discipline and Punish*, Foucault always seemed to take into account the spatial elements of the historical question he was addressing. Second, these historical works – spatial through and through – have been incompletely understood, at least in the English speaking world. This is at least partly due to the fact that a complete translation of *Histoire de la folie* and much of the important material Foucault produced in the early 1970s relating to the project of discipline have never appeared in English. Third, and perhaps most important, Foucault's intellectual heritage has been treated only partially.

When Foucault's historical approach is examined Nietzsche is usually regarded as the principal influence. Nietzsche's understanding of power, the notion of genealogy, and the continued emphasis on Nietzsche in Foucault's works immediately highlight an important relation, but my suggestion is that Nietzsche is continually mediated through Heidegger, and particularly Heidegger's book *Nietzsche*. The general point being made is that, although Nietzsche's influence on Foucault is of great importance, there are a number of central issues in Foucault's work that cannot be explained solely with reference to Nietzsche and Foucault's appropriation of his ideas. Here I argue that several key points – the orientation of history toward the present, the relation between power and knowledge, the issues of technology and the *dispositif* – are prefigured by some of Heidegger's arguments. I suggest that genealogy is historical ontology, a term Foucault himself uses in late works, but which is indebted to the Heidegger of the 1930s and beyond. Most importantly, the aim of this book is to provide a theoretical approach towards a spatial history. I suggest that this is indeed what Foucault does, and that his understanding of space, and his use of a spatialized history, is indebted not so much to his reading of Nietzsche but, most importantly, to his reading of Heidegger.

But Heidegger is not simply of interest in order to show how his work informed and shaped that of Foucault. If Foucault has been badly served by cultural critics eager to get their hands on his theoretical 'toolkit', Heidegger's work on space and place has suffered through simplistic, partial, politically blind, ideologically loaded, or philosophically insubstantial readings. As Heidegger was only too aware, his work was perhaps best characterized as a 'path' [*Weg*], and on the key issues of space and history his work certainly went through a number of changes. First, then, I take three chapters to focus on the work of Heidegger. The first chapter looks at the process that led to the publication of *Being and Time* and examines the working out in lecture courses of parts of unpublished divisions. This chapter ends at the beginning of the 1930s – a crucial time for Heidegger both philosophically and politically. Chapter Two picks up the story at this point, outlining the philosophical points at stake in the Rectorship and its aftermath, concentrating on the key readings of Nietzsche and Hölderlin – two central figures in Heidegger's own development and important in terms of the argument here concerning his influence on Foucault. Concerning the putative *Kehre* (turn), I suggest that the privilege accorded to time in *Being and Time* is corrected in Heidegger's later works, and that the ontology of *Dasein* is historicized to become a historical ontology. These changes may well have been apparent much earlier if Heidegger had published Division III of Part One and Part Two of *Being and Time*. On the issue of space, it is clear from *Being and Time* that Heidegger wants to rethink it as the resolutely non-Cartesian *place*. The use of *Platz* and *Ort* – both words translated here as 'place' – is important in understanding this issue. In some of his later works Heidegger suggests that 'space' can be thought more originally from this understanding of 'place'. Chapter Three then looks at a number of issues in Heidegger's work – art, technology, poetic dwelling and the πόλις – which showcase the application of the theoretical insights into space, place and history traced in the preceding two chapters.

Due emphasis is accorded to the political element in Heidegger's philosophy. Rather than separate the man from the thought or merely dismiss him as a thinker, moves that have tended to dog discussions of Heidegger's Nazism, I follow a number of recent studies in examining the importance of the political to his thought. The relationship of the political and the spatial is examined in detail, particularly through the discussion of Heidegger's rethinking of the πόλις. Such a reading allows us new perspective on Heidegger's retreat from his Nazi allegiance. Though it is possible to provide a picture of Heidegger's path through the works he published in his lifetime – to which Foucault would have had access – this path becomes much clearer and more involved if the lecture courses published in the *Gesamtausgabe* since 1975 are taken into account. These lecture courses shed particular light on Heidegger's readings of Kant, Aristotle and Hölderlin. The first three chapters of this book therefore treat Heidegger in detail, from *Being and Time*, through the crucially important reading of Nietzsche and Hölderlin in the shadow of Nazism, to the later work on art, technology, politics and place. As well as showing the role Heidegger's thought plays in influencing Foucault, the exposition of Heidegger's work also makes a number of claims about his own development.

The second half of the book begins by examining Foucault's historical approach, which falls, on his own designation, into archaeological and genealogical phases. Explicitly in the second, but implicitly in the first, his work was framed by a reading of Nietzsche. This has led many critics to examine the Nietzsche/Foucault relation at length.[15] Such an examination is useful in a number of ways, but most importantly it shows that *Nietzsche alone could not have provided Foucault with the necessary conceptual apparatus to shape his approach*. Because the influence of Nietzsche cannot explain the importance of space to Foucault, a number of issues arise that raise problems about the standard interpretation of Foucault. Why is *Discipline and Punish* framed as a history of the present? Is there a link between Foucault's understanding of the distinction between *connaissance* and *savoir* and the later notion of historical ontology? What is the theoretical base of his discussions of technology and the *dispositif*? Why, too, are his historical studies so overtly spatialized?

On the basis of the earlier detailed discussion of Heidegger, I am able to discuss Foucault's work on history and space from a much stronger perspective. Showing the influence of Heidegger in these areas situates Foucault's work in a much broader intellectual context than is usually recognized. This is not simply a case of asking 'where did he get that from?' which, as Heidegger suggests, stems 'from a shopkeeper's mentality' (GA26, 54). Rather, concepts of Foucault's such as the *connaissance/savoir* distinction, ontology, *dispositif*, technologies, the history of the present, space, knowledge and power become much clearer – *and therefore more useful* – if viewed through a Heideggerian lens. In this reading, the notion of genealogy is recast as a historical ontology, which is framed as a critique of the present. In Foucault's work, this Heideggerian notion is described as a history of the present. Here, with the emphasis on the importance of space, it is re-described as a *mapping of the present*. Such a mapping of the present is a spatial history, rather than a history of space.

With this enriched understanding of Foucault's intellectual heritage we are in a better position to understand his historical studies, because as well as being more attentive to their theoretical foundations, we can better see the role of space within them. To demonstrate this, the final chapter re-reads two of Foucault's most celebrated historical studies – the history of madness, and the history of the disciplined society – as spatial histories. The first of these histories is known to the English reader as *Madness and Civilisation*, which is a greatly edited version of the French original *Histoire de la folie*. As Colin Gordon has pointed out, a number of problems arise from this editing.[16] Re-reading *Histoire de la folie* shows the range of the early Foucault's concerns, and allows us insight into how space has been used politically in relation to the mad, showing the exclusion, ordering, moralization and confinement that were brought to bear on their situation. The second history is *Discipline and Punish*, the central text in a much wider project that encompasses *The Birth of the Clinic* and a number of shorter pieces, lectures and courses at the *Collège de France*. Re-reading *Discipline and Punish* within this wider project allows us to see that the model for the disciplinary society is not punishment, as is usually thought, but the interrelation of a number of mechanisms, notably those of the army and medicine. Such a reading enables us to shift the emphasis of spatial analysis away from the Panopticon, and to recognize the importance of space in a number of other areas.

In re-reading these histories from the perspective of the spatial question, I am able to demonstrate the theoretical insights of the previous chapters in a practical setting. Equally re-reading these two major projects as spatial histories allows their standard interpretations to be *re-placed*, in the light of the argument developed in the previous chapters. In both histories we see the relation between conceptualizations of space and their practical applications; how space and time work together within a historical study; the way understandings of space have changed over time; and how space is fundamental to any exercise of power. Space is inherently political; politics is inherently spatial. In addition, through this practical demonstration, the final chapter provides a reinterpretation of two justly famous and much-referenced texts.

The assertion of space within social theory must not be at the expense of the importance of time and history. In addition, the theorization of space must be philosophically substantial, politically informed, and critically aware. Whilst we can profitably learn from a history of the concept of space, just as we can from a history of the concept of time,[17] simply to undertake this history is, paradoxically, and contrary to the avowed intent of geographers, to continue the modernist occlusion of space. Space simply becomes another term to be examined historically. Rather, we need to *spatialize history*, to inject an awareness of space into all historical studies, to critically examine the power relations at play in the ways space is effected and effects. Understanding the way Heidegger shaped Foucault's historical approach shows this notion of a spatial history to be immanent to Foucault's major works. Foucault's work can therefore be thought of – and potentially employed – as *mapping the present*.

CHAPTER I

Space and History in *Being and Time*

What we know of the early Heidegger has changed dramatically since the mid-1970s. Until relatively recently *Being and Time, Kant and the Problem of Metaphysics* and odd lectures were the only texts available from the 1920s. The incompleteness of *Being and Time* – only two of a projected six divisions were published – and the fact that it appeared after more than a decade of silence on Heidegger's part, has always caused difficulties in understanding its importance and situating its insights. With the publication of Heidegger's lecture courses in the *Gesamtausgabe* and the coming to light of some other pieces several issues become much clearer. At the same time a number of complications arise: some because they require the rethinking of Heidegger's thought; some because of the problematic nature of this edition itself.[1] The lecture courses develop material originally scheduled for the unpublished divisions, situate Heidegger in relation to the tradition of phenomenology in greater detail, and provide closer analysis of key figures in his development, notably Kant and Aristotle. Most of the material covered in this chapter was produced while Heidegger was lecturing at the University of Marburg, the significance of which will be remarked upon below. Recently the wider context of the genesis of *Being and Time* has been discussed in great detail in Kisiel's pathbreaking work,[2] and this study is indebted to it. However, regarding the issues of space and history, some elucidation is still required.

ONTOLOGY, HISTORY AND TIME

Husserlian phenomenology was basically ahistorical,[3] perhaps because of Husserl's background in mathematics and logic. For Heidegger however, as Krell has argued, the *history* of philosophy was an 'essential counterweight to phenomenology': whereas Husserl had once remarked that he had 'forgotten about history', Heidegger never did.[4] In *Being and Time* Heidegger makes some comments indicating the importance of the historical project, though, as shall be seen, his later work suggests that here he did not go far enough. The basic issues at stake can be seen if the distinction Heidegger makes between *ontic* and *ontological* knowledge is examined. Ontic knowledge is knowledge pertaining to the distinctive nature of beings as such, it is the knowledge of the sciences, whereas ontological knowledge is the basis on which any such theory (of *ontic* knowledge) could be constructed, the *a priori* conditions for the possibility of such sciences. Heidegger's own exercise of *fundamental ontology* deals with the conditions of possibility not just of the ontic sciences, but also of the ontologies that precede and found them. This is the question of being (GA2, 11; see GA26, 195–202).[5]

A glimpse of the possibility this insight allows is found in Heidegger's discussion of Newton:

> To say that before Newton his laws were neither true nor false, cannot signify that before him there were no such beings as have been uncovered and pointed out by those laws. Through Newton the laws became true; and with them, beings became accessible in themselves to Dasein. Once beings have been uncovered, they show themselves precisely as beings which beforehand already were. Such uncovering is the kind of being which belongs to 'truth'.
>
> That there are 'eternal truths' will not be adequately proved until someone has succeeded in demonstrating that Dasein has been and will be for all eternity. As long as such a proof is still outstanding, this principle remains a fanciful contention which does not gain in legitimacy from having philosophers commonly 'believe' it. *Because the kind of being that is essential to truth is of the character of Dasein, all truth is relative to Dasein's being* (GA2, 227).[6]

From this, it is clear that Dasein and truth are fundamentally linked, that truth is context dependent. This does not mean that truth is only what an individual thinks, but that truth only has a context dependent on the existence of Dasein (GA3, 281–2). Any eternal truths must rest on an eternal immutability to Dasein. It clearly follows from this that if being changes, or is historicized, so too is truth. It has been remarked by some critics that Heidegger does indeed, in *Being and Time*, suggest such an immutability to Dasein, examining it and its structures as if they were true eternally. Such critics sometimes point to a shift in the later Heidegger towards an understanding of historical nature of being, through a historical sense of Dasein, which would, following the quotation and explication here, lead to a historicizing of truth.[7] The ontic/ontological difference – especially when historicized – is one that Foucault would go on to elaborate and use in the distinction between *connaissance* and *savoir* in *The Archaeology of Knowledge*, where he examined what he called the 'historical *a priori*'.[8]

The idea of the history of being does not appear as an explicit theme until later works, although it would appear that the second part of *Being and Time* would have covered some of this area. However, Heidegger does offer some thoughts on history in what was published of *Being and Time*. These theses are developed in the second division of the work, and are designed for an examination of the historical nature of existence. Lest there be confusion between what Heidegger does in *Being and Time*, and what I will argue he does later, the following point should be considered. In *Being and Time*, Heidegger attempts to understand the structures of Dasein, among which is the sense of history. In his later works, Heidegger historicizes these very structures; in the specific case effectively historicizing the sense of history. If in *Being and Time* Heidegger attempts an ontology of history (for which the ground must be Dasein rather than historiography),[9] in his later work he attempts a history of ontology. This radical shift is central to the influence he was to have on Foucault.

The model of history that Heidegger uses is that of Nietzsche in the second *Untimely Meditation*, 'On the Uses and Disadvantages of Historiography for Life'. This is the only passage of *Being and Time* that treats Nietzsche at any length, a point that shall be returned to. It is worth rehearsing the arguments of Nietzsche here, for Heidegger's reading departs in some important ways. For Nietzsche, history is not capable of objectivity, and where this is aimed for often great harm results. Instead, history has to be subjective, and therefore historians need to be aware of the uses to which their work is being put. In the preface to this work, Nietzsche provides a succinct summary of how he sees the use of historical study:

> For I do not know what meaning classical philology would have for our time if not to have an untimely effect within it, that is, to act against the time and so have an effect on the time, to the advantage, it is to be hoped, of a coming time. (UB II, Preface)

In other words, Nietzsche is aware that studying the past allows us to effect the present, and through this, the future. This much was clear from his *The Birth of Tragedy*, written immediately before this work. Nietzsche sees that there is something fundamentally wrong with the present, that there may be things in the past that may be of interest and illumination, and that knowing these things may be useful to change both how we see the present, and the future. Nietzsche's diagnosis of the cultural malaise of his own time – exacerbated by the threat of war and the Paris Commune – can be cured by seeing how Greece dealt with a parallel problem. Wagner's music dramas can, once reinterpreted in a particular way, provide future benefit.

The *Untimely Meditation* suggests that history is a necessary part of human lives. Unlike the animal, which forgets and is therefore able to live unhistorically, what distinguishes humans is that they remember. Humans live with a sense of time, they remain attached to the past as if chained. The fleeting moment, although it flashes by, can return as a 'spectre' to haunt a later moment. The human therefore has a need of history, but we need to be careful to ensure that it is used to the best advantage of life. This involves a number of balances. First, we must learn that if we remember everything we would never act. Some degree of unhistorical living is necessary (UB II, 1).[10] Nietzsche then distinguishes between three types of history – the monumental, the antiquarian and the critical. As far as humans are active and striving, they have need of monumental history; where they preserve and admire, antiquarian; and where they suffer and are in need of liberation, critical (UB II, 2).

Monumental history is the kind of history needed by someone who aspires to greatness. Nietzsche suggests that by looking back into the past one can see what might be possible again in the future, because what was once possible can be possible again. The question arises as to what difference there is between a monumental past and a mythical fiction. In order to serve its ends, the monumental approach has to generalize and be selective. A dominance of this mode of history would be dangerous because of the fear that some things might be forgotten, and because this mode deceives by analogies, as things will not be the same again (UB II, 2). Antiquarian history is for use by those who preserve and revere – who give thanks for their existence by acknowledging their debt to the past. However, like monumental history, antiquarian history has its problems. It has a tendency to inflate the past, runs the risk of nostalgia and is possibly not entirely critical. Without some critical perspective there is the danger that all is equally revered – without selection – and that the new is despised in relation to the past. Nietzsche suggests that this could mean that life is no longer preserved but is mummified (UB II, 3). The antiquarian and the monumental thus both complement and contradict each other: one takes the spirit from the past in order to elevate the future whereas the other praises heritage.

To accompany these modes of history Nietzsche thinks that the human 'must have the strength, and use it from time to time, to shatter and dissolve something to enable them to live'. As he would repeatedly stress in his later work, he who wishes to create must first destroy. This is the critical attitude to the past (UB II, 3). It is clear from this early essay that Nietzsche sees each of the three modes of history as having its particular context. He suggests that much harm is caused by thoughtless transplanting of the modes. Out of their native soil they will grow as weeds (UB II, 2). At the start of the essay Nietzsche had quoted from Goethe: 'Moreover I hate anything which merely instructs me without increasing or directly enlivening [*beleben*] my activity' (UB II, Preface). Nietzsche uses this quotation to suggest that we need history, but for life [*Leben*] and action, in order to serve life, rather than for narrow, scholarly, scientific goals. Given the choice of life ruling over knowledge, over science, or knowledge ruling over life, we should choose life, for any knowledge that destroys life would also have destroyed itself: knowledge presupposes life (UB II, 4).[11]

Heidegger suggests that although Nietzsche 'distinguished three kinds of historiography – the monumental, the antiquarian, and the critical', he failed to explicitly point out 'the necessity of this triad or the ground of its unity' (GA2, 396). In fact, although his later genealogical approach is arguably a fusion of these three types of historiography, Nietzsche never explicitly states that the three *should* be conflated.[12] Given Heidegger's purpose, this joining together is of key importance. '*The threefold character of historiography* [Historie] *is adumbrated in the historicality* [Geschichtlichkeit] *of Dasein* . . . [which] enables us to understand to what extent these three possibilities must be united factually and concretely in any historiography which is authentic [*eigentliche*]' (GA2, 396). It is important to note the distinction Heidegger draws between *Historie* and *Geschichte*. *Historie* is, for Heidegger, the writing of history, the discipline of historiography; *Geschichte* is history as it actually happens [*geschieht*], the events.[13]

Heidegger reads these three types of historiography as having distinct attitudes to time. The antiquarian approach orientates itself to the past, the having been; the monumental to the future; and the critical to the present. It is in the reading of the last of these that Heidegger departs from Nietzsche, for Nietzsche used the critical approach as an orientation to the *past*.[14] As far back as 1922 Heidegger had suggested this: 'The *critique* of history is always only the critique of the present [*Kritik der Gegenwart*]' (PIA 4). As Bambach notes, this may be due to Heidegger's reading Kierkegaard's *Two Ages* in the German translation *Kritik der Gegenwart*.[15] We find this critical attitude exemplified in Heidegger's reading of philosophy:

> *Ruthlessness toward the tradition is reverence toward the past*, and it is genuine only in an appropriation of the latter (the past) out of a *de-struction* of the former (the tradition). On this basis, all actual historiographical work, something quite different from historiography in the usual sense, must dovetail with philosophy's research into the matters themselves. (GA19, 414)

In other words, the 'tradition' as received in the present covers over the past. This notion of de-struction is therefore far from negative: it is an uncovering, a de-structuring, an archaeology of the levels of interpretation, the layers of sedimentation of the tradition that have obscured the issues at stake, the matters themselves.[16] This ties back into the project of the first two divisions of *Being and Time*:

> Dasein temporalises itself in the way the future and having been are united in the present . . . As authentic, the historiography which is both monumental and antiquarian is necessarily a critique of the 'present'. Authentic historicality is the foundation for the possibility of uniting these three ways of historiography. (GA2, 397)[17]

These three temporal dimensions come together, as will be examined later, in the reading of the Nietzschean moment [*Augenblick*].[18]

Given this, it is surprising that in *Being and Time* Heidegger neither mentions Nietzsche in his discussion of the moment, nor makes the linkage clearer. The notion here is not developed in great detail, and, at least on the surface, seems to owe more to Kierkegaard.[19] The moment is linked to the existential situation [*Situation*] which Heidegger defines thus:

> The existential attributes of any possible resolute Dasein include the items constitutive for an existential phenomenon which we call a *situation* . . . [in which] there is an overtone of a signification that is spatial. (GA2, 299)

Heidegger uses the German *Situation* to mean a temporal/spatial 'there', and opposes it to the solely spatial *Lage* [position] (see PIA 10). Each situation is a *place* in time and space, where existentially Dasein has acted authentically:

> When resolute, Dasein has brought itself back from falling, and has done so precisely in order to be more authentically 'there' in the 'moment of *vision*' [*Augen*blick] as regards the situation which has been disclosed. (GA2, 328)

Regardless of the existential baggage that was later marginalized in his work,[20] these two concepts provide an initial glimpse of what Heidegger, and certainly Foucault, went on to do: the putting into practice of the understanding of the dimensions of time and space concurrently.

One of the intended divisions of *Being and Time* was to be a critique of the Aristotelian notion of time (GA2, 40). Although it never appeared, there are occasional hints of what it may have included, and indeed *The Basic Problems of Phenomenology* discusses some of this area. The Aristotelian view of time was 'as a succession, as a "flowing stream" of "nows", as "the course of time"' (GA2, 421–2).[21] Instead of this temporal sequence, of the now-no-longer, the now, and the not-yet-now (GA24, 348–9), we must, following Heidegger's reading of Nietzsche on history, see the dimensions of past, present and future together, in terms of the authentic 'moment' (see GA29/30, 226).[22] It is notable that although Heidegger praises Kierkegaard's concept of the moment, his main complaint is that it is equated with the now in the common sense (GA2, 338niii; GA24, 408).[23] Heidegger's development of this idea is far too inchoate in what was published of *Being and Time*, and even in the later *The Basic Problems of Phenomenology* and *The Basic Concepts of Metaphysics*, but again there are several hints of where it may lead. It will be suggested that it is in Heidegger's extended reading of Nietzsche in the later 1930s and beyond that these ideas come to greater fruition, and that this formulation becomes clearer:

> When historicality is authentic, it understands history as the 'return' [*Wiederkehr*] of the possible, and knows that a possibility will recur only if existence is open for it fatefully, in a moment, in resolute repetition. (GA2, 391–2)

Understanding Heidegger's use of the three types of historiography helps to explain his comments earlier in *Being and Time*. At one point he writes

> thus 'the past' has a remarkable double meaning; the past belongs irretrievably to an earlier time; it belonged to the events of that time; and in spite of that, it can still be present-at-hand 'now' – for instance, the remains of a Greek temple. With the temple, a 'bit of the past' is still 'in the present'. (GA2, 378)[24]

For the historical structure of Dasein, it is therefore clear that the past is 'present' in the present, a claim Foucault would make many times in his writings. For our current purpose it is worth bearing in mind that Heidegger tends to assimilate the meanings of two German words for presence, which mean the presence of someone in a place or at an occasion [*Anwesenheit*], and presence in the temporal sense [*Gegenwart*]. 'For what the Greeks mean by being is being as presence, being in the present [*Anwesendsein, Gegenwärtigsein*]' (GA19, 34; see 466–7; GA24, 305ff).[25] Heidegger makes this idea of presence clearer in the following passage, which highlights a point Foucault would later elaborate in his reading of Nietzsche:

> What we next have in mind with the term 'history' is not so much 'the past' in the sense of that which is past, but rather *descent* [Herkunft] from such a past. Anything that 'has a history' stands in the context of a becoming. In

such becoming, 'development' is sometimes a rise, sometimes a fall . . . Here 'history' signifies a 'context' of events and 'effects', which draws on through 'the past', the 'present', and the 'future'. On this view, the past has no special priority. (GA2, 378–9)

Although Heidegger's remarks in *Being and Time* are generally limited to the historicality of Dasein, at times he does hint at the direction of his thought to come. Dreyfus has suggested that the sketchy and hurried nature of Division Two should be attributed to the rush in which it was appended to the more polished first division: this may explain its partial nature.[26] Heidegger suggests that

> what is *primarily* historical is Dasein. That which is *secondarily* historical, however, is what we encounter within-the-world . . . also the environing *nature* as the 'very soil of history'. (GA2, 381)[27]

Usually the comments on the more general nature of history are those that directly relate the history of things to their use in reading the history of Dasein, such as the following example: 'Remains, monuments, and records that are still present-at-hand, are *possible* 'material' for the concrete disclosure of the Dasein which has-been-there' (GA2, 394). At one point Heidegger remarks:

> equipment and work – for instance, books – have their 'fates' [*Schicksale*]; buildings and institutions have their history. And even nature is historical. It is *not* historical, to be sure, in so far as we speak of 'natural history'; but nature is historical as a countryside, as an area that has been colonised or exploited, as a battlefield, or as the site of a cult [*Kultstätte*]. (GA2, 388)

In some ways then, rather than being the soil of history, nature might be tentatively designated as the site of history, a claim that will be discussed in Chapters Two and Three.

THE SPACE OF DASEIN AND EQUIPMENT

It is not difficult to immediately find clues that would appear to show the spatiality of Heidegger's thought. Right from his earliest works, he uses the German word *Dasein*, which, as a noun, means 'existence', but that also, as a verb, means 'to be *there*'. If this word is broken apart, or is, as Heidegger often does, hyphenated to *Da-sein*, it literally means 'there-being', 'being-there'. It has regularly been translated as the latter of these in English, and in French has often been rendered as the equivalent *être-là*, most famously in the works of Sartre.[28] Contemporaneous to this use of the word is another of Heidegger's important terms, *In-der-Welt-Sein*, 'being-in-the-world'. A privileging of the spatial over the existential overtones of the preposition in this phrase would seem to underline the importance of space and place in Heidegger's early works. However, such a reading of these terms would be both too simplistic, and in certain respects inaccurate.[29] Indeed, as will be shown, Heidegger's early works often appear to go out of their way to condemn such ideas. Understanding the Heideggerian attitude to space is a more difficult and delicate task.

Early in *Being and Time* Heidegger makes it quite clear that a spatial reading of several of his key terms is not the *primary* sense intended. For example, on the term being-in-the-world, Heidegger asks specifically 'what is meant by "*being-in*"?' (GA2, 53). In contrast to the spatial being in [*Sein in*], such as we might conceive of the water 'in' the glass, or the garment 'in' the cupboard, Heidegger sets up the 'existentiale' being-in [*in-Sein*]: ' "*Being-in" is thus the formal existential expression for the being of Dasein, which has being-in-the-world as its essential state*' (GA2, 54; see GA20, 211–13). Heidegger goes on to suggest that this does not deny every kind of spatiality to Dasein, but that an understanding of being-in-space is only possible *after* an understanding of being-in-the-world as an essential structure of Dasein (GA2, 56). A similar distinction is made some pages later, around the concept of environment [*Umwelt*]: 'The spatial character which incontestably belongs to any environment can be clarified only in terms of the structure of worldhood' (GA2, 66).

As Heidegger believes that 'Dasein does not fill up a bit of space as a real thing or item of equipment would' (GA2, 368), the spatiality of Dasein is not a *primary* characteristic. Even its spatiality in a secondary way is not what would ordinarily be termed spatial,[30] and does not, compared to other analyses of Heidegger's, much further the purpose here. That which Dasein encounters – things, locations and equipment [*Zeug*] – has, on the other hand, very important spatial characteristics. Many of Heidegger's most interesting and perceptive comments on the first two of these three are found in his work of the 1930s and later, but his meditation on the last, equipment, begins much earlier. Heidegger explains that equipment 'always is *in terms of* [*aus*] its belonging to other equipment: writing equipment, pen, ink, paper, blotting pad, table, lamp, furniture, windows, door, room' (GA2, 68). He continues:

> what we encounter as closest to us . . . is the room; and we encounter it not as something 'between four walls' in a geometrical spatial sense, but as equipment for dwelling [*Wohnzeug*]. (GA2, 68; see GA24, 414)

Another example perhaps upsets our customary notions:

> When, for instance, someone wears a pair of spectacles which are so close to them distantially that they are 'sitting on their nose', they are environmentally more remote from them than the picture on the opposite wall ... Equipment for seeing ... has what we have designated as the inconspicuousness of the proximally ready-to-hand. (GA2, 107)

This highlights an important point: for Heidegger, we encounter things in space in a way that stands in opposition to Descartes' view. Heidegger's thoughts on the spatiality of the ready-to-hand suggest that our encounters with equipment are not *primarily* determined by geometry and measurable distance, but by the more prosaic notions of closeness or nearness [*Nähe*], de-distancing [*Ent-fernung*] and directionality [*Ausrichtung*].

> The 'above' is what is 'on the ceiling'; the 'below' is what is 'on the floor'; the 'behind' is what is 'at the door'; all 'wheres' are discovered and circumspectively interpreted as we go our ways in everyday dealings; they are not ascertained and catalogued by the observational measurement of space. (GA2, 103)[31]

In the earliest lecture course we have from Heidegger, from 1919, he makes just such a claim about space in order to illustrate the issue of time:

> I come to Freiburg for the first time on a walking tour and, on entering the town, ask, 'which is the shortest way to the cathedral?' This spatial orientation has nothing to do with the geometrical as such. The distance to the cathedral is not a quantitative stretch [*Strecke*]. Nearness and farness are not a 'how much'; the nearest and shortest way does not mean also something quantitative, or merely extended [*Ausgedehntes*] as such. This is analogous to the phenomenon of time. (GA56/57, 86)

What Heidegger has given here is a more common-sense understanding of how we relate to space. As he notes, 'space is neither in the subject nor is the world in space' (GA2, 111). Space is encountered in everyday life, and lived in, not encountered in geometrically measurable forms and shapes and distances.

A very striking example of this is found in the 1923 course *Ontology: The Hermeneutic of Facticity*. Heidegger draws on the everyday situation of being in a room with a table. What is being encountered here?

A thing in space – as a spatial thing, it is also material. It has such and such a weight, such and such a colour, such and such a shape, with a rectangular or round top – so high, so wide, with a smooth or rough surface. The thing can be dismantled, burned or dissolved in some other way . . .

But the table is more than such calculable attributes. 'When seen more closely, it is not only a material thing in space, but in addition is furnished with definite valuative predicates: beautifully made, useful – it is a piece of equipment, furniture, a part of the room's décor'. This leads Heidegger to suggest that the total domain of what is real can be divided into two realms – things in nature and things of value. The second is dependent on the first, a natural thing in its being is the foundation of value. Therefore the basic determinant of the table is as a material thing in space (GA63, 88–9).

To understand things in this way is apparently true, but only apparently. Heidegger suggests a phenomenological reading will reveal things that are missed by a reading of the table as a thing in nature or a thing of value. It will also reveal the limitations of these readings themselves. First, Heidegger notes that what is there in the room is *the* table, not just any table, but a particular one, which serves particular purposes. It is one 'at which one sits *in order to* write, have a meal, sew, play'. To see it as a writing table or as a dining table is the primary way in which the table is encountered. The table is playing a particular role. We can note that one part is damaged, that there are lines on the table. But these are not just interruptions in the paint. Rather they hold a significance entirely other: they were caused by Heidegger's sons playing at the table and therefore still contain that in them.

> This side is not the east side, and this narrow side so many cm. shorter than the other, but rather the one at which my wife sits in the evening when she wants to stay up and read, there at the table we had such and such a discussion that time, there that decision was made with a *friend* that time, there that *work* written that time, there that *holiday* celebrated that time.

All of these things are *the* table, 'as such it is there in the temporality of everydayness'. Many years from now, when the table is taken apart and unusable, it will still have these significations. Just as the old pair of skis lying broken in the basement are not material things of different lengths, but rather skis from a particular time from a trip with someone, the table cannot be understood in terms of calculation: either physical or aesthetic (GA63, 89–91).

To take the table as a thing in space, a material thing, with a particular weight, colour, shape, dimensions, and so forth, is to miss the way the table is encountered and used. When we sit at the table we do not worry about such things – only if the table is unstable would we wonder if the legs were of different lengths. Only if the lighting were unsuitable for reading, or the table were in the way would we worry about its placing in the room. Mathematical, scientific understandings of the table's situation in the room miss what is essential about our encounter with it. The table is part of the structure of our being-in-the-world. As with Heidegger's thoughts on using equipment and coping with life, he believes that standard investigations begin at the level of abstraction, rather than at the level of everyday *action*. Just as he believes that we encounter a hammer only as a hammer if there is a problem with it, we encounter the room or space geometrically only when something is wrong, when we purposively think of it in that way (see GA2, 109, 361–2).

Heidegger's examples in *The Basic Problems of Phenomenology* are tailored to the situation of the lecture course: 'Sitting here in the auditorium, we do not in fact apprehend walls – not unless we are getting bored. Nevertheless, the walls are already present even before we think of them as objects.'

> When we enter here through the door, we do not apprehend the seats, and the same holds for the door-knob. Nevertheless, they are there in this peculiar way: we go by them circumspectly, avoid them circumspectly, stumble against them, and the like. Stairs, corridors, windows, chair and bench, blackboard, and much more are not given thematically. We say that an equipmental contexture environs us. (GA24, 231–3; see GA20, 229–31; GA29/30, 499–504)[32]

All of this links to his thoughts on place [*Platz*]. Heidegger suggests that all things have their place, but that often 'the region [*Gegend*] of a place does not become accessible explicitly as such a region until one fails to find something in *its* place' (GA2, 104).[33] The notion of place is – for the early Heidegger – most fully explored in the course he gave in 1924–5 on Platonic dialogues. In fact, although the original aim was to explicate a number of dialogues, the course as delivered concentrated on just one, the *Sophist*. But as a way into the reading of Plato, Heidegger provides a detailed reading of Aristotle, particularly the *Nicomachean Ethics*. In an excursus on the nature of the mathematical Heidegger makes some points regarding place that are worth noting here.[34]

Heidegger stresses the τόπος where being and presence [*das Sein und die Anwesenheit*] are determined (GA19, 102), and warns us that 'the modern concept of space [*Begriff des Raumes*] must not at all be allowed to intrude here' (GA19, 105). Aristotle provides an outline of the concept of τόπος in *Physics* IV, and Heidegger claims that the assertions made here are 'self-evident, and we may not permit mathematical-physical determinations to intrude'. We can therefore see a hint that the modern, Cartesian understanding of the spatial is alien to Greek thought. Importantly, Heidegger discusses Aristotle's suggestion that place has a δύναμις. Rather than opting for the standard translation of this as force or power [*Kraft*], Heidegger argues it must be understood in an ontological sense. Place is more fundamental; to say it has a δύναμις

> implies that the place [*Platz*] pertains to the being itself, the place constitutes precisely the possibility of the proper presence [*eigentlichen Anwesendseins*] of the being in question . . . every being has *its* place [*Jedes Seiende hat seinen Ort*] . . . Each being possesses in its being a prescription toward a determinate location or place. *The place is constitutive of the presence of the being* [*Jedes Seiende hat in seinem Sein die Vorzeichnung auf einen bestimmten Platz, Ort. Der Ort ist konstitutiv für die Anwesenheit des Seienden*]. (GA19, 105–6)[35]

If place is indeed, as Heidegger suggests, so essential to being, we are tempted to ask what place actually is. Heidegger recognizes the difficulty of this task, and by way of a response here he quotes lines he will use over 40 years later to preface his essay 'Art and Space': 'It appears that to grasp place in itself is something great and very difficult.'[36] The temptation of determining place in a Cartesian way – to take the extension of the material [*die Ausdehnung des Stoffes*] or the limit of the form as the place – is strong, but must be resisted (GA19, 108). This understanding of the concept of place is therefore summarized by remembering that place has a δύναμις. Δύναμις is a basic ontological category. Place is something belonging to beings as such, it is their capacity to be present, it is constitutive of their being. 'The place is the ability a being has to be there [*Dortseinkönnen*], in such a way that, in being there, it is properly present [*dortseiend, eigentlich da ist*]' (GA19, 109).

Heidegger's comments here are tantalizingly brief. He recognizes that a thorough elucidation 'would have to take up the question of place and space', but here he can only indicate what is necessary for the issue of mathematics (GA19, 104). Generally, then, it is clear that our coping with space in life is essential, but is usually understood at a level removed from the everyday. When Heidegger starts to relate these thoughts on equipment to the structure of being-in-the-world, he again uses these everyday notions: 'We say that to go over yonder is a good walk, a stone's throw, or "as long as it takes to smoke a pipe"' (GA2, 105). A more detailed statement of this situation is found in the 1923 *Ontology* course:

> *Spatiality*, which is saturated in a factical manner with concern, has its distances – it is there as: too far, nearby, through this street, through the

kitchen, a stone's throw, behind the cathedral, and the like. In this spatiality is found a familiarity with its references which prevails for a while at the particular time, and these references are always those of concern. (GA63, 101)

Heidegger also extends his consideration to nature, a point he will return to in his later work on technology:

Nature is not to be understood as that which is just present-at-hand, nor as the *power of nature*. The wood is a timber forest, the mountain a rock quarry; the river water-power, the wind is wind 'in the sails'. As the 'environment' is discovered, the 'nature' thus discovered is encountered too. (GA2, 70)

Several of these key ideas are developed in Heidegger's important later essays.

READING KANT PHENOMENOLOGICALLY

In his genealogy of *Being and Time*, Kisiel suggests that the 1924 lecture and manuscript *The Concept of Time* was directed to the question 'what is history?' and was indebted to Dilthey; the summer semester course of 1925, *History of the Concept of Time: Prolegomena*, was directed to the question 'what is being?' and was Husserlian; and the published version of *Being and Time* asked 'what is time?' Kisiel called this the kairological (from the Greek καιρός – right time, opportunity, crisis, moment), or Kantian version.[37] What is the relationship of Heidegger to Kant, especially round the questions of ontology, history, time and space?

It should immediately be noted that Heidegger's reading of Kant does not claim to be a piece of neutral and objective scholarship but a reading designed to illuminate his own project. He makes two important remarks on this point. In 1928 he tells his students that

when some years ago I studied the *Critique of Pure Reason* anew and read it, as it were, against the background of Husserl's phenomenology, the scales fell from my eyes; and Kant became for me an essential confirmation of the accuracy of the path which I took in my search. (GA25, 431)

Some years later, in response to critiques of his *Kant and the Problem of Metaphysics*, he admitted 'it may not be good Kant, but it is awfully good Heidegger'.[38] These two accounts jar slightly, but the overall intent is quite clear: a phenomenological reading of Kant, and in particular of the *Critique of Pure Reason*, can further the early Heidegger's project. We might note in passing here that the same intent is later applied to Nietzsche and Hölderlin, a point to which I return below.

There are two central issues that I wish to examine in Heidegger's reading of Kant. The first is that Heidegger sees Kant as recognizing the ontic/ontological difference; the second is the role of space and time, and in particular the privileging of time over space. First then, it will be recalled that ontic knowledge is knowledge pertaining to particular beings; ontological knowledge is the condition of possibility for such ontic knowledge. Ontological knowledge is the *a priori* conditions for ontic knowledge, it concerns *being* rather than *beings*, and is the major concern of the early Heidegger, especially in *Being and Time*. The predominant strain of Kant interpretation in Heidegger's time was the neo-Kantianism of the Marburg school, which argued that the *Critique of Pure Reason* was a work of epistemology. This view, put forward by Cohen, Rickert and Natorp, amongst others, held sway from the late nineteenth and early twentieth century. Heidegger – lecturing at Marburg – tackles this interpretation head on: the *Critique of Pure Reason* is a theory of knowledge, but it is not a theory of *ontic* knowledge (i.e. experience), epistemology, but rather of *ontological* knowledge – transcendental philosophy, ontology (GA3, 17; GA24, 180–1; GA25, 186).[39] Ontic knowledge (of beings) must conform to ontological foundations (being). This is the real meaning of Kant's Copernican revolution – that instead of our knowledge conforming to objects, objects must conform to our knowledge (GA25, 55–6).[40]

What was for Kant the examination of the transcendental possibility of experience, becomes in Heidegger's terms an examination of the ontological possibility of the ontic. Heidegger continues, 'with the problem of transcendence, a "theory of knowledge" is not set in place of metaphysics, but rather the inner possibility of ontology is questioned' (GA3, 16–17). Ontology is seen as the laying of the ground for metaphysics as a whole (GA3, 124–5; see GA29/30, 306). This interpretation has a number of effects and forms the basis for Heidegger's reading of Kant throughout his career. For example, in the *Critique of Pure Reason*, as in other places, Kant demolished the proofs for an existence of God, arguing that being was not a real predicate. Heidegger draws a conclusion from this wholly in keeping with his wider interpretation: 'Being, as being possible, being actual, being necessary, is not, to be sure, a real (ontic) predicate, but it is a transcendental (ontological) predicate' (GA9, 294). In other words, in order for something to be something, it must first be. Being in general is the condition of possibility for being in particular.

What is particularly important in this discussion, though, is that Heidegger's reading of the ontic/ontological difference runs almost parallel to Kant's discussion of synthetic *a priori* knowledge. Kant's search for a foundation for such knowledge is his reply to Hume's scepticism: synthetic *a priori* knowledge allows the foundation of a mathematical system, science to proceed by means of experiment, and the establishment of a ground for an ethics. Kant suggests that although experience is a *necessary* condition for knowledge, it is not a *sufficient* condition for knowledge. For any knowledge that is not merely an explication of the meaning of something already known – analytic knowledge – some synthesis of experience and reason is necessary. Kant puts this famously as 'thoughts without content are empty, intuitions without concepts, blind'.[41] The central question of the *Critique of Pure Reason* was 'how are synthetic *a priori* judgements possible?; the central question of *Being and Time* could be rephrased as 'how is ontological knowledge possible?'[42] Synthetic *a priori* knowledge is possible on the basis of the original synthetic unity of the pure productive power of imagination, on the basis of temporality. As temporality is the basic constitution of human Dasein, humans have the possibility of having a pure understanding of being. The understanding of being in general (ontological knowledge) is possible on the basis of the temporality of Dasein (GA25, 424–5).[43]

In Kant, as in *Being and Time*, this is a radically ahistorical question. In Nietzsche and the later Heidegger this question, the problem of metaphysics, or the question of being (GA3, 249), is posed historically. Nietzsche suggests that Kant's answer to the question 'how are synthetic *a priori* judgements possible' is 'by faculty of a faculty [*Vermöge eines Vermögens*]'. These faculties – Kant's perceptual manifold and the categories – continue into his moral thought, with the 'discovery' of the categorical imperative. Nietzsche suggests that this is not really an answer, or an explanation, but rather a repetition of the question. Nietzsche suggests such replies should remain in comedy, and that therefore we should replace the Kantian question 'how are synthetic *a priori* judgements possible?' by the question 'why is belief in such judgements *necessary*?' (JGB 11).[44] This question is, I suggest, the key to understanding the genealogical approach of Nietzsche's work; the later Heidegger's historical ontology; and Foucault's appropriation of these notions. For what Nietzsche, Heidegger and Foucault share is a realization that the structures of knowledge that are taken as absolutes at a particular time are contingent, and that they must be examined historically.

Heidegger again explicitly distances himself from the Marburg school in his reading of the Transcendental Aesthetic. The prevalent interpretation, characterized by Natorp, is that the placing of the Transcendental Aesthetic at the beginning of the *Critique* is a 'well-meant mistake', giving, as it does, priority to time and space over the categories.[45] Natorp wants, Heidegger suggests, to dissolve the Transcendental Aesthetic into the Transcendental Logic, to rethink time and space as *categories* (GA25, 122). In contrast Heidegger does not wish to dissolve the Transcendental Logic into the Transcendental Aesthetic, but to examine the relation between the two: something Kant was not able to do. Heidegger continues, pointing to his interpretation:

> what the Transcendental Aesthetic deals with is not simply turned off in Transcendental Logic . . . rather, the Transcendental Logic takes up what the Transcendental Aesthetic deals with as a necessary foundation and a central clue. From a purely external perspective this shows itself in the fact that the time which is interpreted in the Transcendental Aesthetic in a preliminary fashion functions in all the crucial sections of the Transcendental Logic – and indeed as something fundamental. (GA25, 79)

What is central here is that not only does Heidegger read Kant as providing the ontological foundation of the Transcendental Logic in the Transcendental Aesthetic, he sees the examination of time in the latter as the fundamental clue to the former.[46]

It is worth thinking this through in some detail. Reading the problematic of synthetic *a priori* knowledge as the question of an ontological foundation leads Heidegger to reinterpret the Transcendental Aesthetic in an important way. For Heidegger, 'the "Transcendental Aesthetic" has as its task to set forth the ontological αἴσθησις which makes it possible 'to disclose *a priori*' the being of beings' (GA3, 51). The two elements of the Transcendental Aesthetic, time and space, are, in Kantian terms, the principles to which all objects we perceive must conform. Space and time are the horizon within which we encounter all things: experience must take a spatio-temporal form. Heidegger explains the implications of this by suggesting that the employment of space (and time) as pure intuition is transcendental, because space is understood as being constitutive for the enabling of a pure *a priori* knowledge with respect to things themselves. In this usage space is 'transcendental', which means that it is ideal and not real. 'Therefore the Transcendental Aesthetic investigates such intuitions which, as pure intuitions, first make possible the empirical intuition of what is spatially and temporally present-at-hand' (GA25, 187–8). The transcendental makes possible the experience of present-at-hand objects.

Now, although Kant opens up this fundamentally important avenue, he remains trapped in the conceptions of modern thought. Kant is, in certain key respects, Cartesian (GA2, 24, 204). Previous sections of this chapter have shown how Heidegger was keen for time to be thought more originally than as a now-point, and for space to be thought otherwise than by extension. Yet Kant remains in this position. As Heidegger notes, in the *Groundwork for the Metaphysic of Morals* Kant suggests 'the idea of a twofold metaphysics: a metaphysics of nature and a metaphysics of morals'.[47] Heidegger interprets these as an ontology of *res extensa* and an ontology of *res cogitans* (GA24, 197–8) – precisely the Cartesian formulation Heidegger is trying to escape, through a rethinking of space without a basis in extension, and through a rethinking of Dasein that is not reducible to a subject (see GA20, 237ff, 322). A central distinction between Heidegger's interpretation of Kant and Kant himself therefore arises. To take the example of time: in Kant we intuit through time, in Heidegger temporality is the basic constitution of that which intuits (GA25, 368). We might expect this, given the title of *Being and Time*, and the fact that, for Heidegger, 'and' often functions as a copula.[48] Heidegger explains, 'Dasein, conceived in its most extreme possibility of being, *is time itself*, not *in* time' (CT 13–14). This is well illustrated in a remark Heidegger made in *The Basic Problems of Phenomenology*: 'perhaps it is precisely time which is the *a priori* of the I [*Ich*] – time, to be sure, in a more original sense than Kant was able to conceive it' (GA24, 206).[49]

In the Transcendental Aesthetic Kant discusses time and space in turn, only to accord priority of time over space. In *Being and Time* Heidegger argues that the 'temporality of being-in-the-world thus emerges, and it turns out, at the same time, to be the foundation for the specific spatiality of Dasein' (GA2, 335). To what extent are these two positions linked? In the *Critique*, Kant argues that space is the formal condition of the physical. In order to encounter beings other than ourselves, we must have outer intuition – an experience of the outside. Therefore space is the pure form of outer intuition. However, in order to experience the outside, we must first be able to experience: we must be able to be self-aware. Self-awareness is in no way spatial, for Kant, but is rather a sequence of states – representations, volitions and moods. This shows that time is crucial, and time is both the formal condition of the psychical, and the pure form of inner intuition. Kant continues from this that 'time is the formal *a priori* condition of all appearances whatsoever'.[50] It follows from this, Heidegger suggests, that 'time has a pre-eminence over space' (GA3, 48–9; GA25, 145ff).

As Heidegger recognizes, it is not immediately apparent why this should be so. As he notes, 'already in the Transcendental Aesthetic there comes to light a peculiar priority of time over space. And in subsequent and more decisive sections of the *Critique* time emerges again and again at the centre piece of the transcendental, *viz.* ontological, problematic' (GA25, 111–12). Heidegger reads this problematic in a way that certainly furthers his own project, if not Kant scholarship generally. Time is not a feature of physical objects in an *immediate* sense, but when represented to us, they become temporal in a *mediated* way. Because then both the external world and the internal world are dependent on the temporality of the perceiver, time is the formal condition of outer, spatial appearances, and therefore has priority over space (GA25, 148).[51]

This hierarchical ranking is continued throughout Heidegger's early work. We can now perhaps understand Heidegger's suggestion that 'Dasein's spatiality is "embraced" by temporality in the sense of being existentially founded upon it . . . [but this] is also different from the priority of time over space in Kant's sense' (GA2, 367). For Kant time has priority over space as it is the formal requirement for the experience of all objects; for Heidegger temporality is the basic constitution of Dasein and therefore spatiality is founded upon it. Heidegger claims that this does not mean that space is deduced from, or dissolved into, time (GA2, 367). Whilst this is *perhaps* in itself true, it is not revealed in *Being and Time* how this is the case.[52] Indeed, Heidegger suggests in *History of the Concept of Time* that he has thought the notions of de-distancing, region and orientation in a way that suffices 'in relation to what we need for *time* and the *analysis of time*' (GA20, 322). It is possible that had Heidegger been more interested in space itself in his early career, he would have made good this claim. However, on the evidence of his early work, Heidegger has perpetuated the primacy of time over space found in, amongst others, Kant.[53] It is worth noting that the section this claim is made in is one that Heidegger would refute in later life (see ZSD 24; TB 23) – a point discussed in Chapter Three – and that in several places in *Being and Time* Heidegger warns against founding time on space, even when it appears that time is measured by movement in space, by, for example, observation of the sun or shadow clocks (GA2, 412ff; see CT 18).

Throughout his early work, Heidegger uses the notion of time as the point of departure for his analyses. In *Being and Time*, for example, the analyses of being-toward-death, the attunement *Angst*, falling prey, understanding and discourse are fundamentally temporal analyses (see GA2, 335ff). In the 1929/30 lecture course *The Basic Concepts of Metaphysics*, where Heidegger provides an analysis of the fundamental attunement of boredom, this too takes its departure from an analysis of time. This is perhaps not surprising given that the German word for boredom is *Langeweile*, which literally means 'long-while'.[54] Whilst I would not wish to suggest that these analyses should have been made from the point of view of space, it is notable that Heidegger continually concentrates on the temporality of Dasein.[55]

It is also worth noting, although there are exceptions, that *Being and Time* is concerned almost exclusively with Dasein and, moreover, Dasein as an ahistorical idea. In his later works Heidegger encompasses other areas and realizes the history of being. It is these works, particularly, that are central to understanding Foucault. Glimpses of his later work can be seen in his thoughts on the duality of the situation and the moment, and the hint that they may be linked to the study of history. However, in his thoughts on the spatiality of equipment, Heidegger does set up some important distinctions, specifically with the Cartesian notion of space. Descartes' view of space was that it should be seen as mathematical, geometric, viewed in terms of spatial location, measurable by co-ordinates. On the other hand, Heidegger realizes that for the living of space – space as actually experienced – notions of near/far or close/distant are more practical and better reflect life.[56] However, Heidegger's neglect of the important question of the body is well known: another point he aims to address later in his work.[57]

TOWARDS HÖLDERLIN AND NIETZSCHE

Being and Time is still the foundation of Heidegger's entire *oeuvre*, although it is but a fragment of the intended whole, and is, as even Heidegger would come to accept, radically flawed in certain respects. One of the missing divisions was entitled 'Time and Being', and was intended to discuss time in relation to being as a whole, not simply to Dasein. Villela-Petit has even suggested that this section would also have dealt with 'the third term that the dyad *being* and *time* had, in a certain manner obscured, namely space'.[58] Whatever, it is certain that Heidegger's later writings in this area differ in certain key respects from what had gone before. It will be suggested that the later Heidegger, from the mid-1930s on, is far more sympathetic in his treatment of space, for, despite his attempts to explain otherwise, in *Being and Time* Heidegger remains overtly Kantian in his belief in the inherent primacy of time over space.

At the very end of the year *Being and Time* was published, Heidegger replied to a letter from Rudolf Bultmann:

My work is directed toward a radicalisation of ancient ontology and at the same time toward a universal structuring of this ontology in relation to the region of history. The fundament of this problematic is developed by starting from the 'subject', properly understood as the human Dasein, so that with the radicalising of this approach the true motives of German idealism may likewise come into their own. Augustine, Luther, Kierkegaard are *philosophically* essential for the cultivation of a more radical understanding-of-Dasein, Dilthey for a radical interpretation of the 'historical world', Aristotle and scholasticism for the strict formulation of certain ontological *problems*. All this in a methodology guided by the idea of a scientific philosophy as it has been grounded by Husserl, not without the influence of the logical investigations and philosophy of science of H. Rickert and E. Lask.[59]

The correspondence with Bultmann is of marginal use, as Kisiel notes, because it was a response to loaded questions about how an encyclopaedia article on Heidegger might run. What is interesting is less the choice of names – Bultmann had mentioned most in the original letter – than those left out: notably, *contra* Kisiel, Nietzsche.[60] In *Being and Time* it is notable that there are minimal references to Nietzsche. Compared to Kant and Aristotle, who both receive over thirty direct references, Nietzsche is only referred to three times, and only one of these references is of any substance.[61] Not mentioned at all is Hölderlin.[62]

Yet not only does Heidegger turn to Nietzsche and Hölderlin in such detail – six courses on the thinker, three courses on the poet, and one entitled *Thinking and Poeticising* – but most of the thinkers seemingly so influential in the years leading up to *Being and Time* are rarely discussed after it. After the summer semester 1931 Aristotle is never the subject of a course again, there is only one course on Kant, there are no more courses on religion, and Heidegger rarely describes himself as a phenomenologist.[63] Instead the principal thinkers Heidegger discusses – other than Nietzsche and Hölderlin – are the pre-Socratics Anaximander, Parmenides and Heraclitus; and the German Idealists, particularly Schelling. In terms of the themes so far discussed, it is only when Heidegger devotes several years to reading, thinking and writing about Nietzsche and Hölderlin that his thoughts develop and clarify. Crucially the ontology is no longer universal in relation to the region of history, but is itself historicized as a historical ontology. This is a history of ontology and an ontological history rather than an ontology of history. Historicizing his own Kantian impulses, effectively following Nietzsche, Heidegger becomes a historical ontologist. Like the attempted shift from the essence of truth to the truth of essence (GA9, 96–7), this move in the sense of the genitive is the true meaning of the *Kehre*, the *hinge* between the published *Being and Time* and the promised four divisions, from being and time to time and being, from the analytic of Dasein to the de-struction [*Destruktion*] of the tradition (see PIA 17–18). But in the 1930s this de-struction of the tradition is no longer pursued with temporality as the clue – which implicitly allowed the predominance of time over space – but *historically*, which allows for a fundamental rethinking of the time/space, or time/*place*, relation.[64]

CHAPTER 2

In the Shadow of Nazism: Reading Hölderlin and Nietzsche

EINFÜHRUNG: *INTRODUCTION*

The 1930s are the years when Heidegger's life and thought are most radically altered. They see his turn [*Kehre*] around from the published *Being and Time*;[1] the beginning of his lengthy encounters with Nietzsche and the poet Hölderlin; several important lecture courses and texts – some of which have only been recently published – and, certainly not least, his involvement with the Nazi movement. Heidegger became Rector of Freiburg University in April 1933 and resigned in early 1934. The facts of his tenure are now relatively well known (he himself called it his 'greatest act of stupidity' [*die grösste Dummheit*]),[2] and in the last few years have occasioned a number of articles and books detailing the case against him.[3] The 'Heidegger controversy' has sometimes been used as a way of avoiding the difficult and important task of engaging with Heidegger. This is not to absolve Heidegger from blame, nor to suggest that his thought and his practice are sufficiently divorced that we can condemn the man and applaud his writings; far from it. As Janicaud suggests, to maintain our previous faith and admiration, on the one hand, or to dismiss Heidegger out of hand are false options. What must be done is to examine how the political intrudes in the thought.[4]

For the purpose here, it is most important to see how Heidegger's political thought relates to his ideas of history, and centrally, space. It has been suggested in the previous chapter that Heidegger's attitude to space in *Being and Time* undergoes a fundamental change in his later thought. In situating that change it must be ascertained whether the change is in tandem with his political thought, entirely divorced from it, or a reaction to it. The place I choose to begin is the 1935 lecture course *An Introduction to Metaphysics*, published in 1953. Not only was this the first lecture course from this time to appear, but Heidegger also stresses its importance in the preface to the seventh edition of *Being and Time* (again, 1953), which was the first to drop the designation 'First Half'. Heidegger suggests the basic problematic for him remains, even though the first half would have to be re-presented were the second now to follow. However, he refers the reader to *An Introduction to Metaphysics*, which provides an elucidation of the question of being. Its importance is clear.

Three initial themes present themselves for consideration within this course: Heidegger's reaction to the use and abuse of Nietzsche at the time of the lectures, and to Nazi philosophy as a whole; the importance of the historical to the study of being, and not merely as a part within it; and the increasing importance of early Greek thought, with the implications this has for the understanding of space. I shall briefly sketch out the issues involved in each of these, before moving on to the central task of the chapter, Heidegger's readings of Hölderlin and Nietzsche.

It is within this course that Heidegger first starts to engage with Nietzsche's thought at length. Heidegger was at this time following a common trend, as the philosopher of the 'superman' and the will to power appeared, on a cursory reading, to lend himself ideally to the National Socialist movement.[5] Heidegger was desperately keen to avoid being seen as part of the same trend. Indeed as shall be seen, he would later claim that his work on Nietzsche was a confrontation with Nazism. Nietzsche was, for Heidegger, able to withstand the pressures of poor interpretation:

> Even now [in 1935] this philosophy holds its ground against all the crude importunities of the scribblers who cluster round him more numerous with each passing day. And so far there seems to be no end in sight to this abuse of Nietzsche's work. In speaking here of Nietzsche, we mean to have nothing to do with all that . . . (GA40, 39; IM 36; see GA43, 276)

This was written barely a year after Heidegger's attempt *den Führer zu führen* – to lead the leader, to head the philosophical movement heading National Socialism – had collapsed with his resignation as Rector.[6] We are surely not mistaken if we note the German title of this course – *Einführung in die Metaphysik* – certainly a leading into metaphysics, but is it a leading *from* National Socialism or *to* its true heart?[7]

Heidegger's own answer would appear to lie in the words that he speaks towards the end of the lecture course:

> The works that are being peddled about nowadays as the philosophy of National Socialism but have nothing whatever to do with the inner truth and greatness of this movement (namely the encounter between global

technology and modern humans) – have all been written by men fishing in the troubled waters of 'values' and 'totalities'. (GA40, 208; IM 199)

It would seem that Heidegger is claiming that Nazi philosophy is not merely flawed, but has gone away from the true core of what, he believes, the movement should be about. Perhaps this is merely Heidegger's *Angst* at losing out in the battle for intellectual supremacy, or perhaps he genuinely believed that a movement was needed that would confront the problems and possibilities of the 'encounter between global technology and modern humans'. To claim that the remainder of Heidegger's work is an examination of this encounter would be an accurate description. On the other hand, this quotation is seized upon by some commentators because, if we follow Heidegger's note (GA40, XI; IM xi), we see that 'matter in parentheses was written while I was reworking the text'. It is only *later* (and not in 1935) that Heidegger clarifies what he means or, to put it less kindly, explains an incriminating remark.[8] If one thing counts more against Heidegger than his actions 1933–4, it is his lies, evasions and reworkings of his own history after that date.

In *An Introduction to Metaphysics* there is the first clearly evident use of the historical approach I have argued is implicit in *Being and Time*. Whereas, there, history was a structure of Dasein, one that could be examined ontologically, now the question of being is itself historicized, becoming the *history* of being, or a historical ontology. National Socialism has proved to be not the solution to the problems facing humans but rather their culmination. The problematic of nihilism 'manifests itself with increasing clarity under the political form of fascism' (HC 65; see GA6.2, 33n). How did this happen? As Heidegger states, 'we maintain that this preliminary question [about being] and with it the fundamental question of metaphysics are historical questions through and through' (GA40, 46; IM 43).[9] He then suggests that even the human's relation to history is itself historical: an example of the historicizing of the (in *Being and Time*) ahistorical structures of Dasein. With his regular references to the etymology of key terms, the historical references to the Greek beginnings, and the more oblique allusions to tracing a path of thought, Heidegger allows this historicizing to pervade this and practically all future work. Once again there is a reference to the concurrent nature of the dimensions of time, joining together in the study of history: 'History as happening [*Geschichte als Geschehen*] is an acting and being acted upon which pass through the *present*, which are determined from out of the future, and which take over the past' (GA40, 48; IM 44). The importance of the historical for Heidegger's purpose is shown when he sets out his aim of the present study: '1. The determination of the essence of the human is *never* an answer but essentially a question . . .

2. The asking of this question is historical in the fundamental sense that this questioning first creates history' (GA40, 149–52; IM 140–3).[10]

In *Being and Time* Heidegger argues for the importance of presence. In this later work he sets up an opposition between being as presence and being as substance. The former is, he argues, the correct understanding of the Greek παρουσία, which is usually translated as the latter. The German word for presence, *An-wesen*, 'also designates an estate or homestead' (GA40, 65; IM 61).[11] What we have here is another break with the Cartesian and indeed the modern tradition. Heidegger consistently argues that the translation of Greek thought into Latin has had serious consequences for the understanding of what the ancients intended (for example GA40, 15–16; IM 13; GA5, 13; BW, 149; VA 50ff; QCT 165ff; GA5, 303; EGT 19).[12] Most European languages are, because of their descent from Latin, inextricably linked to this misunderstanding, which has coloured the entirety of modern philosophy. German, because it has non-Latinate resources, is however perhaps able to avoid the problems that other languages fall into: Heidegger believes it to be, along with the Greek, 'at once the most powerful and spiritual of all languages' (GA40, 61; IM 57). We can see this in a number of places in Heidegger's work: the distinction between *Geschichte* and *Historie*, or between *Zeitlichkeit* and *Temporalität*. Heidegger even argues that 'in the Greek language what is said *is* at the same time in an excellent way what it is called', alone among languages it is λόγος (WP, 44/5; GA5, 313; EGT 28). Throughout much of his later work, Heidegger will go back to original texts, often dispensing with accepted translations, seeking to think back to the Greek terms and to provide more fundamental renditions.

There are two interesting discussions related to this point in *An Introduction to Metaphysics*. In the first, Heidegger argues, through an examination of Plato's *Timaeus*, that there has been a fundamental shift in notions of spatial location and place. Heidegger begins by suggesting that

> the Greeks had no word for 'space'. This is no accident; for they experienced the spatial on the basis not of extension but of place [*Ort*] (τόπος);[13] they experienced it as χώρα, which signifies neither place nor space but that which is occupied by what stands there. (GA40, 71; IM 66)[14]

The whole Cartesian approach to space is founded upon this notion of bodies extended in space, but Heidegger here suggests that this concept was not found in early Greek thought: rather there was a conception of space that is far closer to the notions Heidegger suggested in *Being and Time*. The Greek understanding of place is far closer to experiential than mathematical. Heidegger goes on to suggest that the shift from τόπος and χώρα to a 'space' [*Raum*] defined by extension was initiated by Platonic philosophy because of its interpretation of being as ἰδέα (GA40, 71; IM 66; see GA55, 335–6; WHD 174; WCT 227).[15]

The second important discussion of place occurs later, this time in an analysis of Sophocles' *Antigone*. Heidegger focuses particularly on line 370, 'ὑψίπολις ἄπολις', a line that hinges on the Greek word πόλις, which is translated in a standard English version as 'city'.[16] Heidegger suggests that this does not capture the full meaning: 'Πόλις means, rather, the site [*die Stätte*], the there [*Da*], wherein and as which historical Da-sein is. The πόλις is the historical site [*Geschichtsstätte*], the there *in* which, *out of* which, and *for which* history happens [*Geschichte geschieht*]' (GA40, 161; IM 151–2). These brief remarks are greatly developed in courses on Hölderlin and Parmenides, and are discussed at length in Chapter Three.

This brief outline of this lecture course has therefore introduced us to, and led us into, several themes that will be important in our understanding of Heidegger's later work. It has especially highlighted four important things: Heidegger's disenchantment with Nazism; his wish to save Nietzsche from his interpretation at the hands of this movement, in order to prepare the ground for his own reading of him; his growing understanding of the importance of the historical approach he had developed for understanding Dasein's historicity to his actual project; and a return to early Greek thought in order to see how and where things and ideas have changed. It is in this Greek thought that Heidegger finds much that supports the way he wishes to go forward. For my purposes this is especially true concerning place/space, and this important notion of 'historical site'. He is not alone in this. Two fundamentally important figures paved the way. As Heidegger himself says, Nietzsche 'understood the great time of the beginning of the entire Greek Dasein in a way that was surpassed only by Hölderlin' (GA40, 135; IM 126; see GA45, 125–6).

I: HÖLDERLIN

In Heidegger's lifetime, the principal outlet for his reading of Hölderlin was the book *Commentaries [Erläuterungen] on Hölderlin's Poetry*, which was continually updated to include new pieces on the poet. Other essays appeared in the collections *Holzwege*, *Vorträge und Aufsätze*, and *Unterwegs zur Sprache*. Heidegger also delivered three courses on Hölderlin at the University of Freiburg which have appeared in the *Gesamtausgabe* posthumously. The first, given in the Winter Semester of 1934–5 was dedicated to the hymns 'Germania' and 'The Rhine'; the second, given in the Winter Semester of 1941–2, looked at the 'Remembrance' hymn; and the final course, given in the Summer Semester of 1942, examined 'The Ister' hymn and Sophocles' *Antigone*.

A number of important aspects of Heidegger's work become much clearer in the light of this reading, though the emphasis here is largely on the issue of space, or rather place.[17] Heidegger describes his *Commentaries* as having their place in the dialogue between thought [*Denken*] and poetry [*Dichten*] (GA4, 7). As is evident from his later work, he sees thought and poetry, thinkers and poets, as having a close and special relationship. Though Heidegger discusses other poets – George, Rilke, Trakl, Hebel – Hölderlin is the only one he treats at such length, and the one in which he certainly takes the most interest.[18]

It would be amiss to neglect the political context of these lectures. *Hölderlin's Hymns 'Germania' and 'The Rhine'* is one of the first courses delivered after the resignation from the Rectorship. All of the Hölderlin lectures post-date the explicit political career, but they are all written by a card-carrying Nazi, as he remained in the Party until 1945. Various links become evident. The visit to Karl Löwith in Italy in 1936 was to deliver the lecture 'Hölderlin and the Essence of Poetry', found in *Commentaries*, and criticized in the Hitler Youth magazine *Wille und Macht* (*Will and Power*).[19] As Löwith remarked to Karl Jaspers, 'what the essential nature of this poetry has to do with the swastika is hard to see'. It seems that Löwith felt there was nothing in common, but on this trip Heidegger famously wore a swastika badge.[20] We should also note that the publication of the first edition of *Commentaries* came on the heels of the publication of a Nazi edition of Hölderlin for the troops on the front. Similarly Heidegger's final lecture as full professor in 1945 – before his ban from teaching under the Denazification laws – was on Hölderlin.[21] Remarks in the lectures on Hölderlin regularly mention the wider political events in Germany and the world. In these texts we must hear the distant roar of battle; we are forced to confront the political in the thought.

THE GERMANIA AND RHINE HYMNS

Heidegger's first course looks at the hymn 'Germania', and, in its second half, 'The Rhine', one of Hölderlin's many hymns to rivers. Though Heidegger considers Hölderlin's poetry, he does not simply see him as a poet. Indeed he suggests that he 'is one of our greatest, one of the most rich prospects as *thinker*, because he is our greatest *poet*' (GA39, 6). The engagement with the poetry opens up many avenues of thought. Right from the beginning of the course it is clear that Heidegger sees in Hölderlin an understanding of being that avoids many of the modern pitfalls:

One considers Hölderlin 'historiographically' and one is unaware of what is essential, the fact that his work – which has not yet found its time-space – has already overcome our historiographical fuss [*historisches Getue*] and has founded the beginning of an-other history [*Geschichte*], that history which starts with the struggle [*Kampf*] deciding the arrival or flight of the gods. (GA39, 1)

This is, of course, the distinction suggested in *Being and Time* between history [*Geschichte*] and historiography [*Historie*], parallel to that between experiential and clock-time. This is regularly emphasized in Heidegger's reading of Hölderlin. Heidegger argues that the standard understandings of time are totally insufficient for mastering the poetically thought experience of time in Hölderlin (GA39, 55ff). Such a critique is made clearer in the 1939 lecture on the poem 'As on a holiday . . .' Here, Heidegger focuses on the first line of the third strophe – 'But now day breaks! [*Jetzt aber tagts!*]'. He suggests that the 'Now' is clearly Hölderlin's time, but that it needs to be understood in a different way to standard understandings of time: 'Such a time can never be dated, and is never measurable in numbers of years or the division of centuries'. This time is historical not historiographical (GA4, 75–6).[22]

'Germania' is a hymn to the German homeland – Heidegger's discussion therefore also looks at the spatial aspects of the poetry. Here too he finds the problem of relying on the modern understanding, in this case geography: 'the earth of the homeland is not simply a space delimited by exterior frontiers, a natural region, a locality [*Örtlichkeit*] destined to be a scene for this and that to take place. The earth which is the homeland is readied for the gods' (GA39, 104). Later Heidegger warns against allowing this space to be thought of as a storeroom [*Abstellraum*] (GA39, 108). What Heidegger is suggesting is that Hölderlin's poetry, and his conception of historical time and of the homeland are more poetic, more experiential, than those of modern metaphysics. This can be designated the lived: 'The poet moulds something . . . which is "lived" [*erlebt*] in his interior and exterior world, a so-called "Experience" [*Erlebnis*]' (GA39, 26).[23]

However, the attitude of *Being and Time* remains, as the passages on space are relatively rare, and the spatial characteristics of the homeland are not considered as important as the passages on historical fate [*Geschick*]. Time and space need to be regarded differently, and there is a linking of these two characteristics – 'neither place spatially [*Ort räumlich*] nor time temporally [*Zeit zeitlich*] understood in the habitual sense' (GA39, 141) – but the hierarchical ranking still remains. Indeed, at one point Heidegger shows that he has not departed from the attitude of *Being and Time*, citing §§65ff as his exposure of the essential constitution of originary temporality (GA39, 109).

Such an attitude is, to an extent, amended in the second part of the course.[24] To make the transition, Heidegger asks what Hölderlin means by the 'waters of my homeland' in line four of the 'Germania' hymn. He suggests that ordinary poets sing of forests and meadows, streams and shrubs, mountains and sky. Why then does Hölderlin's late poetry speak so often of rivers – 'At the source of the Danube', 'The Rhine', 'The Ister', and so forth?[25] These poems, suggests Heidegger, have an intimate relationship with the 'Germania' hymn (GA39, 90–1). It is for this reason that this course moves from a consideration of the 'Germania' hymn to 'The Rhine'. The first is the general topic, the second a particular aspect of it (GA39, 137–8). This leaves us in no doubt that the later lectures on 'The Ister' also fall within this general project.

In the first part of the course Heidegger had quoted a couple of lines from Hölderlin, lines he would continue to quote throughout his entire engagement with the poet. The lines come from a poem known by its first line, 'In lovely blueness . . .'

Full of acquirements, but poetically, the human dwells on this earth.[26]

These lines pinpoint the entire project at stake here. Heidegger suggests that the opening words mean that 'what the human works at and pursues, is through their own endeavours earned and deserved'. The line hinges on the next word:

> But – says Hölderlin in sharp contrast – none of this touches the essence of their dwelling on the earth, all this does not reach the foundation of human existence. The latter is fundamentally 'poetic' . . . To 'dwell poetically' means to stand in the presence of the gods and to be involved in the nearness of the essence of things. (GA4, 42)

Therefore, as Bernstein has noted, in Hölderlin Heidegger finds 'a contrast between a dwelling place and an abstract space'.[27] Space is characterized as Cartesian; place as experiential, lived: it is to be understood *poetically*.

In 'The Rhine' hymn, Heidegger immediately notices that the first strophe of the poem indicates a place, rather than a time (GA39, 167–8). This seems to prefigure an increased stress on the spatial, or rather the *platial*. In these works Heidegger tends to use the word *Ort* and its compounds *örtlich*, *Ortschaft* and *Örtlichkeit*. *Ort* had been relatively rarely used in *Being and Time*, where *Raum* (space) and *Platz* (place) had been used instead. In the lectures on Hölderlin, and earlier on Plato's *Sophist*, Heidegger designates 'space' as conforming to Cartesian notions, and replaces it with a more originary understanding of 'place'.[28] In *Being and Time*, as noted in the previous chapter, the remarks on place were largely confined to the place of equipment, for which the word *Platz* is appropriate; when the discussion has moved on to the place of humans, the word *Ort* is used. *Ort* was seen as '*constitutive of the presence of the being*' (GA19,

106). *Ort* can be variously translated as 'place' or 'locale'; its compounds usually as 'local' or 'locality'. There is something to be said for working with 'place' and 'placing', coining the neologism 'platial' to reflect its use in adjectival forms. This is perhaps particularly apt given the Latin roots of 'local', but the Greek roots of 'place'. Local also gives rise to the misunderstanding that the term is about scale.

The rivers in Hölderlin's poems do not simply have their own place, but also make the places around them. We must not think of the rivers as symbols or images for something else, 'they are themselves in question, and with them the earth of the homeland [*die heimatliche Erde*]' (GA39, 195). This shows the link between 'Germania' and the river poetry. In Heidegger's reading of Hölderlin, 'the river . . . founds the country [*das Land*] as a country, the homeland for the people' (GA39, 259). The links between the founding power of the river, the spatial characteristics it delivers and the notion of poetic dwelling are well illustrated in the following passage:

> The river now founds in the country a characterised space [*geprägten Raum*] and a delimited place [*Ort*] of settlement, of communication, [giving] to the people a developable country which guarantees their immediate Dasein. The river [*Der Strom*] is not a watercourse [*ein Gewässer*] which passes by the place of humans, it is its streaming [*Strömen*], as country-developing [*als landbildendes*], which founds the possibility of establishing the dwelling of humans. (GA39, 264)

It was seen in the earlier part of the course that Heidegger found problems with the standard modern understandings of time and space. In the second part of the course, and in a later essay, he elaborates this in more detail. It is well known that Heidegger felt that the pre-Socratics had understood being in a more fundamental way, and he sees Nietzsche and Hölderlin as being two thinkers who paved the way for this recognition (see GA40, 135; IM 126; and GA39, 269). A particular example of this affinity comes when Heidegger discusses Hölderlin's use of the word 'nature' [*Natur*]. Both English and German come from the Latin *natura*, which is in Greek φύσις. Heidegger suggests that the translation of φύσις by *natura* immediately transfers in later elements and replaces the originary meaning with something alien (GA40, 15–16; IM 13–14). 'Φύσις, φύειν signifies growth [*Wachstum*] . . . Hölderlin's word 'nature' poetises its essence from the basis of the truth reserved for the initial word: φύσις . . . In the word 'nature', Hölderlin poetises the other . . .' (GA4, 56–7).[29]

In this criticism of the modern view of nature, Heidegger is laying the foundation for his later questioning of modern technology. He suggests that because the 'metaphysical sense of nature, *natura*, φύσις, in the originary nominative force of the word, is already an essential interpretation of being, it has little to do with the sciences of nature' (GA39, 195). This is an example of how his later thought recognizes the historical aspects of the question of being. Rather than the attitude of *Being and Time*, which tended to set universal conditions, the later works realize that this is a historical problem. We must therefore leave behind the standard representations of nature: 'Earth and homeland are understood in a historical sense. The river is historic' (GA39, 196).

It must be remembered that this is a course delivered only a few months after Heidegger had resigned as Rector. Throughout the course there is a stress on the national character and words that cannot fail to carry political overtones in mid 1930s Germany – people [*Volk*], homeland, soil [*Boden*], earth. That said, towards the end of the course he criticizes the 'contemporary snivelling about national character, blood and soil' (GA39, 254).[30] The tension in the course is illustrated in the conclusion to a 1939 lecture: 'Hölderlin's word calls the Holy and also names a unique time-space [*Zeit-Raum*] . . . This word, is, however, still unheard, and is stored in the Western German language' (GA4, 77). Here we have a statement both of the philosophical project – the possibility of a different understanding of time and space – and of its potential political overtones – the uniqueness of the German. If the Rectorship address was a politicizing of the philosophy of *Being and Time*, in these lectures we find a philosophizing of the Rectorship's politics. In particular, Dasein is now taken to refer to a *Volk*, rather than an individual (GA39, 8; see SDU; HC).

Heidegger cannot have failed to realize that the political situation he was lecturing within – even without his own political involvement – charged the language he used. For someone so attentive to the use of particular words it defies belief that he was not aware of this. His remembrance of Norbert von Hellingrath, editor of Hölderlin's works, who fell at the age of 28 at Verdun in 1916 (GA39, 9) has noticeable echoes of the praise of the war dead found in mainstream Nazi discourse.[31] His evocation of Hölderlin as 'the poet of the poet and of poetry' and 'the poet of the Germans' (GA39, 214), even when he suggests that the latter should be understood 'not as subjective genitive, but as objective genitive: the poet who has poetised the Germans' (GA39, 220),[32] is understood as a political project: to make Hölderlin a 'power in the history of our people [*die Macht in der Geschichte unseres Volkes*]' (GA39, 214). In the discussion of the 'Germania' hymn poet and thinker are joined by State-Creator as the three creative forms of the historical Dasein of a people (GA39, 51; 144).[33] These cannot fail to stress the nationalist and political overtones of the course.

However uncomfortable Heidegger's nationalism is, he does engage in criticism of the uses to which it is being put in contemporary interpretations of Hölderlin. Hölderlin himself was made, like Nietzsche, part of the mythologized pantheon of Nazism. In his work was found elements of the leadership principle, division of the German race from others, the notion of the hero and recurrent references to the fatherland. Heidegger is critical of this partial interpretation (GA45, 126). As Megill notes, Heidegger's 'attachment was not to the mighty fatherland but to the more intimate and personal native region, not to the *Vaterland*, but the *Heimat* [home, homeland]. Instead he emphasizes the notion of Hölderlin as seer and prophet'.[34] Heidegger suggests that the 'patriotic' element [*das Vaterländische*] is that which is emphasized, but argues that this is one strand [*Inhalt*] among others, and that the praise of Greece and the apparent censure of the German could equally be emphasized (GA39, 224). He is unequivocal in his critique of the racist, biologizing aspects attached to contemporary German nationalism. Heidegger's nationalism is cultural and linguistic, praising the landscape of the Black Forest and the poetry of Hölderlin; it is not the same as the race-based nationalism of Alfred Rosenberg. This trades on Heidegger's important lectures on biology in 1929/30, published as *The Basic Concepts of Metaphysics*. This lecture course shows that accusations of vitalism, biologism and scientific racism cannot be applied to Heidegger. In the Hölderlin course, Heidegger quotes Kolbenheyer's 1932 pronouncement that 'poetry is a necessary biological function of the people',[35] and sarcastically remarks that 'the same observation is as true for digestion: that too is a necessary biological function' (GA39, 27).[36]

Heidegger's failure as Rector seems to be attributed not to an error of his judgement, but to a failure on the part of the movement as a whole. Heidegger sees his Hölderlin and Nietzsche lectures as a 'confrontation with National Socialism'.[37] It is worth making two remarks on this. First, the word Heidegger uses for confrontation is *Auseinandersetzung*, which is literally *Aus-einander-setzung*, a setting apart from one another.[38] Second, the decisive political situation still exists, yet Heidegger thinks the movement misguided as to its true aims: the reassertion of the national and cultural aspects; the confrontation with global technology (GA40, 208; IM 199). Heidegger's letter to the Academic Rectorate of Albert-Ludwig University is useful here:

> I thought that Hitler, after taking responsibility in 1933 for the whole people, would venture to extricate himself from the Party and its doctrine . . . This conviction was an error that I recognised from the events of 30 June 1934 [the Night of the Long Knives]. I, of course, had intervened in 1933 to say yes to the national and the social . . . the social and the national, as I saw them, were not essentially tied to a biologist and racist ideology.[39]

Heidegger however, ends this course with a dangerously prophetic call to arms: 'The hour of our history has struck' (GA39, 294).[40]

THE ISTER HYMN

It was to be six years before Heidegger returned to lecturing on Hölderlin. But, as we have seen, he wrote a number of shorter essays, some of which were published in the intervening years. Other courses, notably *An Introduction to Metaphysics*, and the Nietzsche courses discussed in the next section, furthered the overall project at stake here: more so than the second course on the poet, which discussed the 'Remembrance' hymn (GA52). The third course, however, both broadens and deepens the understanding developed in the first. In this course Heidegger again looks at a 'river hymn', one that Hölderlin himself never published, that was given the title 'The Ister' (the Danube – *die Donau*) by von Hellingrath (GA53, 2). 'The Ister' begins with what Heidegger describes as a calling [*ein Rufen*]: 'Now come, fire!' (GA53, 5). Once again Heidegger suggests that Hölderlin's 'Now' cannot be grasped 'historiographically' and that it cannot be related to historical dates of well-known historical events: 'No calendrical date can be given for the "Now" of his poetry'. However, though the poem begins with a 'Now', in line 15 there also follows the naming of a 'Here': 'Here, however, we wish to build' (GA53, 8–9).

Before I examine the way in which the 'Now' and the 'Here' work together, which is an important element of this course, it is worth devoting a little more space to the discussion of place, an understanding that is enriched here. From both 'The Rhine' hymn, and now from 'The Ister' hymn, Heidegger suggests that we learn that 'the rivers are a distinctive and significant place [*Ort*] at which humans [*der Mensch*], though not only humans, find their dwelling place [*Wohnstatt*]' (GA53, 12). The river determines the dwelling place of humans upon the earth, but this dwelling is not to be understood as the possession of accommodation and housing. Whilst such things are indeed dwelling, they do not fulfil or ground its essence: 'Dwelling takes on an abode and is an abiding in such an abode, specifically that of humans upon this earth'. The crucial thing pertaining to the abode is its place, and the placing of the place [*die Ortschaft des Ortes*]. Therefore, 'the river "*is*" the placing that pervades the abode of humans upon the earth, determines them to where they belong and where they are homely [*heimisch*]' (GA53, 23). As Heidegger later notes, 'the river does not merely grant the place [*Ort*], in the sense of the mere place [*bloßen Platzes*], that is occupied by humans in their dwelling. The place is intrinsic to the river itself. The river itself dwells' (GA53, 41).

Heidegger suggests that Hölderlin's other poetry emphasizes the 'Now', a moment [*Augenblick*], but that in this poem 'equal intonation' is given to the 'Here'. Slightly further on he suggests that the river 'abandons the Now', by which he means not that space is prioritized over time, but that the time does not remain static, it 'passes into what is bygone, or into what lies in the future' (GA53, 16). This helps us to understand the sense of the following passage:

> The river is simultaneously vanishing and full of intimation in a double sense. What is proper to the river is thus the essential fullness of a journey. The river is a journey in a singular and consummate way. We name the consummate essence of the journey [*Wanderung*] a journeying [*Wanderschaft*], corresponding to the placing [*Ortschaft*] of the place [*Ort*]. The river is the journeying . . . Becoming homely and dwelling upon this earth are of another essence. We may approach it in giving thought to the essence of the rivers. The river is the place for dwelling. The river is the journeying of becoming homely. To put it more clearly: the river is that very place that is attained in and through the journeying. (GA53, 35–6)

What is obvious here is that not only has the prioritization of time over space been abandoned, but space and time – as placing and journeying – are understood as an 'originary unity . . . the one belongs to the other'. Journeying has resonances of space as well as time; place, in the sense of an abiding, is also temporal. In order to understand them there is a temptation to look back to the unity of space and time, understood in their modern sense. It is this temptation that Heidegger tries to avoid. The reason for this is linked to one of the major themes in the later Heidegger: the question of technology. As Heidegger suggests:

> via our calculations and machinery, we have such convincing power over its 'spaces' and 'times' that the space of our planet is shrinking and the annual seasons and years of human life are being condensed into diminutive numerical values for the purposes of our calculative planning far in advance. (GA53, 46–7)

In these terms, space is understood as coordinates – x, y, z – and if the spatial element is understood as being in motion, changing its location through time, the fourth coordinate, one-dimensional time – t – is added (GA53, 47–8; see GA65, 377–8). These coordinates, which Western philosophy, modern science and technology have used to designate the unity of time and space, allow the exploitation of the world. They are considered to be so clear that to further explain them, to question them, is looked at as a worthless pursuit. There is therefore a great temptation to reduce place and journey back to this understanding. To avoid this is Heidegger's aim (GA53, 50).

Heidegger is not yet successful in this aim, but he lays the foundation for one of the major projects of his later thought: the overcoming of metaphysics.[41] First

Heidegger questions whether time and space are objective – gigantic containers in which all positions (spatial and temporal) are accommodated. If so, he asks, *where* is space – the container? And, *when* is time – the container?

> Or is space itself to be found nowhere, and time itself not to be found at any time? So long as we continue to think space and time as appearing within a space and time, we are not yet thinking space itself or time itself.

Second, Heidegger asks if time and space are subjective. He suggests that if people fight wars over space – a comment that cannot fail to have resonance in 1942 with the talk of *Lebensraum* and the Russian campaign – space is unlikely to be something they subjectively imagine. Heidegger is therefore reluctant to see them as subjective – as constructs. Time and space are something that

> cannot be accommodated within the schema of 'either objective' – 'or subjective'. And in that case the unity of space and time cannot consist in space and time being thought together in the representational activity of the thinking subject either, as is the custom.

Therefore, resorting to space and time to understand placing and journeying does not help, as 'that which is meant to shed light here is itself obscure' (GA53, 55–6).[42]

Heidegger's conclusion is that neither time nor space in Hölderlin's hymnal poetry – which post 1799 'is not concerned with symbolic images at all' – can be understood by metaphysics, or by the metaphysical doctrine of art – aesthetics (GA53, 20–1). Why then do we turn to metaphysics at all, 'why are we even becoming involved in these representations [*Vorstellungen*] of space and time that have prevailed now for two thousand years?' The answer is that we cannot free ourselves overnight, and

> simply because only an explicit look at the commonplace representations of space and time and their metaphysical (rather than historiographical) provenance permits us initially to become attentive to that other than Hölderlin poetizes. In poetizing the rivers, Hölderlin thinks his way into the essential realm of placing and journeying. (GA53, 58)

Heidegger concedes that Hölderlin himself never speaks of placing and journeying, but suggests that it could be 'that the essential origin of space and time lies concealed in what we are attempting to think in a unitary manner in the names placing and journeying' (GA53, 58–9):

Between the spatio-temporal [*raumzeitlich*] grasping that extends toward world domination and the movement of settlement subservient to such domination on the one side, and humans coming to be at home via journeying and placing on the other, there presumably prevails a covert relation whose historical essence we do not know. (GA53, 60)

The river hymns of Hölderlin help in Heidegger's attempt to provide a non-metaphysical understanding of time-space. Time is not understood in terms of calendrical dates, it is understood as the passage, as the journeying of becoming homely. Space is not understood in terms of Cartesian coordinates, extension or, indeed, space, but in terms of locale or place. Neither of these understandings can truly be said to have overcome metaphysics, but the project certainly takes its departure from this point.

Heidegger's reading of Hölderlin therefore opens up a number of the paths in his later thought. The project of overcoming metaphysics, the questioning concerning technology, and poetic dwelling all become clearer and more developed if we follow the confrontation between thinker and poet. The later essays on technology suggest that humans are attempting to dominate, to challenge nature, partly because they have lost sight of what it means to dwell poetically. The modern understanding of time and space is fit only for world domination. To find a way to overcome metaphysics is the later Heidegger's project: to avoid the nihilism. More broadly, Heidegger's reading of Hölderlin's poetry provides us – in the concepts of journey and place – with a new understanding of temporal and spatial relations. Geography and historiography are no use for understanding these concepts: they are deaf to the other that Hölderlin poetizes. As Dominique Janicaud has noted, we need to use instead the notions of historicity and topology.[43]

II: NIETZSCHE

Heidegger's *Nietzsche* is pivotal in this book's articulation of the influence of these two figures on the work of Foucault. Nietzsche is an absent presence throughout much of Heidegger's early work, but it is only in the mid 1930s that the confrontation is drawn into the open. It is not right to suggest, as Megill does, that this confrontation is when Heidegger begins to take Nietzsche seriously,[44] but it is certainly when the seriousness becomes most evident. My reading will therefore trace a path through what Derrida has called 'the plenums and lacunas, projections and indentations, of a certain Heideggerian landscape', bearing in mind the admonition that 'the arguments of Heidegger's *grande livre* [*Nietzsche*] are much less simple than is generally admitted'.[45]

In 1961, Heidegger considered that his *Nietzsche* volumes provided a view of the path of thought that his work had taken from 1930 to the 'Letter on Humanism' (1947), whereas the *Commentaries on Hölderlins Poetry* 'shed only indirect light on that path' (GA6.1, xii; N I, xl). The previous section has shown how indirect light provides some illumination, but although several other texts have been brought into the open, *Nietzsche* remains of central importance. Heidegger also argued that these collected texts clearly showed his own divergence from Nazism:

> Beginning in 1936 I embarked on a series of courses and lectures on Nietzsche which lasted until 1945 and which represented . . . a declaration of spiritual resistance. In truth it is unjust to assimilate Nietzsche to National Socialism . . .[46]

Perhaps it should also be asked: is it unjust to assimilate *Nietzsche* to National Socialism? Several points of reference for the discussion of this question can be found in *Nietzsche*, but space precludes a full treatment of all of these. As Derrida suggests, these collected lectures and texts on Nietzsche are 'supposed to withdraw him from any biologistic, zoologistic, or vitalistic reappropriation. The strategy of interpretation is also a politics'.[47]

RETURNING TO THE AUGENBLICK

In the reading of *Being and Time* I suggested that the Nietzschean moment, *Augenblick*, was central to the fusion of the temporal, the spatial and the historical. In the *Nietzsche* lectures, particularly the second lecture course – *The Eternal Return of the Same* – Heidegger elaborates and deepens his reading substantially. His main source for the reading is the chapter in *Thus Spoke Zarathustra* entitled 'On the Vision and the Riddle'. Heidegger asks:

> what sort of vision, then, does the riddle which Zarathustra tells have? Again we must pay heed to the way he tells it, to the *where* and *when* and *to whom*, if we are to examine the *what* aright. (GA44, 40; N II, 38)

Aside from the reference to the importance of the temporal and spatial location of the saying, Heidegger has shown that the dramatic situation within the work as a whole is important. The riddle is told aboard ship, at sea, to the crew and two days into the voyage. Having set the scene, Heidegger looks at the riddle itself, where Zarathustra is climbing a mountain with a dwarf upon his shoulders:

In his narrative of the ascent two regions of an essential imagery converge – and, in fact, Nietzsche's transposition of thought into sensuous imagery always haunts these two realms: the sea and the mountain heights. (GA44, 41; N II, 39)

As Zarathustra reaches the top of the mountain path, the dwarf jumps from his shoulders, and he describes the gateway. 'With the description of the image of the gateway Zarathustra brings the riddle to vision' (GA44, 43; N II, 40).

In the chapter in *Thus Spoke Zarathustra* it is not immediately clear why the dwarf has not grasped the riddle when he says 'All that is straight lies . . . time itself is a circle.' It *appears* that he has succinctly said what at this point Zarathustra cannot. However, Heidegger convincingly argues that the usual reading of Nietzsche/Zarathustra's eternal return is close to the dwarf's understanding – too easy, and, in essential respects, wrong. To simply look at the moment, the gateway, from the outside is not to understand the fundamental issue, which can only become clear to 'one who does not remain a spectator but *is himself* the moment, performing actions directed towards the future and at the same time accepting and affirming the past' (GA44, 59; N II, 56). Heidegger suggests that if the eternal return is thought at the basic level – that 'everything turns in a circle' then it is perhaps sheer delusion: but that this is not Nietzsche's thought. He suggests that we must think the eternal return in terms of the moment, and in terms of overcoming nihilism (GA44, 203; N II, 182–3):

Whoever stands in the moment is turned both ways: for him past and future *run up against* one another. Whoever stands in the moment lets what runs counter to itself come to collision . . . But the dwarf keeps to the outside, perches on the periphery . . . That is what is peculiar [*Eigentliche*] to, and hardest to bear in, the doctrine of the eternal return – that eternity *is* in the moment, that the moment is not the fleeting now, not an instant [*Moment*] of time whizzing by a spectator, but the collision of future and past. (GA44, 59; N II, 56–7)

It has been shown from the understanding that Heidegger gives to Nietzsche's three modes of historical inquiry, that the past, present and future should not be seen separately, but together. It can now be seen how this links to the concept of the moment. The moment, *Augenblick*, the eye-glance, is the place, the gateway, *where* these three dimensions come together. The English translation loses many of the overtones of the German word *Augenblick*. This word, a compound of *das Auge*, eye, and *der Blick*, glance, was used by Martin Luther in his translation of the Bible into German, in Paul's first letter to the Corinthians: 'we will all be changed – in a flash, in the twinkling of an eye [*Augenblick*], at the last trumpet'.[48] The usage of this word by Nietzsche lends a visual hint to the temporal that is missing in the English, but which is perhaps better preserved in the word *instant* (used in the French translation),[49] which, deriving from the Latin *instare* (to be present), has at least a distant echo of the double meaning of present, the temporal and spatial signifier. The authentic individual performs actions directed toward the future but remembers the past:

> We define the 'moment' as that time [the omission of the word 'time' in the English translation is an important slip] in which future and past affront one another, in which future and past are decisively accomplished and consummated by humans themselves, inasmuch as humans occupy the point [*Stelle*] of their collision, and *are* themselves that collision. (GA6.1, 318; N II, 98)[50]

Heidegger's reading of the eternal return is perhaps the highpoint of his lectures on Nietzsche, but he does not fully explicate the thought of *Thus Spoke Zarathustra*. It would appear that the key spatial element of this teaching is the gateway, with two faces, where two paths meet, two long lanes which no one has ever followed to the end, both stretching onwards for an eternity. The name of the gateway is inscribed above it: 'Moment'. Whilst this thought is essentially temporal,[51] the message is also couched in both dramatic and spatial terms. Dramatically, Zarathustra has struggled with the thought of the eternal return for the entire first three parts of the book, and it is only at the very end of the third, that, overcoming his nausea, he is able to speak of his love: 'For I love you, O eternity!' (Z III, 16, 1). This cry is repeated seven times, in a dramatic recapitulation of the return.

As a work as a whole, *Thus Spoke Zarathustra* is structured around a spatial return, a circle, with the key high point being Zarathustra's cave and the mountains, and the low point being the depths of mankind in the town. The spatial return is mirrored in the metaphor of the sun, and in a dramatic restatement of dialogue. In the Prologue, Zarathustra's descent to the town follows his speech to the sun, as that morning 'he rose with the dawn' and 'stepped before the sun'. In order to talk to humans, Zarathustra must, like the sun, 'go under', set [*üntergehen*][52] (Z Prologue, 1). Zarathustra then goes down to the forest, and from there to the town. At the dead of night he leaves the town, returns to a forest, and then sleeps under a tree until 'not only dawn passed over his face but the morning too' (Z Prologue, 9). The Prologue ends with Zarathustra declaring his goal as 'the sun stood at high noon', at which point he sees his animals from the mountains overhead. Then Zarathustra again begins to 'go under'. At the end of the first part, Zarathustra returns to the mountains himself, speaking to his followers of 'the great noon when the human stands in the middle of the way between beast and *Übermensch* and celebrates their way to the evening at his highest hope: for it is the way to a new morning' (Z I, 22, 3). What we have here is a *spatial* return – mountains, forest, town, forest, mountains – paralleled by the rising, setting and rising to high noon of the sun. Finally, Zarathustra, setting like the sun, goes down to humans once again.

A similar, yet larger, spatial return takes place in the book as a whole, specifically in the second and third parts. At the beginning of the second part Zarathustra is back in his cave, withdrawn from humans, 'like a sower who has scattered his seed'. He stays here, we are told, for several months and years, before he tells his animals that his 'impatient love overflows in rivers, downward towards sunrise and sunset. From silent mountains and thunderstorms of suffering my soul rushes into valleys' (Z II, 1). Zarathustra is then absent from his cave and mountains for the whole of the second part of the book towards the end of this part he realizes he must return, but as he is a long way from home, having dwelt in the blessed isles, he spends most of the third part undertaking this journey. Zarathustra returns from the blessed isles to the mainland, but does not proceed directly back to his mountains and cave, but takes a winding and circuitous path, encountering various people, an indirect route for which he realizes the end, likening himself to a 'river that flows, winding and twisting, back to its source [*Quelle*]!' (Z III, 5). It would appear that Zarathustra realizes this spatial return before he can cope with the thought of the eternal return. This return is completed in the chapter actually entitled 'The Return Home'. It is after this spatial return, and his overcoming of the nausea, that Zarathustra declares his love for eternity.

The fourth part again shows a similar return, as Zarathustra descends from his cave and meets various people, who then gather at his cave waiting for him to join them. The final chapter, 'The Sign', is both a recapitulation of the theme of the Fourth Part, Zarathustra's struggle with pity, and as a restatement of key themes from earlier neatly serves to tie up the work as a whole. Zarathustra is back in the mountains, and leaves his cave, 'glowing and strong as a morning sun that comes out of dark mountains'. He then speaks to the sun 'as he had said once before', in the Prologue. Thus the chapter returns both to the Prologue, and in its final lines returns to its own start, as Zarathustra once more leaves his cave, 'glowing and strong as a morning sun that comes out of dark mountains' (Z IV, 20).

The eternal return is clearly, and importantly, spatial. Its importance is found in the spatial return of the book as a whole and in the movement of the sun. Heidegger wholly neglects the first of these, though he does recognize something of the symbolism of the eternal return:

> The eagle soars in vast circles in the air. The circling is an image of eternal return . . . The serpent hangs suspended from the eagle, coiled around his throat. Again, the coils of the serpent, wound in rings about the eagle's throat, are symbolic of the ring of eternal return. Moreover, the serpent winds itself about the one who wends his way in great circles in the sky – a proprietary and essential, yet for us still obscure, tangle of coils . . . circling in a ring, coiling in a circle. (GA44, 48; N II, 46)

However, Heidegger does show an awareness of the importance of the sun. At one point he quotes Nietzsche: 'In every ring of human existence in general there is always an hour when the mightiest thought emerges . . . the thought of the eternal return of all things. It is each time, the hour of *midday* for humanity', and then adds his own commentary:

> We know what Nietzsche means by this word *midday*: the moment of the shortest shadow, when fore-noon and after-noon, past and future, meet in one. Their meeting-place is the moment of supreme unity for all temporal things in utterly magnificent transfiguration . . . it is the moment of eternity. (GA44, 149; N II, 139–40)

Heidegger later notes how the second part of Nietzsche's riddle, that of the howling dog, takes place at midnight – 'the most remote time from midday . . . it is the full moon that is shining here; it too is a light, but a merely borrowed light, the most pallid reflection of actual illumination, a diaphanous ghost of light' (GA44, 197; N II, 177).

There is more in Nietzsche than this, but equally there is more in Heidegger. It is instructive to return to an earlier passage from the course, this time reading the lecture manuscript rather than the version published by Heidegger.

> The eternity of return, hence the time of return, and thus return itself, can be grasped solely in terms of the 'moment'. We define by this that time [*damit jene Zeit*] in which future and past affront one another, in which future and past are decisively accomplished and consummated by humans themselves, inasmuch as humans occupy the point [*Stelle*] of their collision, and *are* themselves that (Da-*sein*). (GA44, 103)

There are two important points that arise. In the 1961 version there is a paragraph break between 'moment' and its definition. Beginning the definition is the word 'moment' again (GA6.1, 318; N II, 98). However, in the manuscript there is no break and the sentence begins as I have translated it above. Second, the 1961 edition omits the bracketed Da-*sein*. It is worth juxtaposing these with the continuation of Heidegger's discussion of midday:

> In the word *midday* the propriation [*Ereignis*] of the thought of eternal return within the eternal return of the same is determined in its temporality – as a point of time, but one no clock can measure, as it is a point in being as a whole when time itself *is* as the temporality of the moment. (GA44, 149; N II, 139–40)

The importance of these two changes and the introduction of *Ereignis* is twofold. First we see that here Heidegger has brought the thinking of time into the moment. Time, far from being calculated on a clock, is the moment future and past collide in the present, as the temporality of the moment. Second, the human in the point of this collision *is* its collision, the point of its collision, as Da-*sein*, *being*-that-there, being the moment, being as presence. The human in, *as*, the point of collision is simultaneously future and past in the present. But they are not solely temporal, they are also situated. Likewise, history too must orientate itself toward the future with reference to the past, by becoming, just as the *Augenblick* is the authentic present, *a history of the present*. This history, of the present as presence, is also situated. This is what will be meant by the *mapping* of the present.

SPACE AND THE BODY

Though there are moments of insight such as those outlined above, at other points Heidegger seems to neglect the importance of space within Nietzsche's work. The articulation of space in Nietzsche is unsystematic, but a detailed reading of his work provides many useful insights. For example, in *The Gay Science*, Nietzsche argues that we have built an imaginary world of 'lines, planes, bodies, atoms, divisible time spans, divisible spaces', in order that we can exist in this world built around our image, around how we perceive things (FW 112; see FW 121; WM 487). Tested consistently, says Nietzsche, these perceptions are logically false (MAM 18), and in places, especially in his notes (see WM 515; 516; 530; 553ff), he begins to pick apart the notions behind these constructs. However, sketchy though these notes are, they provide the foundation for some interesting analyses.

Some of the most pertinent of these relate to architecture. Nietzsche feels that we 'no longer understand architecture', and are missing the insights into it that we used to have: 'everything in a Greek or Christian building originally signified something, and indeed something of a higher order of things: this feeling of inexhaustible significance lay about the building like a magical veil' (MAM 218). Reading buildings provides a valuable understanding of our 'cultural architecture' (MAM 276; see also UB II, 3), and indeed Nietzsche sees that

> the architect has always been under the spell of power. His buildings are supposed to render pride visible, and the victory over gravity, the will to power. Architecture is a kind of eloquence of power in forms – now persuading, even flattering, now only commanding. The highest feeling of power and sureness finds expression in a *grand style*. (GD 9, 11)

Like so much else in a Nietzschean analysis, architecture is an exhibition of a will to power at work. Understanding the power relations behind a building – the construction and use of space – can provide useful observations about the culture it is situated within.

The most sustained example of an analysis of the spatial properties of architecture is found in *The Birth of Tragedy*, when Nietzsche provides an insightful reading of the Greek theatre.[53] Nietzsche argues that the 'public of spectators as we know it was unknown to the Greeks', rather than the division into boxes or levels of seats of more contemporary theatres, there was a terraced structure of concentric arcs, without hierarchical division. This seating area, known as the *theatron* (seeing place) was sometimes cut into the side of a hill – like 'a lonely valley in the mountains' – cutting out outside distractions and focusing attention on the *orchestra* (dancing place) – 'at bottom there was no opposition between public and chorus'. This structure made it possible for the public to 'overlook [*Übersehen*]' the spectacle, in both senses of the word – to survey, and to be oblivious to the outside world.[54] 'The architecture of the scene [the backdrop]' was a 'splendid frame' in which the action was revealed. Such an arrangement made the 'men of culture' in the audience much closer – physically, culturally and psychologically – to the symbolism of the performance, and is part of the entire Greek attitude to tragedy and life (GT 8).

Nietzsche's attitudes to the theatre are anticipated somewhat by Wagner's expectations of the 'artwork of the future', where he expects the public to forget 'the confines of the auditorium', so that it 'lives and breathes now only in the artwork which seems to it life itself'.[55] Wagner's Bayreuth project, which built a theatre around a Greek design, was, in its initial stages, the subject of praise from Nietzsche (see UB IV, 9), but the actual Bayreuth festival, where the famous Ring cycle was performed for the first time complete, singularly failed to live up to expectations. However, the Bayreuth theatre is regularly described as having the best acoustics in the world,[56] and other spatial/architectural features of the building are also praised. One famous example is the hidden orchestra – no visual distraction, and no orchestra pit to distance the audience from the dramatic action – but it also makes it impossible to *locate* the source of the sound.[57] Clearly, the use of space, both in Athens and Bayreuth, had social consequences and, most evidently in the latter case, exhibited the signs of a will to power at work.

Religious buildings are also open to such an analysis, and Nietzsche talks of 'enclosed domains to which divine right denied entry except under certain conditions: in the first instance these were simply areas of ground, inasmuch as certain places were not to be stepped upon by the feet of the uninitiated, who were seized with fear and trembling when they approached them'. This exclusion is then extended by religion to other things, for example to sex, which becomes a 'privilege and adytum [innermost chamber of a temple, where oracles are developed] of maturity', from which 'the gaze of youth must for its own advantage be directed away'. In this passage, Nietzsche links the ideas of 'shame' and 'mystery', saying that the Arabic word for chamber is 'harem', meaning both sanctuary and the forecourt of a mosque (literally forbidden place), as well as having the sexual connotations (MAM 100). There are a number of other analyses of religious spaces (see, for example, Z II, 4; A 17, 21; MAM 130).

However, despite Heidegger's neglect of passages such as these, within *Nietzsche* the anti-Cartesian project is enriched in a number of ways. The following passage of Heidegger's showcases the neglect:

> Zarathustra begins the episode 'On the Great Longing' with the words: 'O my soul, I taught you to say 'Today' like 'One Day' and 'Formerly', I taught you to dance your round-dance beyond every Here and There and Yonder'. The three words 'Today', 'One Day' and 'Formerly' are capitalised and placed in quotation marks. They designate the fundamental features of time . . . 'One Day' and 'Formerly', future and past, are like 'Today' . . . today is like what is past and what is to come. All three phases of time merge in a single identity, as the same in one single present, a perpetual 'now'. (VA 105; N II, 218)

What is perhaps worthy of note is that Heidegger only explicates the first half of the quoted passage. Whilst he has made clear his reading of Nietzsche on time, why does he not explicitly remark on the fact that the Here, There and Yonder are the fundamental features of space?

In the *Nietzsche* volumes Heidegger makes the link between the Cartesian view of space as extension, criticized, as has been shown, in *Being and Time*, and the wider Cartesian method.

The certitude of the principle *cogito sum* (*ego ens cogitans*) determines the essence of all knowledge and everything knowable; that is, of *mathesis*; hence, of the mathematical . . . The mathematically accessible, what can be securely reckoned in a being that humans themselves are not, in lifeless nature, is *extension* (the spatial), *extensio*, which includes both space *and* time. Descartes, however, equates *extensio* and *spatium*. In that way, the nonhuman realm of finite beings, 'nature', is conceived as *res extensa*. Behind this characterisation of the objectivity of the nature stands the principle expressed in the *cogito sum*: Being is representedness [*Vorgestelltheit*]. (GA48, 204–5; N IV, 116)

Heidegger has spent a number of pages within the text criticizing various aspects of the *cogito*, as did Nietzsche before him, and it appears, given the problems he has identified with this thought, that he wishes to discard it and its results. It has been shown, and it will become clearer in the discussion of later essays, that Heidegger wishes to respond to space experientially rather than geometrically. Undermining the *cogito ergo sum* and with it the opposition between *res cogitans* and *res extensa* clearly furthers this purpose. To interpret nature as *res extensa* is one sided and unsatisfactory, but it follows from the principle of *res cogitans*, and it has enormous consequences. When thought and measured metaphysically 'it is the first resolute step through which modern machine technology, and along with it the modern world and modern mankind, become metaphysically possible for the first time'. As Heidegger continues – and it should be remembered that this is *1940*: 'It is not sufficient that one possesses tanks, airplanes and communication equipments; nor is it sufficient that one has humans, who can service them . . . only the Over-man [*Übermensch*] is appropriate to an absolute "machine economy"' (GA48, 204–5; N IV, 116–17; see GA54, 66–7).[58] Nietzsche, and the *Blitzkrieg* National Socialism has become are clearly not solutions but continuations of this. This critique of technology, with Nazism and Ernst Jünger's call for total mobilization looming large, will be picked up in the following chapter.

Abandoning the geometric, the Cartesian, does not resign us to disorder, or to chaos. In a discussion of Nietzsche on schematizing a chaos, Heidegger gives the following practical example:

If we simply look around, knowingly, here, in the lecture hall, on the street, in the forest, and elsewhere, do we, knowing and taking notice, encounter 'chaos'? Do we not rather find an ordered, articulated region out of which objects that pertain to one another stand over against us in a surveyable, handy, available and measurable way?

Heidegger continues to suggest, through reading Nietzsche on this point, that our

> regulating forms are imposed ... by our *'practical needs'*. Thus practical behaviour, the *praxis* of life, not 'theoretical' re-presentation is the attitude from which the knowing mode of behaviour arises and is determined. (GA47, 138–9; N III, 72)

Now this may help to make clear a remark Heidegger made in the previous lecture course:

> Space is therefore an imaginary, imaginative bit of imagery, formed by force and the relations of force *themselves*. Which forces and relations of force it is that instigate the formation of space, that is to say, the self-formation of a representation of space, and *how* they do so, Nietzsche does not say ... Nevertheless, with this remark Nietzsche is on the trail of an essential nexus, one that he never thought through, however, and never mastered. (GA44, 94; N II, 89)

Of course, as shall be seen later, the interrelations of space and force, or power, are central to Foucault's work. Though we may indeed wish to agree with Heidegger's opinion that 'viewed as a whole, Nietzsche's meditations of space and time are quite meagre' (GA44, 94–5; N II, 90), it is perhaps not unjust to suggest that Heidegger does neglect some important points. Though Heidegger finds Nietzsche invaluable in his de-struction of the tradition, on the critical notion of space and place he appears to owe more to Hölderlin.

One issue that is furthered in the Nietzsche lectures however is the issue of the body.[59] Nietzsche's treatment of the body, found in many of his unpublished notes, but also in some sections of *Thus Spoke Zarathustra*, often relies on nineteenth century physiology,[60] and can lead him to several of his most ill-judged passages (see for example M 241), but there are still some potentially useful ideas to be found. Nietzsche sees it as an important advance of the nineteenth century that 'more and more decisively the question concerning the *health of the body* [*Leibes*] is put ahead of that of "the soul"' (WM 117; see also WM 491; 532; Z I, 4; and Z III, 10), and as well as berating philosophers for their lack of historical sense, he also attacks them for their neglect of the body (GD 3, 1), and of physiology (WM 408).

'Taking a large view', Nietzsche wonders if 'philosophy has not been merely an interpretation of the body [*Leibes*] and a *misunderstanding* of the body', and he looks to the day when 'a philosophical *physician*' will read the 'symptoms of the body' (FW Preface, 2), as his own work in this area clearly does not go this far. 'We can analyse our body spatially', says Nietzsche (WM 676), and this can lead us to understanding our senses 'inside' and 'outside' (WM 500), and, the inference is drawn, of the culture we are within. In two of Nietzsche's notes, he sketches some ideas about the body as a 'political structure [*Herrschaftsgebilde*]' (WM 660) 'in which the most distant and most recent past of all organic development again becomes living and corporeal, through which and over and beyond which a tremendous inaudible stream seems to flow' (WM 659).

Heidegger's discussion of the body is somewhat limited, but the issue is of crucial importance given Heidegger's attempt to rescue Nietzsche from the crudely reductionist reading that found traits of biologism and racism in his works. This reading finds its sources in several places in Nietzsche. The readings of the blond beast and the overman as biologically racist models have been convincingly destroyed in recent scholarship, and so need not detain us here.[61] An area that is perhaps more problematic is that of the body. If Nietzsche pursues a vitalist line, can he do so without being reduced to the Nazi reading? Heidegger understands these problems in looking at Nietzsche on the body.

> We cannot deny that the things physiology grapples with – particular bodily states [*bestimmte Leibzustände*], changes in internal secretions, muscle flexions, occurrences in the nervous system – are also proper to affects, passions, and feelings. But we also have to ask whether all these bodily states and the body itself are grasped in a metaphysically adequate way, so that one may without further ado borrow material from physiology and biology, as Nietzsche, to his own detriment, so often did. The one fundamental point to realise here is that no result of any science can ever be applied *immediately* to philosophy. (GA43, 52; N I, 45)[62]

Heidegger's understanding of the body does not conform to the Cartesian mind/body dualism. It was shown in *Being and Time* that Dasein did not take up a bit of space like a thing did. Dasein is not a body, and its spatiality is understood in fundamentally different ways. Heidegger tries to explain:

> Bodily being does not mean that the soul is burdened by a hulk we call the body. In feeling oneself to be, the body is already contained in advance in that self, in such a way that the body in its bodily state permeates the self. We do not 'have' a body in the way we carry a knife in a sheath. Neither is the body [*Leib*] a body [*Körper*] that merely accompanies us and which we can establish, expressly or not, as also present-at-hand. We do not 'have' a body [*Leib*]; rather, we 'are' bodily [*leiblich*]. (GA43, 117; N I, 98–9)

Heidegger understands the body not as a noun, as an object, but as an adjectival state or even a verb, *to body*. This idea is expressed in one of the later lecture courses:

> Life lives in that it bodies forth [*Das Leben lebt, indem es leibt*]. We know by now perhaps a great deal – almost more than we can encompass – about what we call the body [*Leibkörper*], without having seriously thought about what *bodying* [*Leiben*] is. (GA47, 152–3; N III, 79; see GA47, 158–9)

These lines hint at the notion that as beings-in-the-world we are bodily – that embodiment *mediates* our existence. Such ideas would be developed in the work of Merleau-Ponty.[63] Heidegger then suggests the sense in which the body can be seen as power. ' "Body" is the name for that configuration of will to power in which the latter is always immediately accessible, because it is always within the province of the human identified as "subject" ' (GA50, 48; N III, 223). Now this does not appear to further the purpose of understanding the body as space, as a site of history, shaped by forces, as Nietzsche seemed to begin. However, Heidegger argues that Nietzsche's thought of will to power was 'ontological rather than biological' (GA6.2, 278; N III, 231), an attitude that is aimed at disputing the reading of Nazi ideologues.[64] This distinction adds to the earlier formulation of the difference between *der Körper* and *der Leib*, two German words that are close to synonyms and are both translated by the English body. *Der Körper* is closer to the understanding of body as mass, and is used for animals and humans. *Der Leib* is used only for humans, and can mean body in a less tangible way.[65] The following passage seems to link these ideas into a more useful formulation:

> The bodying of life is nothing separate by itself, encapsulated in the 'body' [*Körper*] in which the body [*Leib*] can appear to us; the body [*Leib*] is transmission and passage at the same time. Through this body flows a stream of life of which we feel but a small and fleeting portion, in accordance with the receptivity of the momentary state of the body. Our body itself is admitted into this stream of life, floating in it, and is carried off and snatched away by this stream or else pushed to the banks . . . Nietzsche declared often enough in his later years that the body must be made *the guideline* of observation not only of humans but of the *world*. (GA47, 153, 509; N III, 79–80)

This perhaps advances us further in the understanding that Nietzsche gives to the body, in that we should see the body in historical – transmission and passage – terms. Foucault's major essay on Nietzsche will elaborate some of these ideas. Heidegger does not fully support Nietzsche, however, as he quotes

The Will to Power paragraphs 489 and 491, and argues that, although Nietzsche founds his thought on the body and not on the 'I', he is still fundamentally following Descartes. This is because

> the body is to be placed first '*methodologically*'. It is a question of method . . . That the body is to be placed first methodologically means that we must think more clearly and comprehensibly and still more adroitly than Descartes, but to do so wholly and solely in his sense. The method is decisive. (GA48, 247; N IV, 133)

This provides a good example of how Heidegger's later work on Nietzsche (these particular lectures date from 1940) sees him as the last thinker of metaphysics, reversing several key points, but still from within a metaphysical framework.[66] Whether Heidegger is any more able to escape from metaphysics is a much-debated point.

EXCURSUS: THE BEITRÄGE

It is with some hesitation that I venture a few words here on the 1936–8 manuscript *Beiträge zur Philosophie (Vom Ereignis)* [*Contributions to Philosophy: Of Propriation*].[67] This manuscript contains a wealth of ideas – many developed from lecture courses Heidegger had delivered between *Being and Time* and its writing; many that would not appear in public work (either lectures or publications) for several years. Of its many themes, I will here treat but one, which is referred to in some notes appended to the *Gesamtausgabe* version of the first lecture course on Nietzsche: the notion of time-space (see GA43, 286). Within the *Beiträge* Heidegger sketches the broad terrain of his inquiry:

> One must first generally attempt to think the essence of time so originally (in its 'ecstasis') that it becomes graspable as the possible truth for being [*Seyn*] as such. But already thinking time through in this way brings time, in its relatedness to the *Da* of Da-sein, into an essential relationship with the spatiality of Da-sein and thus with space (cf. Grounding [Part V of the *Beiträge*]). But measured against their ordinary representations, time and space are here more originary; and ultimately, they are time-space, which is not a coupling of time and space but what is more originary in their belonging together. (GA65, 189)

In this manuscript we find a far more explicit formulation of the insight I suggested can be found in the reading of the eternal return: 'As joining [*Fügung*] truth, time-space is originally the site for the moment of propriation [*Augenblicks-Stätte des Ereignisses*]' (GA65, 30). Time-space is understood as the moment-site [*Augenblicksstätte*] (GA65, 235), and this is the way to understand Da-sein: 'the site for the moment of the grounding of the truth of being [*Seyn*]' (GA65, 323). To understand time-space – *Zeit-Raum*, and not *Zeitraum*, timespan, i.e. the spacing of time – we need to think through time and space in a more fundamental sense, in a way other than the mathematically calculative understanding holding sway in the modern age. Now as I have shown this project has been important throughout Heidegger's work, and will be developed and continued for many years. Here in the *Beiträge* he is anticipating a position he will not feel able to articulate publicly until 1962.

There is much more that could be looked at here: the relation of mathematical conceptions of time and space to the oblivion of being; the importance of measure and calculation to this; the interlinked nature of machination and lived experience; and an anticipation of the way this paves for modern technology and totalitarianism. But most of this is dealt with in some way in Heidegger's later work or lecture courses, and the material here in the *Beiträge* often has the appearance of claims he has yet to fully work through. A number of questions remain unanswered, but one will take centre stage in the following chapter: if space is tied up with Cartesian extension, and was a concept not found in Greek thought, how do we think space more originally?

However, before that treatment it is worth examining some other themes discussed in the Nietzsche lectures, which will also be picked up in Foucault's work.

POWER AND PERSPECTIVISM

What a revelation it was for the mass of people who were unfamiliar with actual thinking and its rich history when two decades ago, in 1918, Oswald Spengler announced that he was the first to discover that every age and every civilisation has its own world view! Yet it was nothing more than a very deft and clever popularisation of the thoughts and questions on which others long before him had ruminated far more profoundly. Nietzsche was the most recent of these. (GA44, 106; N II, 101)

With these words, Heidegger links Nietzsche to the philosophical tradition – the reference to Spengler's appropriation, and the suggestion that Nietzsche is the most recent profound rumination – and suggests an attitude that was to become important in some of his own works, and absolutely central to the work of Foucault on the *episteme*, most obviously in *The Order of Things*. This historical understanding of understanding links to important ideas such as the space of possibilities and to earlier Heideggerian concepts such as the difference between ontic and ontological knowledge. The key issues at stake are those of power and perspectivism.

By the time of the Nietzsche lectures Heidegger has realized that his own project of 'de-struction [*Destruktion*], like "phenomenology" and all hermeneutical-transcendental questions, has not yet been thought in terms of the history of being' (GA6.2, 378; EP 15), and that, fundamentally, though these critical approaches can be useful, these must be used alongside that of history. 'History is the history of *being*' (GA47, 294; N III, 182), and much of his later work is taken up in an investigation of the history of philosophy, that in many ways, like Hegel, though with clearly divergent results, becomes a meditation on the philosophy of history.[68] In the third lecture course on Nietzsche, Heidegger reaches the stage it was suggested was implicit in his formulation of the import of Newtonian physics: 'In its own being, therefore, truth is historicised' (GA50, 3; N III, 187; see GA45, 27). Truth is now seen as historical, as plural. There is no one truth, but this does not preclude the possibility of truths. Within this formulation of history and truth, Heidegger also sees the central importance of Nietzsche's idea of power: 'In the sense of Nietzsche's interpretation of history, the question asks, what configuration of the will to power was at work here?' (GA48, 123; N IV, 75). So, questions must be asked bearing in mind the historical dimension, and considering the power relations at stake.

Whilst Heidegger thinks Nietzsche is onto something fundamentally important, he is far from being uncritical. In Nietzsche's understanding, Heidegger suggests, 'knowledge in general – science, for example – is a configuration of will to power. Thoughtful reflection . . . about knowledge – and science in particular – must make visible what will to power is' (GA47, 27; N III, 19). Some pages later he notes that, for Nietzsche, 'the essence of knowledge, that is, the essence of truth, must be defined in terms of the will to power' (GA47, 34; N III, 24). Indeed this lecture course on Nietzsche has, for Heidegger, one question: 'the question of the essence of knowledge and truth as a configuration of will to power' (GA47, 222; N III, 122).

These formulations are ones that Foucault later elaborates, and in Chapter Four I shall argue that Foucault's understanding of the Nietzschean concept of power/knowledge is impossible without the mediation of Heidegger. But Foucault's understanding is of *power* and its relation to knowledge and truth, rather than *will to power*. Crucially, it is Heidegger's critique of will to power as essentially will to will (GA50, 14; N III, 196) that allows Foucault to take forward power analysis without the voluntarism remaining in Nietzsche's conception. It is important to note in this regard that Heidegger regards Nietzsche's conception of will to power as still tied within the subjectivist Cartesian tradition both he and Foucault wish to escape. Nietzsche is the last metaphysician of the

West (GA47, 8; N III, 8; see GA47, 10). 'Will to power' might be Nietzsche's 'name for the essence of power' (GA48, 29–30; 35), but it is a way of thinking power that is essentially Cartesian:

> In order to grasp Nietzsche's philosophy as metaphysics and to circumscribe its place in the history of metaphysics, it is not enough to explain historiographically a few of his fundamental concepts as being 'metaphysical'. *We must grasp Nietzsche's philosophy as the metaphysics of subjectivity.* What was said concerning the expression 'metaphysics of will to power' is also valid for the phrase 'metaphysics of subjectivity'. The genitive is ambiguous, having the sense of a subjective and objective genitive, in which the words *objective* and *subjective* maintain emphatic and rigorous significance. (GA48, 266; N IV, 147)

These thoughts on power and history provide a link into the thought that underpins them – that of perspectivism:

> Is there anything at all like an observation of history that is not one-sided but omni-sided? Must not every particular present always examine and interpret the past in terms of *its own* horizon? Won't its historiographical knowledge be more 'alive' the more decisively the given horizon of that particular present is taken as a guide? (GA48, 119; N IV, 71)

In a reading of a passage in *The Gay Science* (374), Heidegger argues that Nietzsche 'achieves waxing clarity concerning the fact that humans always think within the confinements of their little "corner" of the world, their tiny angle of space-time' (GA44, 126; N II, 117). Nietzsche argues that we cannot see around our own corner, and Heidegger elaborates this and other scattered remarks on perspectivism in some of the most useful passages of his lectures. 'Nietzsche thinks tacitly as follows: All thinking in categories, all nascent thinking in schemata, that is, in accordance with rules, is *perspectival*' (GA47, 194; N III, 102). Will to power itself is perspectival, and as every being occurs essentially as will to power it too is perspectival. The 'will to power is in its innermost essence a perspectival reckoning with the conditions of its possibility, conditions that in itself posits as such. Will to power is in itself value positing' (GA50, 18; N III, 199). Heidegger's example of perspectivism is powerfully simple, and is often emulated in descriptions of this idea.

> Assuming that we frequently come across a lone tree outside on a meadow slope, a particular birch, the manifold of colours, shades, light, atmosphere has a different character according to the time of day and year, and also

according to the changing perspective of our perception, our distance and our mood; and yet it is always this 'identical' birch. (GA47, 178; N III, 95)

Several of these ideas are put to practical use in the contemporaneous essay 'The Age of the World Picture'. The following passage shows the main thrust of Heidegger's argument.

When we use the word 'science' [*Wissenschaft*] today, it means something essentially different from the *doctrina* and *scientia* of the Middle Ages, and also from the Greek ἐπιστήμη. Greek science was never exact, precisely because, in keeping with its essence, it could not be exact and did not need to be exact. Hence it makes no sense whatever to suppose that modern science is more exact than that of antiquity. Neither can we say that the Galilean doctrine of free-falling bodies [*Körper*] is true and that Aristotle's teaching, that light bodies strive upward, is false; for the Greek understanding . . . rests upon a different interpretation of beings and hence conditions a correspondingly different kind of seeing and questioning of natural events. No one would presume to maintain that Shakespeare's poetry is more advanced than that of Aeschylus. (GA5, 70–1; QCT 117)

Whilst arguing that different conceptions of what we now call 'science' have existed over time, and that we could trace these changes historically, Heidegger warns us as to how such an investigation would have to run. 'If we want to grasp the essence of modern science, we must first free ourselves from the habit of comparing the new science with the old solely in terms of degree, from the point of view of progress' (GA5, 71; QCT 117–18). Teleology is out, but a revised Nietzschean genealogy would be more successful. As Krell notes, the investigation of boredom in *The Basic Concepts of Metaphysics* is not *Kulturdiagnostik*, phenomenology or fundamental ontology, but closer to genealogy than anything else.[69] Given the suggestions propounded in the previous chapter I suggest that it is historical ontology, a term almost synonymous with genealogy. This notion of historical ontology is at work in Heidegger's readings of technology, the housing crisis in post-war Germany, the πόλις in the early 1940s and other later concerns. All of these are orientated as critiques of the present. Indeed, in *Being and Time*, Heidegger talks of the 'ontological task of constructing a non deductive genealogy of the different possible ways of being' (GA2, 11). In other words, like Foucault, through his investigation of the ontic phenomena of history, Heidegger is exposing the metaphysical assumptions behind the systems of thought that condition their possibility. We have seen how the ideas of power and perspectivism would be important.

Heidegger considers the modern view of the world: 'When we reflect on the modern age, we are questioning the modern world picture [*Weltbild*]. We characterise the latter by throwing it into relief over against the medieval and ancient world pictures' (GA5, 81; QCT 128). However, medieval and ancient world pictures are modern inventions reimposed on those ages, as it is only in the modern age [*der Neuzeit*] that the world is conquered and conceived of as a picture. Heidegger suggests that this view occurs at the same time that the human is conceived of as a *subiectum* and that therefore 'observation and teaching about the world change into a doctrine of humans, into anthropology' (GA5, 86; QCT 133). This is of course a reference to philosophy after Descartes. Heidegger continues: 'it is no wonder that humanism first arises where the world first becomes picture. It would have been just as impossible for a humanism to have gained currency in the great age of the Greeks as it would have been to have had anything like a world picture in that age' (GA5, 86; QCT 133).

Such a view links to what Dreyfus has called plural realism, a belief that suggests, *contra* Kuhn, that different conceptions within science across time are not all false, but all true. This belief suggests that there is no one truth, but that there are, usually across different times and spaces, various truths. Dreyfus elaborates: 'One can reject the claim that there is *a* correct description of reality and still hold that there can be *many* correct descriptions, including a correct causal description of objectified physical nature.'[70] This belief is shown in one of Heidegger's examples: 'Each historical age is not only great in a distinctive way in contrast to others; it also has, in each instance, its own concept of greatness' (GA5, 88; QCT 135). The idea of plural realism, though the name is Dreyfus' invention, is clearly found in the works of the later Heidegger, and before him, in Nietzsche. In several of his works Foucault takes up these ideas. In *The Order of Things*, Foucault particularly develops this notion that the subject, humanism and anthropology are concepts of the modern age, and famously argues that they may well be nearing their end.[71]

It is important to note that under the shadow of Nazism Heidegger reads two thinkers who have been appropriated by the movement and openly contests much of the official line. Notably, the biologistic, racist appropriations are continually challenged. It is simply inaccurate to suggest that Heidegger turns to these thinkers because of a sympathy with Nazism, or in spite of Nazism. Rather he turns to them because of Nazism, precisely in order to contest their readings, because, as a thinker, this is the best way of showing his 'spiritual resistance'. Hannah Arendt suggests that 'Heidegger himself corrected his "error" more quickly and more radically than many of those who later sat in judgement over him – he took considerably greater risks than were usual in German literary and university life during that period.'[72] This is clearly too strong, but there are signs of a thinking against, a confrontation, an *Auseinander-*

setzung. In the next chapter I return to this issue, looking at Heidegger's rethinking of the πόλις. This is a reading that challenges the notion of the political prevalent in Nazism: one he himself seemed to support in the Rectoral Address.

Heidegger's later work is the product of the twists and turns of the paths of thought he has followed since *Being and Time*. The whole picture comes into view, but all the pieces have been at least glimpsed in the readings of Hölderlin and Nietzsche. It has been shown how Heidegger's work provides the basis for an understanding of history that dispenses with the linearity of time, but that sees the dimensions of past, present and future collide in the gateway of the moment. This makes any history necessarily a critique of the present. And it has been suggested that this history is one that takes a far greater interest in the *spatial*, as opposed to the merely temporal. Through a reading of early Greek thought, Heidegger has convincingly shown up the deficiencies of seeing space in terms of extension, as Descartes does, and has with waxing clarity moved from an understanding of space experientially to dwelling in place poetically. This last notion is particularly evident in the work of the later Heidegger. Following Greek thought, Heidegger has suggested avoiding the concept of space, which is so tied up with ἰδέα and extension, and has argued a return to the notion of place, τόπος, *Ort*. Such a reading, and a rethinking of the time/space relation is particularly evident in the Hölderlin lectures. This has led Janicaud to suggest the duality of topology and historicity, a dyad I would suggest can be condensed into the Anglicized neologism *platial history*. The following chapter will examine how Heidegger puts this notion into practice.

CHAPTER 3

Art, Technology, Place and the Political

This chapter shifts from the chronological approach employed in the previous two chapters, to a more thematic discussion. The theoretical insights that have been traced from *Being and Time* through the readings of Kant, Hölderlin, and Nietzsche can now be used to illuminate the later Heidegger's concerns. The issues of place and history are central to many of the pieces Heidegger would produce: they are evident in one text of the 1930s, *The Origin of the Work of Art*, and in various ways are used in essays and lectures of the 1940s and beyond. These pieces cover many topics, but recurrent themes include the question of language, the confrontation with technology, the meaning of the word πόλις, and the notion of the fourfold, which Heidegger adapts and elaborates from Hölderlin. The question of language itself has only tangential relevance to the purpose here, but in various ways the content of the essays on language and certainly those on technology, the πόλις and the fourfold relate to the main themes of place and history. Many of the essays under consideration in this chapter date from the period after the end of the Second World War, when Heidegger was banned from teaching by the occupying Allies. The ban remained in place until 1951, at which point Heidegger resumed courses at Freiburg. Given the range of Heidegger's interests, and the fact that I am now moving to a thematic approach, an exhaustive treatment is not possible. Those texts that will be considered, however, provide a picture of Heidegger's later concerns, and demonstrate the applications to which he puts his theoretical insights.

THE ORIGIN OF THE WORK OF ART

The Origin of the Work of Art is one of Heidegger's most famous and important works. Originally delivered as a Freiburg lecture in late 1935, it was repeated in Zürich in January 1936, and expanded through the course of that year to its full form, which was given in three parts in November and December, in Frankfurt am Main. This was the text that appeared in the collection *Holzwege*.

After some changes, and the addition of the Epilogue and the 1956 Addendum, the text was republished as a book in 1960.[1] It is therefore obvious that this text, which straddles many times and places, bridges the entirety of the work being considered in this section.[2] Indeed, I believe that it serves as a particularly apposite example of how these ideas can be and are put into practice. It also opens up a number of themes that are considered in the later Heidegger's more 'poetic' work. Early in the first lecture, Heidegger sets out his aim of looking to conceptualize what the origin [*Ursprung*] of a work of art is. Instead of taking the usual, and perhaps obvious, route of claiming that the artist is the origin of the work of art, or the reverse route of claiming that the artist only becomes an artist as a result of the work, Heidegger suggests that both 'artist and work *are* each of them by virtue of a third thing, which is prior to both, namely, that which also gives artist and work of art their names – art' (GA5, 7; BW 143).

Heidegger makes it clear that his investigation is neither abstract nor confined to pictorial art: 'Works of art are familiar to everyone. Architectural and sculptural works can be seen installed in public places [*Plätzen*], in churches, and in dwellings' (GA5, 8; BW 145). This balancing of the various forms of artworks is shown throughout Heidegger's later works, where the plastic arts, which in German includes architecture, are given a ranking equal to the more traditional art forms of literature and painting. Only music seems to be lacking from Heidegger's consideration.[3] It is immediately recognized that any question of art is by its nature historical, especially one that looks at the problematic 'origin'. Heidegger suggests that

> art is historical, and as historical it is the creative preserving of truth in the work . . . Art is history in the essential sense that it grounds history . . . To originate something by a leap, to bring something into being from out of its essential source in a founding leap – this is what the word 'origin' [*Ursprung*, literally primal leap] means. (GA5, 64; BW 202)

As with much of Heidegger's work of this period, there is an important question of truth, and truth, as has been seen, is historicized: 'Can truth happen [*geschehen*] at all and thus be historical [*geschichtlich*]? Yet truth, people say, is something timeless and super-temporal' (GA5, 27; BW 163). There is also an understanding of the spatial implications of the work of art, in part due to the consideration of form:

> The self-contained block of granite is something material in a definite if unshapely form. Form means here the spatial place distribution and arrangement of the material parts [*Form meint hier die räumlich örtliche*

Verteilung und Anordnung der Stoffteile], resulting in a particular outline [*Umriß*], namely that of a block. (GA5, 17; BW 154)

These implications come to the fore in two of the most important passages in Heidegger's study.

Heidegger sets out to describe a piece of equipment, his example being a pair of peasant shoes, particularly as they appear in a painting by Van Gogh, 'without any philosophical theory' (GA5, 22; BW 158). He is being disingenuous here, for, if the argument so far is believed, he is putting into practice his ideas of place and history. Heidegger begins by stating the basic impressions we immediately have of the shoes: the material they are made from, how they are stitched together, their general purpose and the differences that will arise regarding their particular purpose. Heidegger has already hinted at the direction he will take in his analysis of the shoes and the painting in a remark in *An Introduction to Metaphysics*. He is interested in the nature of being that arises in that visual scene, a question of time and space, history and place:

> A painting by Van Gogh. A pair of rough peasant shoes, nothing else. Actually the painting represents nothing. But as to what *is* in that picture, you are immediately alone with it as though you yourself were making your way wearily home with your hoe on a late autumn evening after the last potato fires have died down. (GA40, 38; IM 35)

In *The Origin of the Work of Art* Heidegger elaborates his theme:

> From the dark opening of the worn insides of the shoes the toilsome tread of the worker stares forth. In the stiffly rugged heaviness of the shoes there is the accumulated tenacity of her slow trudge through the far-spreading and ever-uniform furrows of the field swept by a raw wind. On the leather lie the dampness and richness of the soil. Under the soles stretches the loneliness of the field-path as evening falls. In the shoes vibrates the silent call of the earth, its quiet gift of the ripening grain and its unexpected self-refusal in the fallow desolation of the wintry field ... This equipment belongs to the *earth*, and is protected in the *world* of the peasant woman. From out of this protected belonging the equipment itself rises to its resting-within-itself. (GA5, 22–3; BW 159–60)

There are few passages in Heidegger that so clearly show the duality of place and history. This fictive story that Heidegger has created may read more into the painting than should be seen, but it is very much a story in which the spatial dimension is important. As well as providing a useful example of how we cope with equipment in everyday life, it exhibits elements of what Chapter Two tentatively called a platial history. This remains, whether we believe Heidegger or not. Meyer Schapiro, in an essay entitled 'The Still Life as Personal Object', contests Heidegger's reading of Van Gogh's picture, as he claims that the shoes are not those of a peasant but those of a city dweller, perhaps even Van Gogh's own shoes from his time in Paris.[4] Maybe, maybe not – does it matter? Would there be any fundamental difference if Heidegger had eulogized the painting as a vibrant representation of the world of a man in the city, walking the streets, between the buildings, through the rain and the polluted skies? This too would be a possible fictive history, an interpretation of a painting that 'represents nothing'. However the importance of the particular reading that Heidegger makes is suggested by Derrida, and following him Bernstein. They argue that it is significant that, writing in 1935–6, Heidegger should opt for a reading that emphasizes the importance of soil, earth:

> Heidegger's attribution of the shoes to the peasant woman in part licences Heidegger's ideologically loaded description of the shoes, with its embarrassing, heavily coded, 'poetics of the soil', the earth, ground. Derrida sights in this language of soil, earth, ground a still active desire for restitution operative in Heidegger despite, and in the midst of, his critique of the subject.[5]

A few pages later, Heidegger applies the same treatment to the Greek temple, a more obviously spatial artwork.[6]

> A building, a Greek temple, portrays nothing. It simply stands there in the middle of the rock-cleft valley. The building encloses the figure of the god, and in this concealment lets it stand out into the holy precinct through the open portico. By means of the temple, the god is present in the temple. This presence of the god is in itself the extension and delimitation of the precinct as a holy precinct . . . Standing there, the building rests on the rocky ground. This resting of the work draws up out of the rock the obscurity of that rock's bulky yet spontaneous support. Standing there, the building holds its ground against the storm raging above it and so first makes the storm itself manifest in its violence . . . The early Greeks called this emerging and rising in itself and in all things Φύσις. It illuminates also that on which and in which the human bases their dwelling. We call this ground the *earth*. (GA5, 30–1; BW 167–8)

Rather than simply seeing the temple as a political or religious structure, Heidegger also sees the importance of the use of space and place, which will come to the fore in the discussion of the πόλις in the following section. However, Heidegger's attitude to the idea of origins is also open to question, as his praising of the pre-Socratic beginnings sets him up for the damning charge of conservative nostalgia, something that is still evident in his attitude to technology which dominates several later pieces. Along with the language of earth and soil this may well be the enduring legacy in Heidegger's works of his links with Nazism. Heidegger's explanation of how he sees the problematic term comes right at the start of the piece, and colours all that follows: 'Origin here means that from which and by which something is what it is and as it is. What something is, as it is, we call its essence. The origin of something is the descent [*Herkunft*] of its essence' (GA5, 7; BW 143). This notion of 'origin' within the historical approach that Heidegger adapts from Nietzsche is one from which Foucault will depart.

RE-THINKING THE ΠΟΛΙΣ

This notion of the origin is a potential problem in *The Origin of the Work of Art*, in the Hölderlin lectures, and will return as a spectre to haunt other later texts of Heidegger's. Hölderlin himself is said to have remarked that 'nothing is dearer to me than the things that are as old as the world itself',[7] and there appears to be in Heidegger's work a desire to return to an original, rural state (though see WHD 53-4; WCT 23). In one remark in a 1943 piece on Hölderlin, commentating on the poem 'Homecoming', Heidegger suggests that 'homecoming is the return into the nearness of the origin [*Ursprung*] . . . then must not the return home consist chiefly, and perhaps for a long time, in getting to know this mystery, or even first of all in learning how to get to know it' (GA4, 23-4; see GA53, 202). Heidegger's analyses of equipment, of dwelling and building can perhaps all be related to this notion of the origin, one that runs close to the idea of nostalgia. It has been suggested that the 1934-5 lectures are more open to accusations of nostalgia than the later work on Hölderlin,[8] but the rural was clearly a very important element in Heidegger's own life – witness his refusal to move to Berlin for a teaching post in the 1930s, and his eulogizing of his Black Forest existence.[9]

Whilst an element of rural nostalgia is found in Heidegger's work, and perhaps increasingly in the later pieces which further develop the notion of poetic dwelling and introduce the concept of the fourfold [*das Geviert*] of earth, sky, gods and mortals, Heidegger does make a series of important remarks which show the importance of place in areas other than the rural.[10] Throughout his career, Heidegger stressed that looking at the fundamental concepts of Greek thought with our modern eyes was sometimes dangerous. He argues that a fundamental change had been made in the transition from the Greek to the Latin language (GA40, 15–16; IM 13; GA54, 63–4).[11] For example, using our modern understanding of logic could not shed light on the Greek concept of λόγος; that of ethics could not describe the realm of ἦθος; and physics was no use in understanding φύσις.[12] And, perhaps especially, Heidegger made us think of the original meaning of μεταφυσικά – τὰ μετὰ τὰ φυσικά – and used this to point out the problems of the accepted sense of metaphysics (see GA29/30, 55ff; GA9, 15; GA40; IM). It comes as no surprise then that Heidegger also challenges our understanding of politics by rethinking the notion of πόλις. Indeed, Heidegger suggests the πόλις was for the Greeks that which was absolutely worthy of question, and yet for the modern mind the 'political' is unquestioned: not in terms of its content, but in terms of its essence (GA53, 117–18). To question the political then, through a rethinking of the πόλις, is to send us nearer the Greeks.

One of the reasons that Heidegger wants to rethink the πόλις, and through it the notion of the political, is to explicitly distance himself both from the attitude of the time and from his own political involvement. It is notable that *Being and Time* does not discuss the πόλις, the state, or politics. There are only a couple of passing references to the state and to politics in the entire work.[13] However, as has been suggested, the Rectoral Address was in some sense a politicizing of the earlier philosophy and the first lecture course on Hölderlin a philosophizing of these politics. In bringing his thought to the political arena, Heidegger is greatly influenced by Plato's Πολιτεία (known in English as *Republic*),[14] with its call for philosopher-kings or rulers. Heidegger's important treatment of this text is found in the Winter Semester course of 1931–2, *On the Essence of Truth: Plato's Cave Allegory and the Theaetetus*, as well as in the Rectoral Address itself.

In the lecture course Heidegger makes the following remark:

> Concerning the 'state' [*Staat*] (in this way we translate πόλις, not quite adequately), and the question of its inner possibility, according to Plato what prevails as the highest principle is that the proper guardians [*eigentlichen Wächter*] of the being-with-another of humans, in the oneness of the πόλις, must be philosophical humans. This does not mean that Professors of philosophy should become chancellors of the Reich [*Reichkanzler*], but that philosophers must become φύλαχες, guardians. The domination of the state and its ordering must be guided through by philosophical humans who, on the basis of the deepest and widest, freely questioning knowledge, bring the measure and rule, and open the routes of decision. (GA34, 100)

Philosophers are seen here as guardians, guides to the conduct of the state, those who can lead the leader, *den Führer zu führen*. Although Heidegger hints at its inadequacy, he translates πόλις as *Staat*,[15] and uses a word that cannot fail to have nationalistic overtones: *Reichkanzler*. This attitude – here suggested as an interpretation of Plato – is given concrete expression when Heidegger takes over the Rectorship. It is notable that throughout the Rectoral Address Heidegger uses the word 'state', never explicitly linking it to the word πόλις, but never denying this is the reference intended. The first line of the Address suggests that 'assuming the Rectorship means committing oneself to leading [*Führung*] this university *spiritually and intellectually* [*geistigen*]' (SDU 9; HC 29).

This leading calls for a new kind of questioning, one that will

> ground knowledge [*Wissenschaft*] once again directly in the fruitfulness and blessing of all the world-shaping forces of the human's historical Dasein, such as: nature, history, language; *Volk*, custom [*Sitte*], state; poetry, thought, belief; sickness, madness, death; law, economy, technology. (SDU 13–14; HC 33)[16]

Heidegger appropriates Ernst Jünger's concepts of 'military service' and 'labour service', and sets up the idea of 'knowledge service'. In his key work *Der Arbeiter (The Worker)* Jünger likens the worker to the soldier, and opposes them to the security-seeking bourgeoisie.[17] Indeed, Wolin suggests that Heidegger's 'option' for National Socialism was based on the supposition that it was the way toward the society of workers proposed by Jünger.[18] Heidegger sees the role of the university as 'knowledge service', part designed to prepare people for the other two services:

> Because the statesman and the teacher, the doctor and the judge, the pastor and the master builder lead Dasein as a *Volk* and a state [*volklich-staatliche Dasein führen*] and watch over it in its essential relations to the world-shaping forces of human being and keep it focused, these professions and the education for them are entrusted to the knowledge service. (SDU 16; HC 35)[19]

Heidegger's first rethinking of the πόλις appears in *An Introduction to Metaphysics* two years later. It would seem that the most obvious route to understand the concept of the πόλις would be to return to the central texts of Ancient Greek philosophy on politics – Plato's Πολιτεία and Aristotle's Επιστήμη Πολιτική (*The Politics*) – or to political texts, histories or documents.

Instead, Heidegger looks at Sophocles' tragedy *Antigone*, and particularly at the second chorus. The discussion of πόλις forms part of an analysis of the nature of the human as revealed in this choral ode. There are three remarkable lines for Heidegger. The first (line 333-4) describes the human as 'τὸ δεινότατον' – the strangest, uncanniest [*das Unheimlichste*] of all beings,[20] and the second (line 360) sees the human as 'παντοπόρος ἄπορος' – 'underway in all directions, on the way to nothing'.[21] Heidegger explains that πόρος means 'passage through . . ., transition to . . ., route [*Bahn*]'. The human is everywhere a path for being, but is therefore flung out of all paths, essentially homeless, unfamiliar. As Heidegger notes, the παντοπόρος απορος clearly contains an interpretation of δεινότατον (GA40, 157–61; IM 148–52). We might also note that the notion of a path was very important for Heidegger – he called two of his most important collections *Wegmarken* [*Pathmarks*] and *Holzwege* [*Woodpaths* – the type of paths that lead, but not necessarily anywhere in particular][22] and just before his death asked for his collected writings to be known as 'Paths – not Works [*Wege, nicht Werke*]'.[23]

Heidegger then focuses on line 370, which begins 'ὑψίπολις ἄπολις' – translated in a standard English version as 'he and his city rise high – but the city casts out'.[24] The line has a similar construction to παντοπόρος ἄπορος, but instead of speaking of the path it speaks of the place where these paths meet, the πόλις, from which 'political' is derived, and which is usually translated as 'city' [*Stadt*] or 'city-state' [*Stadtstaat*]. Heidegger suggests that this does not capture the full meaning: πόλις is so familiar to us through the words 'politics' and 'political' that we no longer see it as worthy of question. 'Πόλις means, rather, the site [*die Stätte*], the there [*Da*], wherein and as which historical Da-sein is. The πόλις is the historical site [*Geschichtsstätte*], the there *in* which, *out of* which, and *for which* history happens [*Geschichte geschieht*]' (GA40, 161; IM 151–2). To this site and scene of history belong the gods, the temples, the priests, the festivals, the games, the poets, the thinkers, the ruler [*Herrscher*], the council of elders, the assembly of the people, the army and the fleet. All of these do not first belong to the πόλις, or are political through a relationship with a statesman, but through their being constitute the πόλις. This is why the human is both ὑψίπολις – rising high above the site – and ἄπολις – without site. The historical site is the result of human creation: without them it is nothing, without it they are nothing (GA40, 161–2; IM 152–3). In the first instance, then, πόλις means the historical site of Dasein, of human existence. The πόλις is the site or place where history happens: the πόλις is essentially situated and, rather than being spatial, is *platial*.[25] Only afterwards does πόλις take on its *political* meaning.

These remarks have, however, remained unclear and incomplete, that is until the publication of the lectures in the *Gesamtausgabe* on Hölderlin, and pre-Socratic thinkers such as Heraclitus and Parmenides. The lecture course on Hölderlin's hymn 'The Ister', delivered in 1942, is the next interpretation. Once again the source is the choral ode from *Antigone*, and Heidegger again picks the same three lines for analysis, along with one that speaks of the ἑστία [hearth]. In his discussion of τὸ δεινόν as *das Unheimliche* Heidegger accepts that in 'philological' terms, the translation is 'wrong'. It can only be seen as justified, even necessary, on the basis of an interpretation. The points concerning this particular translation need not concern us here, but the general remarks are worth bearing in mind. Heidegger reminds us that we receive our knowledge of words in a foreign language from a dictionary, which is based on a preceding interpretation of linguistic concepts. A dictionary can give us pointers as to how to understand a word, but it is never an absolute authority to which we are bound. All translating must be an interpreting. Heidegger closes:

> this interim remark about the essence of translating is meant to recall that the difficulty of a translation is never merely a technical issue but concerns the relation of humans to the essence of the word and to the worthiness of language. Tell me what you think of translation, and I will tell you who you are. (GA53, 74–5)

Heidegger sees πόρος as 'the passage or the passage through to something' and πόλις as a particular realm of πόρος: 'one field in which the latter emphatically comes to pass'. Heidegger suggests that the contemporary interpretation is that everything in Greek thought is politically determined. This, he suggests, is a mistake, but one that is being put to the cause of National Socialism. Heidegger argues that it is evident that 'the "political" is that which belongs to the πόλις and can therefore be determined only in terms of the πόλις. Yet the converse is precisely not the case'. If the political derives from the πόλις, then we cannot use our understanding of the political to explain the πόλις: '*The πόλις cannot be determined "politically"*. The πόλις, and precisely it, is therefore not a "political" concept' (GA53, 98–9).

Alternatives to seeing it as political would include seeing the πόλις as 'state', or as 'city', but Heidegger argues that the first leads us to relate it to modern state formations; the second is distinguished from village only because it is 'stately', again leading to confusion. Instead, 'perhaps the πόλις is that realm and place around which everything question-worthy and uncanny [*Unheimliche*] turns in an exceptional sense. The πόλις is πόλος, that is, the pole, the swirl or vortex [*Wirbel*] in which and around which everything turns' (GA53, 100). The πόλις is therefore 'neither merely state [*Staat*], nor merely city [*Stadt*], rather in the first instance it is properly 'the stead' ['*die Statt*']: the site [*die Stätte*] of the abode of human history'. The essential thing about the πόλις therefore is this site of abode: which means that the political 'in the originary and in the derivative sense, lies in its being the open site of that fitting destining [*Schickung* – related to *Geschichte*, history] from out of which all human relations toward beings . . . are determined' (GA53, 101–2; see GA4, 88). To be political means to be at the site of history.

Heidegger takes this forward by asking us to question two of the most famous pronouncements in Greek thought. The first is Aristotle's formulation of the human being as 'ζῷον πολιτικόν',[26] which is usually 'translated in a superficial way' as political animal, entity, or being.[27] But as Heidegger has argued, the πόλις is determined through its relationship to human beings, and therefore the human is that being capable of belonging to the πόλις (GA53, 102–3). The second is the suggestion in Plato's *Republic* that either philosophers should become rulers, or the rulers philosophers, or there will be no end of trouble for the πόλις.[28] Heidegger argues that Plato does not mean that philosophers should assume the business of the state, because the πόλις is not the 'state'; nor should rulers ' "busy themselves" with "philosophy", as though it were something like collecting beetles'. Instead, Heidegger argues, Plato's statement means that the πόλις – as the site of abode of human history – is best served by philosophers, who stand in the radiance and light of being. This does not mean that everything is determined in terms of the political, or that the political has priority. 'The doctrine of the unconditional priority of the political on the one hand, and on the other hand the conception of the πόλις as the ground that is worthy of question and as the site of beings, are separated from one another by an abyss'. Neither Greek nor contemporary political thought (by which Heidegger means National Socialism, whose historical singularity is stressed) are served by their conflation (GA53, 105–7). There would therefore seem to be a distancing from the attitude of the Rectoral Address when Heidegger offered his services to National Socialism and the state as a philosopher, to complement the *Führer*'s role as ruler.[29]

The lines 'παντοπόρος ἄπορος' – under way in all directions, on the way to nothing – and 'ὑψίπολις ἄπολις' – towering high above the site, forfeiting the site – show, Heidegger suggests, what is so 'τὸ δεινόν', *Unheimliche*, uncanny, in human beings. And yet *das Unheimliche*, the uncanny, is not to be understood in terms of an impression of fear or terror that humans instil in others, but to be conceived in terms of *das Un-heimische*, the un-homely, 'namely that unhomely that is the fundamental trait of human abode in the midst of beings' (GA53, 113–14). The 'un' of unhomely is not merely a negative – the duality of παντοπόρος ἄπορος and ὑψίπολις ἄπολις show this. Heidegger explicitly links the human's being unhomely to the πόλις, which is not some isolated realm – the so-called 'political' – within a wider realm of πόρος, but 'the site within whose expansive realm every πόρος moves' (GA53, 110-11). This is a reversal of the earlier definition, and a progression from that of *An Introduction to Metaphysics*, but Heidegger is quick to counter that it allows the belief that everything is political. Rather, all human activity that is historical has 'the πόλις as its site, as the place to which it belongs' (GA53, 117). Everything that is historical, is therefore explicitly situated, *platial*.

For modern eyes, the 'political' is the way in which history is accomplished, and as such is itself unquestioned. Heidegger suggests that the failure to question the 'political' belongs with its totality. The totality of the political is not simply based on the arbitrary wilfulness of dictators, but in the metaphysical essence of modern actuality in general. This metaphysical essence is, of course, fundamentally different from the way in which the Greek world was historical. In the last of the Nietzsche courses we find a similar critique made of the notions of 'new order' [*Neue Ordnung*] and *Lebensraum*. Both are symptoms of a much wider malaise – nihilism and the culmination of metaphysics in technology (GA48, 139-41). This critique is therefore not just of National Socialism, but of modern conceptions of the political. Heidegger suggests that the 'political' is unquestioned, yet for the Greeks the πόλις was that which was altogether worthy of question (GA53, 117-18; see GA48, 161). Rethinking the πόλις therefore leads us explicitly to question the 'political', to historicize it, to situate it.

In the following semester, in a course on Parmenides, Heidegger returns again to a discussion of the πόλις.[30] Again Heidegger suggests that we think the Greek πόλις and the 'political' in a totally un-Greek fashion. Much of the discussion replicates that from 'The Ister' course, something we might expect given their proximity. In this course, however, he suggests explicitly that we think the 'political' as Romans, as, since the time of the *Imperium*, the word 'political' [πολιτικόν] has been thought imperially. The only thing left of Greek in the word political is its sound (GA54, 63-7). Plato's dialogue on the essence [*Wesen*] of the πόλις (GA9, 109) is called the Πολιτεία, which is rendered as *res publica* [public business] by the Romans, *Der Staat* in modern German, *Republic* in modern English.[31] Earlier in the course Heidegger had distinguished between the Greek ἀλήθεια, the Roman *rectitudo*, and the modern notion of truth. Ἀλήθεια should not be thought of as 'truth' [*Wahrheit*] but as 'non-concealment' [*Unverborgenheit*].[32] He suggests that there is a similar distinction to be drawn between the πόλις, the *res publica* and the state. This is no surprise, he suggests, given that the essence of the Greek πόλις is grounded in the essence of ἀλήθεια. The πόλις, as the πόλος, the pole, is the site of the non-concealment of beings in general (GA54, 132-3).

This detailed reading of Heidegger's remarks on the πόλις is important both in terms of his overall development and the implications it might have.[33]

Elsewhere in the Hölderlin lectures Heidegger thinks the notions of space and time through the notions of placing and journeying; in these discussions he rethinks them through the notions of site and history. On the charge of rural nostalgia, it is worth noting, in distinction to this emphasis, that the discussion of the πόλις is much wider than simply the rural, even if we bear in mind Heidegger's admonition not to translate πόλις as 'city'.

Second, and perhaps most interestingly – but certainly most speculatively – is the potential for rethinking the political that this discussion provides. In recent years there has been important work distinguishing 'politics' [*la politique, die Politik*] – concrete policy-making – and the 'political' [*le politique, das Politische*] – the frame of reference within which 'politics' occurs.[34] We will recall that Heidegger suggested that 'the "political" is that which belongs to the πόλις and can therefore be determined only in terms of the πόλις. Yet the converse is precisely not the case' (GA53, 98–9). We could not use our understanding of the political to explain the πόλις, but, as the political derives from the πόλις, we can use our understanding of πόλις to rethink the political. As Heidegger notes in a discussion of Plato's Πολιτεία:

> we can call Plato's inquiry into art political to the extent that it arises in connection with πολιτεία; but we have to know, and then say, what 'political' is supposed to mean. If we are to grasp Plato's teaching concerning art as 'political', we should understand that word solely in accordance with the concept of the essence of the πόλις that emerges from the dialogue itself. (GA43, 203; N I, 165; see GA43, 209)

This would enable an explicit distancing from the modern – in Heidegger's time, as well as perhaps in our own – Schmittian, notion of the political. Carl Schmitt, the Nazi jurist we know Heidegger to have read, develops an understanding of the political predicated on the friend/enemy distinction. In Schmitt's understanding, 'the concept of the state presupposes the concept of the political'.[35] Such an understanding risks confusing the political with the polemical, πόλις with πόλεμος, a word that links closely to πολέμιος, the enemy.[36] Indeed in a 1933 letter to Schmitt, thanking him for a copy of *The Concept of the Political*, Heidegger suggested that he was 'in the middle of πόλεμος and all literary projects must take second place'.[37]

In distinction to Schmitt, and with Heidegger's rethinking, we can suggest that the concept of the political presupposes the concept of the πόλις. The political, as the ontological foundation of politics, is where politics *takes place*. This understanding of the political would be very different from much of the recent work on the notion of the political, which takes its lead from Schmitt.[38] Essentially, though, rethinking the notion of the political distances Heidegger from his own political involvement of the Rectorship period, where he understood politics through πόλεμος. We might call this his retreating from/retreating of the political.[39] This issue will be picked up on in the discussion of technology in the following section.

THE QUESTION OF TECHNOLOGY

What does Heidegger understand by technology? Starting with the word itself, he suggests that it derives from the Greek τεχνικόν, which means 'that which belongs to τέχνη . . . τέχνη is the name not only for the activities and skills of the craftsman but also for the arts of the mind and the fine arts . . . the word τέχνη is linked with the word ἐπιστήμη. Both words are terms for knowing in the widest sense' (VA 16; BW 318). This should be borne in mind throughout this reading of Heidegger's readings, although Heidegger's discussions centre around what we would normally understand by technology. This is because technology in the modern sense is a particular attitude towards what is, and what constitutes knowledge. The piece *The Question of Technology* was first delivered as a lecture on 1 December 1949, and was originally called '*Das Gestell*', 'The Enframing'. This lecture was part of a series of four, under the general title '*Einblick in das, was ist*', 'Insight into that which is'. The other lectures were 'The Turning', 'The Thing', and 'The Danger'. Heidegger explains the general title thus: 'Insight into that which is – thus do we name the sudden flash of the truth of being into truthless being' (GA79, 75; QCT 47). These lectures aim for an understanding, a questioning, of the state of affairs in the modern world. There is a fundamental shift, a turn, in the human's relations with technology, a turn that Nietzsche and Nazism were both, albeit for different reasons, unable to comprehend.

Krell has pointed out the importance of the wording of the general title for these lectures: 'Only the flash of an eye can apprehend such an impending turn: *Einblick* is surely related to what Heidegger has earlier called *Augenblick*. The thinker's task is to train his eye on that possible momentary turning, enabling the technological hazard to turn into a kind of rescue.'[40] Heidegger himself makes much of the links between the words he uses in these pieces: '"To flash" [*blitzen*], in terms both of its word and its matter, is "to glance" [*blicken*]. In the glance and as that flash, the essence, the coming to presence, of being enters into its own emitting of light . . . The in-turning that is the flash of the truth of being is the insight [*Einkehr des Blitzes der Wahrheit des Seyns ist Einblick*]' (GA79, 74; QCT 45). Bearing in mind everything that is behind Heidegger's notion of the *Augenblick*, it is clear that these lectures aim to use the new understanding of history, and of place, to shed light on the issues of technology and poetic dwelling. Platial histories, or certainly descriptions, are evident in these lectures. Given the contemporary relevance of the topic, they can equally be seen as critiques, even histories, of the present.

Heidegger's analysis of technology looks at how technological apparatus have changed over time, and, more specifically, how their attitude toward nature has altered. His examples are polarized between those belonging to a rural existence and those of a more modern age. 'A radar station is of course less simple than a weather vane . . . And certainly a sawmill in a secluded valley of the Black Forest is a primitive means compared with the hydroelectric plant on the Rhine River' (VA 10; BW 312).[41] It is suggested that modern technology unlocks the potential of nature to be a source of power that can be extracted and stored. Heidegger refutes the claim that this is what the old windmill did: 'No. Its sails do indeed turn in the wind; they are left entirely to the wind's blowing. But the windmill does not unlock energy from the air currents in order to store it' (VA 18; BW 320). This change over time is one that is particularly evident when the changes in place and landscape are examined. In our modern age 'a tract of land is challenged in the hauling out of coal and ore. The earth now reveals itself as a coal mining district, the soil as the site of mineral deposits [*Erzlagerstätte*]' (VA 18; BW 320).[42]

This concept of 'challenging' or 'setting upon' is found again when Heidegger argues that 'the work of the peasant does not challenge the soil of the field'. By this Heidegger means that the peasant works *with* the field, using it naturally. In contrast, the modern mode of agriculture '*sets upon [stellt]* nature. It sets upon it in the sense of challenging it. Agriculture is now a motorised food industry' (VA 18; BW 320). The use of machines, chemical fertilizers and similar are unnatural ways of working *upon* the field, not working with it. In consequence, 'nature becomes a gigantic gasoline station, an energy source for modern technology and industry' (G 18; DT 50). The opposition that Heidegger finds is made particularly clear when he makes an examination of the Rhine river. Heidegger compares the old wooden bridge over the Rhine with the new hydroelectric plant. Whereas the bridge was built into the river, now the river is dammed up into the power plant. The river has now become a 'water-power supplier', which derives its essence from the power plant.

> In order that we may even remotely consider the monstrousness that reigns here, let us ponder for a moment the contrast that is spoken by the two titles: 'The Rhine', as dammed up into the *power* works, and 'The Rhine', as uttered by the *art*-work in Hölderlin's hymn by that name. But, it will be replied, the Rhine is still a river in the landscape, is it not? Perhaps. But how? In no other way than as an object on call for inspection by a tour group ordered there by the vacation industry. (VA 19–20; BW 321)

Nature has become standing-reserve [*Bestand*], a designation that means something more than merely stock. This, argues Heidegger, is a fundamental shift from the previous attitude to nature, found, of course, in the rural setting. But even this is changing irrevocably. 'The forester who measures the felled timber in the woods and who to all appearances walks the forest path in the same way his grandfather did is today ordered by the industry that produces commercial woods, whether he knows it or not.' His work is subordinate to the demand for cellulose, for paper, which is then turned into newspapers and magazines which 'set public opinion to swallowing what is printed' (VA 21–2; BW 323). There is even talk of the idea of human resources, although the human is never merely standing-reserve, as it is humans, in part, that drive technology forward. However Heidegger cautions against simply seeing the human as leading technology: 'It seems time and time again as though technology were a means in the hands of humans. But, in truth, it is the essence of the human that is now being ordered forth to lend a hand to the essence of technology' (GA79, 68; QCT 37). The question of technology is not simply and purely technical, but is something that shapes the whole attitude of our age, 'not only for humans, but also upon all beings, nature and history' (ID 34/98).

Now such an understanding of technology would be one thing, but if we consult the transcript of '*Das Ge-stell*', rather than the version published as 'The Question of Technology', we find that the text has been edited. The published version suggests that the modern mode of agriculture '*sets upon* nature. It sets upon it in the sense of challenging it. Agriculture is now a motorised food industry' (VA 18; BW 320). In the transcript published in the *Gesamtausgabe* Heidegger continues to compare the role of technology in modern agriculture with events on a wider world stage: 'Agriculture is now a motorised food industry, the same thing in its essence [*im Wesen das Selbe*] as the production of corpses in the gas chambers and extermination camps, the same thing as blockades and the reduction of countries to famine, the same thing as the production of hydrogen bombs' (GA79, 27).[43] Lacoue-Labarthe has described this remark as 'scandalous and lamentably inadequate', something it clearly is, given Heidegger's compliance with the Nazi regime in its nascent years, but it should not *merely* be the cause for accusations.[44] I am aware that I am on dangerous ground because a reading of this passage that does not condemn it outright could be seen as a tacit acceptance, but it is worth thinking a little more about it.

In terms of the four examples Heidegger gives – the motorized food industry; the gas chambers and extermination camps; the blockades and the hydrogen bomb – what they, on his terms, have in common is the essence of technology. The essence of modern agriculture is something entirely apart from agriculture — it is the *Ge-stell* that frames agriculture, that of modern technology, the modern ethos. In Heidegger's terms this is the inevitable result of the world made picture, the Cartesian objectification of the world. What Heidegger fails to realize — and this is the scandal, the inadequacy — is that there is something essentially *different* between agriculture and the Holocaust. What many of his critics fail to realize is what that difference is. This is exhibited most obviously in de Beistegui's book *Heidegger and the Political*. He suggests that the thinking of the Holocaust in the same terms as the hydrogen bomb or the Berlin blockade is the problem. Does not, he suggests, the Holocaust force 'thinking outside of itself'?[45]

This absence, or indeed failure, is particularly obvious in de Beistegui's work because his is a book expressly dealing with the political, and yet what links the last three examples is a particular concept of the political. As was noted in the discussion of the πόλις earlier in this chapter, Heidegger suggests that the failure to question the 'political' belongs with its totality. He suggests that the totality of the political is not simply based on the arbitrary wilfulness of dictators, but in the metaphysical essence of modern actuality in general (GA53, 117–18). The modern concept of the political is, like the modern attitude to technology, not merely a regionalized, historically limited event, but one that has its essence in modern ways of being. The gas chambers and extermination camps, the blockades and the hydrogen bomb, all exhibit the political thinking of the friend/enemy distinction. There is clearly something in Heidegger's critique of the political that aims at Schmitt, yet notably de Beistegui's book contains no reference to Schmitt. Whereas before a problem of an enemy was resolved by pogroms and 'conventional' weapons, modern technology allows the possibility of a much more devastating response. The potential of modern technology allows the resolution of a friend/enemy problem in a way as distinct from previous solutions as modern agriculture is from the peasant in the field.[46]

It was noted above that Heidegger's understanding of modern technology rests upon his understanding of *Ge-stell*. This was a word that appeared in *The Origin of the Work of Art*, where he suggests that the figure [*Gestalt*] of the work of art needed to be understood 'in terms of the particular setting [*Stellen*] and *Ge-stell* as which the *work* occurs when it sets itself up and sets itself forth' (GA5, 52; BW 189). In German, *Stelle, -n* is a word with a range of meanings, including place, position, department, and passage in a book; similarly *Gestell* means stand, rack, frame, framework, and chassis, amongst other things. The verb *stellen* means to set upon, to challenge — as in the way modern technology sets upon (*stellt*) nature — but also producing and presenting (*Her- und Dar- stellen*). The prefix *Ge-* means bringing together — *Gebirg*, mountain range; *Gebiß*, set of teeth; *Gemüt*, disposition, i.e. a gathering of feelings — therefore, in Heidegger's usage, *Ge-stell* does not only mean the support or frame around something, but the bringing together of the setting, the en-framing (VA, 23–4; BW 324–6; GA79, 26–7, 32–5). As will be suggested in the following chapter, Foucault's important notion of *dispositif* – as the ensemble of discourses and practices of a given era – is closely related to this concept.

Such an understanding leads to Heidegger's radical claim that the essence of technology is before, and not a consequence of, the scientific revolution: a claim he makes by opposing historiological chronology [*historische Zeitrechnung*] to history.

> For historiological chronology, modern physical science begins in the seventeenth century. In contrast, machine-power technology develops only in the second half of the eighteenth century. But modern technology, which for chronological reckoning is the later, is, from the point of view of the essence holding sway within it, historically earlier. (VA 26; BW 327)

This is because the modern physical theory of nature prepares the way not simply for technology but for the *essence* of modern technology, which is not in itself technological, but is a way of seeing things as calculable, mathematical, extended and therefore controllable (see also WHD 155; WCT 135–6).[47] This claim will not be further examined here, but it is worth noting the similarity to some of Foucault's claims about historical development. *The Question of Technology* itself will be left at this point, in order to discuss the influence of Ernst Jünger on Heidegger's attitudes to technology. This also provides the space for a recapitulation of some of the more problematic and intertwining themes from the previous discussions of Heidegger and Nazism.

We have seen how in his Rectoral Address Heidegger had taken Jünger's concepts of 'military service' and 'labour service', and linked them to the idea of 'knowledge service'. However, as has been seen, Heidegger did turn away from this. Similarly, although around 1933 he did seem to support Jünger, by the mid 1930s he was distancing himself from Jünger's attitudes on, amongst other things, technology. Jünger believed that the way out of nihilism was a wholehearted embrace of technology, which would lead us deep into nihilism, but then out the other side. There are noticeable parallels with some of Nietzsche's thought on the subject.[48] In the later volumes of *Nietzsche*, Heidegger is critical of Nietzsche's attitude to nihilism, suggesting that it is thought nihilistically. Similar accusations could be made of Jünger and Nazism.

It is instructive to compare the following two passages from *Der Arbeiter* with the analysis in *The Question of Technology*, discussed above. 'There is no region left that has not yet been chained by streets and railways, by cables and wires, by airlines and fairways';[49] 'the field that is ploughed by machines and fertilised by nitrogen produced in factories is no longer the same field'.[50] The parallels are clear, and the immediate reaction might be to suggest Heidegger is appropriating Jünger's ideas. Whilst an influence is there, and Heidegger accepts this (GA9, 219), this does not mean to say that the influence is without dispute. Where Jünger praises and wishes to embrace technology, Heidegger, already in the mid 1930s, more clearly in the later Nietzsche lectures and certainly by 1949, has purged his work of any trace of this. Heidegger's attitude to technology is far more critical. In the 1950s, Heidegger and Jünger exchanged articles in *Festschriften* for each other's sixtieth birthdays; Jünger's entitled *Über die Linie*, Heidegger's *Über 'Die Linie'*. Jünger's article looks at the nihilistic consequences of technological domination, implicitly criticizing his own ideas of the 1930s. Heidegger explains that Jünger's *über* signifies 'across, *trans*, μετά' (GA9, 214). Jünger is therefore concerned with the passage *over* the line of nihilism, with the consequence of passing through nihilism: *Across the Line*.

In contrast, by introducing the quotation marks, Heidegger liberates the *über* from the line. His interpretation of *über* is in terms of *de*, περί. His treatment is '"of" the line itself, of the zone of self-consummating nihilism' (GA9, 214): *Concerning 'The Line'*.[51] Like Nietzsche, suggests Heidegger, Jünger is taking a medical approach: 'prognosis, diagnosis, therapy' (GA9, 215). Heidegger suggests that a cure is not possible for the *essence* of nihilism, only for the results and symptoms: 'The essence of nihilism is neither healable nor unhealable: It is the heal-less, and yet, as such, a unique pointer into health' (GA9, 216). For this reason Heidegger offers his piece as an explanation that 'seeks an encounter with the medical assessment of the situation that you [Jünger] have provided. You look and cross over the line; I simply look at the line you have represented'. As has been seen, Jünger's earlier work believed that it could, as Nietzsche believed he could, overcome nihilism by nihilism: '*The Worker* belongs in the phase of "active nihilism" (Nietzsche)' (GA9, 217). The later Jünger seems to recognize that this approach is shot down in flames: 'Total mobilisation has entered a stage which is even more threatening than what has gone before.'[52]

Heidegger's approach, once again, tends toward the descriptive rather than, as Jünger's does, towards the prescriptive, and notably uses spatial terms to clarify the difference:

In the article *Across the Line* you give an *Ortbeschreibung* [a description of the place/platial description] of nihilism and an estimation of the situation [*Lage*] and of the possibility of the human's movement in respect to the place [*Ort*] described and designated by the image of the line. A topography of nihilism, of its process and of its overcoming is certainly needed. Yet the topography must be preceded by a topology: the discussion of that place [*Ortes*] which gathers being and nothingness into their essence, determines the essence of nihilism, and thus makes known the paths on which the ways of a possible overcoming of nihilism are indicated. (GA9, 240)

If topology is understood as the study of the limit, and topography as the writing of place, Heidegger's intent becomes clearer. Whereas Jünger is looking over the line, Heidegger is concerned with the line, the demarcation, a *delineation*.[53] This does not mean that Heidegger holds out no hope. He is fond of quoting the following lines of Hölderlin:

> But where danger is, grows
> The saving power also[54]

Heidegger expressly sees this in terms of technology, a point he makes several times in his works. 'Thus the essential unfolding of technology harbours in itself what we least suspect, the possible rise of the saving power' (VA 36; BW 337). Though he is deeply sceptical about the advances of technology, Heidegger, contrary to how his critics have often characterized him, suggests that outright rejection is absurd. Instead, Heidegger suggests that we must give it a trial:

> For all of us, the arrangements, devices and machinery of the technological world are to a greater or lesser extent indispensable. It would be foolish to attack the technological world blindly. It would be short-sighted to condemn it as the work of the devil. We depend on technical devices; they even challenge us to ever greater advances. (G22–3; DT53)

What is important is to work with technology, but not surrender ourselves to it, so that it affects our inner and real core. Heidegger suggests that this 'yes' and 'no' is best summarized as releasement toward things [*Die Gelassenheit zu den Dingen*] (G 22–3; DT 54; see ID 40/105). Unlike the early Jünger he neither sees technology as a solution, nor looks to a new mode of thought over the line. What we have to do is understand and think: where there is danger, there is the potential of salvation; where there is power there lies the means of its resistance. This leads Heidegger to one of his most famous formulations: 'The closer we come to the danger, the more brightly do the paths into the saving power begin to shine and the more questioning we become. For questioning is the piety of thought' (VA 40; BW 341).

DWELLING POETICALLY AT THE PLACE OF THE FOURFOLD

In his consideration of the poet Hebel, Heidegger declares that 'the human "dwells", *if* they dwell, in the words of *Hölderlin*, "poetically . . . upon this earth" (GA13, 147). It has been argued that the model of poetic dwelling is very close to the anti-Cartesian understanding of space begun in *Being and Time*. Perhaps now a return to an etymological formulation found in this early work can be properly understood: '"In" is derived from *"innan"* – "to reside" [*wohnen*], *"habitare"*, "to dwell" . . . The expression *"bin"* is connected with *"bei"*, and so *"ich bin"* ["I am"] means in its turn "I reside" or "dwell alongside" the world' (GA2, 54). The formulation, although now clear, was anything but in *Being and Time*, where the spatiality of being was sacrificed to the wish to ground existence on temporality, and to derive spatiality from temporality. The shift in understanding has been outlined throughout these chapters.[55] As an example, it is worth considering Heidegger's discussion of fragment 119 of Heraclitus: ἦθος ἀνθρώπῳ δαίμων.

> This is usually translated, 'The human's character is their daimon' [Jonathan Barnes has it as 'a man's character is his fate']. This translation thinks in a modern way, not a Greek one. ἦθος means abode, dwelling place. The word names the open region in which the human dwells. The open region of their abode allows what pertains to the essence of the human, and what is thus arriving resides in nearness to them, to appear. The abode of the human contains and preserves the advent of what belongs to them in their essence. According to Heraclitus's phrase this is δαίμων, the god. The fragment says: The human dwells, insofar as they are human, in the nearness of god. (GA9, 185)[56]

It is worth noting the fact that the notion of dwelling that Heidegger wishes to reintroduce is found (at least by Heidegger) in Greek thought. This of course links back to Heidegger's praise of Hölderlin and Nietzsche for understanding the great age of Greek beginnings. Heidegger goes on to suggest that ἦθος is found in the word ethics and that therefore ethics ponders the abode of the human. The truth of being is therefore an original ethics, but first an *ontology* (GA9, 186–7). The understanding of moral or ethical systems in metaphorically spatial terms is also evident in the works of both Foucault and Nietzsche.

However, the notion of poetic dwelling is not intended to be, at least not primarily, metaphorical. This therefore begs the question as to *where* do humans dwell poetically? The lines of Hölderlin already quoted suggest 'on the earth', something that Heidegger suggests counters the accusation that poetic dwelling is in the realm of fantasy. That said, I have already cautioned against the idea of earth alone. The answer is found in many of Heidegger's pieces, such as in the following passage: 'If the verb "to dwell" is thought deeply and essentially enough, it shows us the manner in which humans, upon the earth and beneath the sky, complete the passage from birth to death' (GA13, 138–9).[57] Humans dwell poetically at the place of the fourfold. What this means is made clear if the lines of Hölderlin that Heidegger is so fond of quoting ('poetically the human dwells') are returned to their true context:

> As long as kindliness [*Freundlichkeit*], which is pure, remains in his heart not unhappily the human may compare himself with the god [*Gottheit*]. Is God unknown? Is he manifest as the sky [*Himmel*]? This rather I believe. It is the measure of the *human*. Full of acquirements, but poetically, the human dwells on this earth.[58]

These lines are absolutely key, and are worth repeating, with added emphasis to four words.

> As long as kindliness, which is pure, remains in his heart not unhappily the human may compare himself with the *god*. Is God unknown? Is he manifest as the *sky*? This rather I believe. It is the measure of the *human*. Full of acquirements, but poetically, the human dwells on this *earth*.

These four words, 'human', 'god', 'sky' and 'earth' are the constituent parts of the fourfold, the gathering of the four [*Geviert*]. Therefore, the human's dwelling poetically on the earth is also under the sky, before the gods, and with other humans:

> 'On the earth' already means 'under the sky'. Both of these *also* mean 'remaining before the gods', and include a 'belonging to humans' being with one another'. By an *originary* oneness the four – earth and sky, gods and mortals – belong together in one . . . The simple oneness of the four we call *the fourfold*. Mortals *are* in the fourfold by *dwelling*. (VA 143; BW 351–2)

Heidegger has now clearly shown the site, the place of poetic dwelling. This site or place is the truth of being, and the fundamental links between the different thoughts in Heidegger's work seem to come together. Heidegger claims that 'we have thought the truth of being in the worlding of world as the mirror play [*Spiegel-Spiel*] of the fourfold of sky and earth, mortals and gods' (GA79, 74; QCT 45; see GA65, 310).

If the above argument is followed, it can be seen that the history of being must work in tandem with the notion of poetic dwelling. This is made clear in the essay on Jünger discussed earlier. It will be remembered that Heidegger is debating with Jünger on the notion of nihilism. Here, instead of opposing being to nothingness, the void, nihilism, Heidegger instead effaces the word itself. This is because Heidegger argues that

> a thoughtful glance ahead [*Vorblick*] into this realm can only write 'being' as ~~being~~. The drawing of these crossed lines initially has only a preventative role, namely, that of preventing the almost ineradicable habit of representing 'being' only as something standing somewhere on its own that then on occasion first comes face-to-face with humans. (GA9, 238–9)

The purpose of this peculiar typographical device is not difficult to understand:

> The symbol of crossing through [*Durchkreuzung*] cannot, however, be the merely negative sign of crossing out [*Durchstreichung*]. It points, rather, toward the four regions of the fourfold [*Geviert*] and of their gathering at the place of crossing through [*Ort der Durchkreuzung*]. (GA9, 239)

The place of intersection is ~~being~~, and therefore any history of being must take into account the crossed lines of poetic dwelling, of platial significance.

Within these four-crossed lines, at their intersection, the human dwells, poetically. Despite Krell's worry that 'Heidegger's preoccupation with "the holy" is indeed discomforting',[59] and despite the fact that a potentially romantic reading of the fourfold (i.e. anti-technology) might be apparent,[60] there is something of fundamental value in what Heidegger is suggesting here. I am not suggesting that histories should henceforth take notice of the fourfold in quite the same way that Heidegger suggests, but that they can feed on the insight this reading of Hölderlin allows. Foucault, for example, is heavily indebted to the way Heidegger has fused the concepts of history and space and yet he never discusses the prison, the hospital or the plague town in terms of the gods, the human, sky and earth.

PLATIAL DESCRIPTIONS

Having gained these insights, Heidegger undertakes some studies that could be seen as platial. However, important though the historical is to these pieces, it would be pushing credulity to describe them as histories. What they do instead is examine, although with a historical backdrop, the significance of space, place and location. Indeed, throughout Heidegger's later works the importance of space and place is evident, turning up in some unusual places. For example, in an essay entitled 'Language', Heidegger discusses Georg Trakl's poem 'A Winter Evening'. His commentary is especially of interest when he looks at the line 'Pain has turned the threshold to stone', the second line of the third stanza: 'The threshold is the ground-beam that bears the doorway as a whole. It sustains the middle in which the two, the outside and the inside, penetrate each other. The threshold bears the between . . .' (GA12, 24; PLT 204). This understanding of the threshold as a place of transition is recurrent in several places in Foucault's work. But in the context of this chapter, and to draw together some of the strands, the focus will be on three places: the bridge in 'Building Dwelling Thinking'; the jug in 'The Thing'; and, in a return to an earlier theme, a discussion of art and space.

Heidegger's lecture 'Building Dwelling Thinking' is geared toward investigating two questions. First, 'what is the relationship between place [*Ort*] and space?' and second 'what is the relationship between the human and space?' (VA 149; BW 357). As with many of his later essays, Heidegger uses etymology to penetrate the words.[61] He begins by looking at the word space itself: 'What the word for space, *Raum*, designates is said by its ancient meaning. *Raum, Rum,* means a *Platz* that is freed for settlement and lodging'. Space is freed, liberated, for a purpose:

> A space is something that has been made room for [*Eingeräumtes*], something that has been freed, namely within a boundary, Greek πέρας. A boundary is not that at which something stops but, as the Greeks recognised, the boundary is that from which something *begins its essential unfolding.* That is why the concept is that of the ὁρισμός, that is boundary [*Grenze*].

A freed space within a boundary, a threshold. Heidegger continues: 'Space is in essence that for which room has been made, that which is let into its bounds' (VA 149; BW 356). There is an important shift in Heidegger's overall argument here. Rather than place being opposed to space, understood as Cartesian, Heidegger is suggesting that space can be rethought through its relation to place, in order to return us to a more originary understanding. But this is space as *Raum*, a word which unlike the English has no etymological kinship with the Latin *spatium*. Such an attitude is clearly evident in the late lecture 'Art and Space', dealt with in detail in the final section of this chapter. To further his purpose here Heidegger decides to examine something that has been built, a built thing, and to assess how this relates to space and place. The example for Heidegger's reflection is a bridge:

> The bridge ... does not just connect banks [*Ufer*] that are already present-at-hand. The banks emerge as banks only as the bridge crosses the stream. The bridge expressly causes them to lie across from each other. One side is set off against the other by the bridge. Nor do the banks stretch along the stream as indifferent border strips of the dry land. With the banks, the bridge brings to the stream the one and the other expanse of the landscape lying behind them [*Uferlandschaft*]. It brings stream and bank and land into each other's neighbourhood ... Bridges initiate in many ways. The city bridge leads from the precincts of the castle to the cathedral square; the river bridge near the country town brings wagons and horse teams to the surrounding villages. The old stone bridge's humble brook crossing gives to the harvest wagon its passage [*Weg*] from the fields into the village and carries the lumber cart from the field path to the road. The *Autobahn* bridge is tied into the network of long-distance traffic, paced and calculated for maximum yield. (VA 146–7; BW 354)

The investigation of the question of technology showed that there Heidegger opposed the bridge in its relationship with nature to the hydroelectric plant. Both are related to the river, but in fundamentally different ways. The bridge Heidegger has in mind here is a site for the fourfold:

> To be sure, the bridge is a thing of its *own* kind; for it gathers the fourfold in such a way that it allows a *site* [*Stätte*] for it. But only something *that is itself a place* [*Ort*] can make space [*einräumen*] for a site. The place is not already present-at-hand before the bridge ... *Accordingly, spaces receive their essential being from places and not 'from' space* [*Demnach empfangen die Räume ihr Wesen aus Orten und nicht aus «dem» Raum*]. (VA 148–9; BW 355–6)

The bridge is such a place. It can therefore, as such a thing, function to situate 'a space into which earth and sky, gods and mortals are admitted' (VA 149; BW 357).[62]

This all links back into the project outlined above, of finding a more truthful way of characterizing the human's relationship with, and perception of, space. Heidegger suggests that we should pay heed to the relations between places and spaces, especially as these come together in buildings. Space should not be seen as something 'over and above' humans, because inherent in the concept of the human is that of dwelling. Instead of the abstracting Cartesianism, Heidegger suggests space as locales, places. Numerical magnitudes can never be the '*ground* of the essence of spaces and places' (VA 150; BW 358). Heidegger explains: 'The human's relation to places, and through places to spaces, inheres in his dwelling. The relationship between the human and space is none other than dwelling, thought essentially' (VA 152; BW 359). 'Because building produces things as places, it is closer to the essence of spaces and to the essential descent "of" space than any geometry and mathematics. Building puts up places that make space for the site of the fourfold' (VA 153; BW 360). Having attained this insight, Heidegger comes back to the purpose for his talk, the housing crisis in Germany. As with many of his essays of this period – the work on technology and the πόλις are striking examples – this is a critique of the present. Building is not simply architecture or construction, but a letting dwell. Heidegger suggests that Germany is not just facing a crisis of housing, but of dwelling and thinking too (VA 156; BW 363).[63]

Indeed, Heidegger thinks that the crisis of thinking is perhaps the greatest crisis facing mankind: 'Most thought-provoking in our thought-provoking time is that we are still not thinking' (WHD 3; WCT 6). As a concluding comment to the remarks on this essay, it is worth noting that understanding the German word *bauen*, to build, enables us to understand better Heidegger's notion – already there in *Being and Time*, of *Destruktion*. This has been continually rendered as 'de-struction'. Like the English destruction, *Destruktion* derives from the Latin *destruere*, to pull down, literally *de-struere*, to un-build. To translate *Destruktion* as 'destruction' emphasizes the violence rather than the de-structuring. Violence may well be a part, but it is a violence of excavation, unbuilding rather than obliteration. Nietzsche, Foucault and Derrida (who most obviously borrows and creatively translates this term as *deconstruction*) all undertake this project in various ways. As Heidegger himself clarifies: 'De-struction does not mean destroying [*Zerstören*] but unbuilding [*Abbauen*], liquidating [*Abtragen*], putting to one side the merely historical assertions about the history of philosophy' (WP 70–2/71–3; see Q IV, 426).

Heidegger's discussion in the lecture 'The Thing', part of the 'Insight' series, begins by discussing the way the modern world is making all distances in time and space shrink. Now we can reach the other side of the world overnight, hear news as it happens across the world, watch speeded up footage of a plant growing and see sites from ancient history on film. But, as has been shown, Heidegger does not always equate shortness of distance with nearness. Via a brief passage that suggests that the atom bomb is the culmination of humanity's attitude to science, Heidegger claims that so far humanity has 'given no more thought to the thing as a thing than we have to nearness'. Just as the bridge served as the example of a built thing, Van Gogh's painting was a representative work of art, and the shoes he painted an example of equipment, Heidegger this time chooses a jug to stand as his case-study: 'The jug is a thing. What is the jug?' (VA 158; PLT 166).

The jug is a holding vessel, something that holds. The holding is done by the base and sides, and the jug can be held itself by its handle. The jug is made by the potter from the earth. 'The jug's thingness resides in its being as vessel. We become aware of the vessel's holding nature when we fill the jug'. But, asks Heidegger, what does filling the jug mean? We fill the jug, which can hold, and which does so by the base and sides. This does not mean that we fill the base and sides, but rather pour between the sides and over the bottom. Therefore, rather than filling anything of the jug, we fill the emptiness of the jug. 'The emptiness, the void [*die Leere*], is what does the vessel's holding. The empty space, this nothing of the jug, is what the jug is as the holding vessel.' It follows from this that the potter who 'forms sides and bottom on his wheel' does not strictly speaking make the jug; rather, he shapes the void (VA 161; PLT 169).

Of course, modern science will tell us that there is no void in the jug, but that it is filled with air, and that pouring anything else into the jug merely displaces what is already there. Heidegger does not dispute that this scientific view is correct but he does argue that it tells us little about the jug. This is because 'science always encounters only what *its* kind of representation has admitted beforehand as an object possible for science' (VA 162; PLT 170). This is what Heidegger was arguing back in *Being and Time* – that usual theories relate to things at a level abstracted from everyday action. The ontological foundation of modern science acts to limit the ontic phenomena it is able to experience and to encompass. Science can give us an interpretation, which can even be correct, but it does not help in understanding the jug. We can place a stone on a balance, but this merely brings its heaviness into the form of a calculated weight; the weight's burden has escaped us (GA5, 35; BW 172). Similarly, Kant's thing-in-itself means 'an object that is no object for us' because it is thought apart from the human encounter of it (VA 169; PLT 177; see GA41).

Although Heidegger does not mention it, there has also been a subtle revision of his view in *Being and Time* on the idea of 'in', for now it is significant that the gift, the wine, is 'in' the jug. For Heidegger believes it is important that the character of the jug consists 'in the gift of the outpouring' (VA 164; PLT 172). This thing, in its place, in its context, holding the gift, is another site for the fourfold of gods, humans, sky and earth: 'In the gift of the outpouring earth and sky, gods and mortals dwell *together all at once*' (VA 165–6; PLT 173). Heidegger continues, and makes clearer the spatial implications:

> What is gathered in the gift gathers itself in appropriatively staying the fourfold. This manifold-simple gathering is the jug's essence. Our language denotes what a gathering is by an ancient word. That word is: *thing*. The

jug's essence is the pure, giving gathering of the one-fold fourfold into a single stay. The jug essences as a thing. (VA 166; PLT 174)

Just as we use a hammer, and experience space, we must look at the jug in a way akin to poetic dwelling. To understand the jug as a jug we must avoid the abstraction of modern science.

ART AND SPACE

One of Heidegger's very last pieces is a lecture entitled 'Art and Space', published in 1969. It picks up several of the themes about space that have been discussed in these chapters, and therefore serves well to summarize the argument. It also leads us into the arguments concerning Foucault in the following chapters. It is very precise in its use of certain key terms, a fact obscured in part by the existing English translation. It was shown in the discussion of the bridge that Heidegger thought that a space is something that has been made room for, something that has been freed, namely within a boundary. This idea is found in a few places within his work, notably when he looks at elements of the rural existence. In one example he talks of the cabinet-maker's apprentice learning to 'answer and respond . . . to all the different kinds of wood and to the shapes slumbering within wood . . . this relationship to wood is what maintains the whole craft' (WHD 50; WCT 14–15). In another example, Heidegger speaks of the idea of a pathway: a recurrent theme in his work. 'To clear a way [*Einen Weg bahnen*] – for instance across a snow-covered field – is still today in the Alemannic-Swabian dialect called *wëgen* [waying]. This transitive verb means to form a way, giving shape to it and keeping it in shape (GA12, 249; WL 129–30). We will remember the titles of *Holzwege* and *Wegmarken*. A path through the woods may need to be cleared before it can be seen.

It seems to be the same with sculpture, the art-form that is the basis for the 'Art and Space' lecture. Heidegger begins by suggesting that even those remarks of his that are uttered as assertions are actually questions, but it seems as if what he is doing is gradually exposing the flaws in some of his initial formulations of the question of sculpture, and that the path of thought is becoming increasingly clear. At the outset, Heidegger suggests that

> sculpted forms [*Die plastischen Gebilde*] are bodies [*Körper*]. Their mass, consisting of different materials, is variously fashioned. The fashioning happens by limitation through an inclusionary and exclusionary limit.

Through this, space comes into play; occupied by the sculpted form as a closed, breached and empty volume.

This seems fair enough, and perhaps a usual initial reaction. Then Heidegger remarks that 'art and scientific technology consider and treat space toward various purposes in various ways' (GA13, 204). This much has been made clear in his opposition of experiential and mathematical space. Heidegger rehearses that argument again here, suggesting that 'physically-technologically ordered space, however it may be determined' should not be held 'as the sole true space'. This is due to the fact that this view of space, of uniform extension, determined by Galileo and Newton, is the correlate of modern European subjectivity (GA13, 205) – i.e. of Descartes. The question of history is central.

However Heidegger then outlines what appear to be the three spaces involved in an understanding of sculpture: 'Space, within which the sculptured form can be met as a present-at-hand object; space, which encloses the volume of the figure; space, which persists between volumes.' Even if calculative measurement cannot be applied to artistic figures, asks Heidegger, are these three spaces still not merely derivative of physical-technological space? For an answer to the question of the propriety [*Eigenes*] of space, Heidegger returns to language – so often the preoccupation of his late essays. In 'space' [*Raum*], the word 'making space' [*Räumen*] is spoken. 'This means: clearing out [*roden*], to make free from wilderness. Making space brings forth the free, the openness for the settling and dwelling of humans' (GA13, 206). This much has been seen in the essays that looked at the idea of poetic dwelling. As Heidegger then goes on to suggest, 'making space is, thought in its propriety, the release [*Freigabe*] of places [*Orten*]' (GA13, 206).

Shifting the emphasis onto place recalls the insights of the essays on the jug and the bridge. These places are important to humans in terms of a home, in terms of the gods, in terms of dwelling. We are reminded that 'place always opens a region, in which it gathers things in their belonging together' (GA13, 207), and that we must 'learn to recognise that things themselves are places, and not only occupy a place'. This notion of place is now, as before, opposed to technological, Cartesian space: 'Place is not found within a pre-given space, such as that of physico-technological space. The latter unfolds only through the reigning of places of a region.' What this enables is the potential for rethinking the notion of space otherwise than extension. Although in these chapters I have often introduced an opposition between space and place, this is in order to distance myself from space understood as extension. Here – as in 'Building Dwelling Thinking' – Heidegger collapses the terms back together, by hinting at their originary bond. This was clearly the intent of the understanding of time-space in the *Beiträge*. As shall be suggested in the following chapter, the French *espace* holds this association with place better than the English 'space'.

Returning to the subject of the lecture, Heidegger suggests that the initial direction of the piece was misguided, as 'the interplay of art and space must be thought out of the experience of place and region'. Where art is sculpture, there is 'no occupying of space. Sculpture would have no confrontation [*Auseinandersetzung*] with space', instead 'sculpture would be the embodiment of places' (GA13, 208). In thinking of sculpture we should abandon the idea of volume, 'the signification of which is only as old as modern technological natural science', which would make sculpture 'an embodying bringing-into-the-work of places . . . the embodiment of the truth of being in its work of instituting places' (GA13, 209). The link to the truth of being, which has been seen to be an inherently historical question, makes the suggestion complete. Place is historical: history is platial.

In a 1958 essay on language, Heidegger again returns to the rural, and argues that two farmsteads an hour apart can have greater neighbourhood than two townhouses. Nearness is not outside and independent of space and time, but it does not depend on space and time as *parameters* (GA12, 198–9; WL 103). Understanding space and time in a non-mathematically calculated way is precisely what Heidegger has been shown to do throughout these three chapters. Struggling for a way to express what he means, Heidegger resorts to creating new verbs: time times, space spaces. 'Space: makes space for placing and places, vacates them and at the same time gives them free for all things and receives what is simultaneous as space-time.' This notion of space-time – anticipated and outlined in the *Beiträge*, but only fully elaborated and made possible by later work – brings to completion the path that Heidegger has been walking. The Kantian primacy of time is gone; time is resolutely non-Aristotelian; the understanding of space by extension is discarded. Timing and spacing [*Zeitigend einräumend*] 'move the time-play-space of the encounter of the four world regions: earth and sky, gods and the human – the world play' (GA12, 201–2; WL 106). This is clarified in the lecture 'Time and Being'. As has been shown, Heidegger wishes to conceive of time not in terms of the now but of the Moment, in terms of presencing. Here, he suggests that presencing 'opens up what we call time-space'. Time-space does not mean the distance between two points in time, it is not a time-*span*, but the 'openness which opens up in the mutual self-extending of futural approach, past and present. This openness exclusively and primarily provides the space in which space as we usually know it can unfold' (ZSD 14–15; TB 14; see GA41, 16; GA65, 371–88).

These chapters have attempted to trace the trajectory of the concepts of history and space through the works of Heidegger, in order to illuminate both Heidegger's own work, and to demonstrate his influence on Foucault. In the lecture 'Time and Being', Heidegger concedes that 'the attempt in *Being and Time*, section 70, to derive the spatiality of Dasein from temporality is untenable' (ZSD 24; TB 23).[64] To think space fundamentally requires insight into 'the properties peculiar to place' (ZSD 24; TB 23). This half of the book has shown how and why Heidegger came to realize this. The consequences of this realization are readily apparent in the work of Foucault, whose own path of thought had begun at the time of this lecture. Following that path leads into the territory of the second half of this book.

CHAPTER 4

Towards a Spatial History

Foucault was never keen for his work to be analysed as a method, a theory, or worse, as a system, but suggested that those interested in his work should do genealogies, as he had done.[1] But whilst Foucault felt that his work provided a set of conceptual tools, a toolbox (DE III, 427; P/K 145) for use by others, these tools have sometimes been used uncritically, without due attendance to their theoretical underpinnings.[2] It is a principal claim of this book that to understand how to use Foucault's work it is necessary to understand its theoretical background, and, therefore, his intellectual heritage.

This chapter therefore looks at Foucault's works in the light of the understanding of Heidegger established in the previous chapters. It deals with the theoretical formulations of Foucault's work, with emphasis on his methodological works, looking at his historical approach, and the role of space within it. The following chapter uses the insights gained from these analyses to recast the readings of two of Foucault's most important studies: *Histoire de la folie*; and the genealogy of modern discipline in hospitals, schools, the army and prisons found in *The Birth of the Clinic*, *Discipline and Punish* and numerous shorter pieces.

I: A HISTORY OF LIMITS

The preface to Foucault's first major work, *Folie et déraison: Histoire de la folie à l'âge classique*, tried to set out some methodological concerns.[3] Foucault argues that what he is writing is a 'history of *limits* [*limites*]' (DE I, 161), a history of boundaries. His research examines a realm 'where what is in question are the limits rather than the identity of a culture' (DE I, 161; MC xiii). Each limit-experience — an experience, such as madness, which inhabits the frontiers of our culture — 'marks a limit which signifies, at the same time, an original division' (DE I, 161).[4] This interest in the limits of experience — of transgression, of the crossing of boundaries, of the mapping of uncharted space, of the path between the known and the unknown — works on two main levels, the level of the imaginary and the level of the real. Foucault stresses that he undertakes his inquiry 'under the sun of the great Nietzschean search' (DE I, 162), and the link to the approach of *The Birth of Tragedy* is clear throughout. In an interview around the same time he also indicates the influence of the historian of religions, Georges Dumézil. Dumézil is important because of his understanding of structure, of social segregation and exclusion. In *Histoire de la folie* Foucault is interested in seeing how the physical divide of segregation and exclusion interrelates with the experience of madness, with science and rationalist philosophy (DE I, 168; FL 8). This relationship of the real and the imaginary – of the practical and the theoretical – underpins his studies throughout.[5]

The language that Foucault uses in works of his archaeological period – *Histoire de la folie, The Birth of the Clinic, The Order of Things, The Archaeology of Knowledge* – is often overtly spatialized, making use of terms such as limit, boundary, transgression, and threshold.[6] In its understanding of the conceptualization of knowledge – of discourse and *episteme* – it bears comparison with the spatialized conceptions of Nietzsche and Heidegger. The particular terms that Foucault uses are also found in his contemporaneous essays on literature – mainly in the journal *Critique* – on figures such as Bataille, Blanchot, Hölderlin and Flaubert.[7] As a particular example of the links between his literary and historical work, it is instructive to compare the books *The Birth of the Clinic* and *Raymond Roussel*, both published in May 1963.[8] The opening line of the former – 'This book is about space, about language, and about death; it is a question of the gaze' (NC v; BC ix) – could easily stand as a description of the latter (see RR 209; DL 166).[9]

What is important about Foucault's use of overtly spatialized language is that it enables him to free his histories from the teleological bias of alternative accounts. By conceiving of historical periods or epochs as bounded areas, he is able to investigate their limits or thresholds, and trace the potential of transgression, or egress.[10] Foucault is occasionally described, therefore, as a thinker of discontinuity, in that he tries to locate abrupt shifts, or 'breaks' in the history of thought.[11] Instead, Foucault argues that he recognizes what appear to be obvious breaks, but tries to analyse how the shift occurred. For example, *The Birth of the Clinic* is concerned with less than half a century, but it is 'one of those periods that mark an ineradicable chronological threshold' (NC 199; BC 195). The work of Bayle seems like a 'hilarious object of folklore', whereas Pomme's work, even if it contains errors, is 'nevertheless part of the same type of knowledge as our own' (PPC 100; see DE III, 142–4; FR 53–5). His work is therefore a critical operation to investigate this, aiming:

> *To establish limits,* where the history of thought, in its traditional form, gave itself an indefinite space ... I would like to substitute the notion that the

discourses are limited practical domains which have their boundaries [*frontières* – borders/frontiers], their rules of formation, their conditions of existence ... to which one can affix thresholds, and assign conditions of birth and disappearance. (DE I, 683–4; FL 41)

Similarly he conceives of madness and reason, sickness and health in spatial terms, and then examines the groups that inhabit the liminal areas. I will return to the analyses of actual spaces below, but first it is worth dwelling on Foucault's use of spatialized language in his work on history, designated by two main rubrics – archaeology and genealogy.

ARCHAEOLOGY

Foucault uses the word archaeology in a number of early works, and it at first appears, as Sheridan suggests, to be almost just an alternative to 'history' as a means of distinguishing his approach.[12] Over the course of his work in the 1960s it becomes a central concept in his work. Foucault's choice of the term 'archaeology', however, immediately invites misunderstanding. It is neither the search for an origin – in Greek *arche* – nor does it relate to geological excavation. Foucault claims that he is justified by 'the right of words – which is not that of the philologists' in using the term *archaeology* to describe his researches, as they examine the *archive*: 'Archaeology describes discourses as practices specified in the element of the archive' (AS 173; AK 131). In the sense that he understands his research it is closer to being an *archiveology*.

Foucault describes the archive as 'the general system of the formation and transformation of statements [*énoncés*]' (AS 171; AK 130). An *énoncé* is a technical or formal statement, made within a particular discipline – Linnaeus' *Genera Plantaruma* is made up of *énoncés*, the forms of a verb in a book of Latin grammar are *énoncés*, as are algebraic formulae (AS 109; AK 82). The *énoncé* is neither the same kind of unit as a sentence, a proposition, or a speech act, nor is it the same as a material object. It is 'neither entirely linguistic, nor exclusively material ... it is caught up in a logical, grammatical, locutory nexus' (AS 114–15; AK 86). This last definition is important as the rules of discourse function in a similar way to those of logic and grammar. Just as in ordinary speech we need to obey the rules of grammar and logic, within a technical conversation we have to situate our *énoncés* within the rules of the discourse. 'An *énoncé* belongs to a discursive formation as a sentence belongs to a text, and a proposition to a deductive whole' (AS 152; AK 116). The *énoncés* actually permissible at any given time are only a fraction of those logically and grammatically possible: the discursive formulation of the subject also acts as a limit. This is why, for example, Bayle makes sense to us today, whilst Pomme 'speaks to us in the language of fantasy' (NC v–vi; BC ix–x); why Borges' 'certain Chinese Encyclopaedia' provokes such laughter (M&C 7; OT xv).

For an *énoncé* to be accepted within a discipline – even before it can be pronounced true or false – it must 'fulfil complex and serious demands', it must be, in Canguilhem's phrase, 'within the true' (OD 35–6). This is an important point, as it proves that a discourse conditions the possibility of all *énoncés* – whether they are true or false. We cannot judge Pomme's *énoncé* as true or false, it fails at a lower level than that, it is simply 'fantasy'. This becomes clearer in Foucault's discussion of the 'positivity of a discourse' that 'characterises its unity throughout time ... it defines a limited space of communication ... positivity plays the role of what might be called the *historical a priori*' (AS 166–7; AK 126–7). Foucault accepts that juxtaposing these two words produces a 'rather startling effect', as the standard understanding of *a priori* is that it is ahistorical, absolute. Foucault's term does not simply mean that the *a priori* is also endowed with a history, rather he is introducing a notion of pluralism into the history of ideas, in that there have been several *a priori* structures in various disciplines, that conditioned possibilities in those subjects.[13] This bears definite comparison with the understanding of the history of science found in Nietzsche and Heidegger. Foucault is, like Nietzsche and the later Heidegger, historicizing the Kantian question. Foucault's understanding of the historical *a priori* does not function as 'a condition of validity for judgements, but a condition of reality for *énoncés*' (AS 167–9; AK 127–8).[14] In other words he is not looking to see whether *énoncés* are true, but how they are possible.

In *The Birth of the Clinic* Foucault examines the area of physical illness, and argues that there has been a shift in how things have been seen. Today, medicine is generally accepted to be based upon clear, objective, scientific knowledge: the body and diseases seen with an unblemished empirical eye. However, it has not always been so, and medicine is not based on pure experience free of interpretation, but is structured by a set of beliefs relative to the period, a grid of *a priori* conceptions. For the nineteenth century physician the patient (their age, sex, and personal history) got in the way of the disease, so this interference has to be bypassed, through the abstraction of the gaze [*le regard*]. *The Birth of the Clinic* is therefore the archaeology of this 'medical gaze', it looks to establish how it arose and what made it achievable.[15]

In *The Order of Things* this understanding is put to work across a sweep of disciplines, examining the knowledges of life, language and wealth through three broad historical periods, which Foucault calls *epistemes*. Interestingly, he finds examples of the shift from one *episteme* to another in literary works.[16]

Between the Renaissance and the Classical epoch, Don Quixote's adventures 'form the boundary [*tracent la limite*]: they mark the end of the old interplay between resemblance and signs and contain the beginnings of new relations' (M&C 60; OT 46). The birth of modern culture is found in the work of the Marquis de Sade, especially in *Justine* and *Juliette* (M&C 222; OT 210). Foucault is concerned with:

> In what way, then, our culture has made manifest the existence of order, and how, to the modalities of that order, the exchanges owed their laws, the living beings their constants, the words their sequence and their representative value; what modalities of order have been recognized, posited, linked with space and time, in order to create the positive basis of knowledge [*connaissances*] as we find it employed in grammar and philology, in natural history and biology, in the study of wealth and political economy. Quite obviously, such an analysis does not belong to the history of ideas or of science: it is rather an inquiry whose aim is to rediscover on what basis knowledge [*connaissance*] and theory become *possible* [emphasis added]; within what space of order knowledge [*savoir*] was constituted; on the basis of what historical *a priori*, and in the element of what positivity, ideas could appear, sciences be established, experience be reflected in philosophies, rationalities be formed, only, perhaps, to dissolve and vanish soon afterwards. I am not concerned therefore, to describe the progress of knowledge [*connaissances*] towards an objectivity in which today's science can finally be recognised; what I am attempting to bring to light is the epistemological field, the *episteme* in which knowledge [*connaissances*], envisaged apart from all criteria having reference to its rational value or to its objective forms, grounds positivity and thereby manifests a history which is not that of its growing perfection, *but rather that of its conditions of possibility* [emphasis added]; in this account what should appear are those configurations within the *space* of knowledge [*savoir*] which have given rise to the diverse forms of empirical science [*connaissance empirique*]. Rather than a history in the traditional meaning of the word, this is an 'archaeology'. (M&C 13; OT xxi–xxii)

The archaeological analysis allows Foucault to trace the change in these knowledges, examining how the seventeenth and eighteenth centuries had general grammar, natural history and the analysis of wealth; whilst the nineteenth century had philology, biology and political economy:

> Archaeology, addressing itself to the general space of knowledge, to its configurations, and to the mode of being of the things that appear in it,

defines systems of simultaneity, as well as the series of mutations necessary and sufficient to circumscribe the threshold of a new positivity. (M&C 14; OT xxiii)

The use of spatial language throughout these works is pronounced. Rather than conceive of historical changes as a linear development, Foucault suggests that the 'domain of the modern *episteme* should be represented rather as a volume of space open in three dimensions . . . [an] epistemological trihedron' (M&C 358; OT 346–7). These examinations lead Foucault to one of his most celebrated formulations, suggesting that 'the human is an invention of recent date. And one perhaps nearing its end'.

> If those arrangements [*dispositions*] were to disappear as they appeared, if some event of which we can at the moment do no more than sense the possibility . . . were to cause them to crumble, as the ground of Classical thought did, at the end of the eighteenth century, then one can certainly wager that the human would be erased, like a face drawn in sand at the edge [*limite*] of the sea. (M&C 398; OT 387)

Some key issues arise from Foucault's archaeological period: first, does his analysis of *epistemes* constitute a global study, and is he able to escape the problem of subjectivity; and second, are his studies structuralist? Concerning the first, Foucault suggests that archaeological analysis is always limited and regional: 'Far from wishing to reveal general forms, archaeology tries to outline particular configurations' (AS 206; AK 157). Whilst it is true that most of his studies do look at limited areas – historically and geographically bounded – at times he does try to make the broad sweep. *The Birth of the Clinic*, looking at medicine, for about 50 years, and at the French example, is arguably a more successful study than *The Order of Things*, which studies three areas, across almost 400 years, and across the Western world. Foucault denied this, but the comparative study in the latter work set him up for refutation by counter-examples that did not follow the same epistemic shifts (see AS 207–8; AK 158–9).

Foucault suggests that 'instead of exploring the consciousness/knowledge [*connaissance*]/science axis (which cannot escape subjectivity), archaeology explores the discursive practice/knowledge [*savoir*]/science axis' (AS 239; AK 183). It is clear that a distinction between *connaissance* and *savoir* is essential, although they are both usually translated as 'knowledge' in English. To explain his understanding of these terms, Foucault adds a note to the English edition:

By *connaissance* I mean the relation of the subject to the object and the formal rules that govern it. *Savoir* refers to the conditions that are necessary in a particular period for this or that type of object to be given to *connaissance* and for this or that enunciation to be formulated. (AK 15n)[17]

We can see how this understanding parallels the distinction Heidegger makes between ontic and ontological knowledge in *Being and Time*. For Heidegger, the question of being is an ontological question, which aims 'at ascertaining the *a priori* conditions ... for the possibility of the sciences which examine entities' – ontic knowledge (GA2, 11).

Just as Heidegger read Kant's *Critique of Pure Reason* not as a theory of *ontic* knowledge (an epistemology) but rather of *ontological* knowledge (an ontology), so too must we understand Foucault's archaeology as a theory of ontological knowledge (*savoir*) rather than of ontic knowledge [*connaissance*]. As I noted in Chapter One, in Kant and the early Heidegger, this investigation of the conditions of possibility is a radically ahistorical question. But Nietzsche's hints in *Beyond Good and Evil* and the later Heidegger show that this investigation must be posed historically. This is precisely what Foucault's research is concerned with: his refusal to set universal conditions means that this ontology is historicized as a historical ontology. One of Foucault's most revealing pieces in this regard is his preface to the English edition of *The Order of Things*. Here he makes some important points about how his investigation should be seen. First, he notes that the history of science gives pride of place to rigorous sciences such as mathematics, cosmology and physics, but other disciplines – such as those Foucault examines here – are perhaps thought of as too tinged with empirical thought: their history is thought to be irregular.

> But what if empirical knowledge, at a given time and in a given culture, *did* possess a well-defined regularity? If the very possibility of recording facts, of allowing oneself to be convinced by them, of distorting them in traditions or of making purely speculative use of them, if even this was not at the mercy of chance? If errors (and truths), the practice of old beliefs including not only genuine discoveries, but also the most naïve notions, obeyed, at a given moment, the laws of a certain code of knowledge? (OT ix)

But instead of working at the levels usual for the historian of science, Foucault works at a lower level. The basic level of investigation for such historians is that of tracing the progress of discovery, the formulation of problems and the clash of controversy, a level that examines theories in their internal economy. This is what Foucault calls the 'processes and products of the scientific consciousness'. However, the history of science also tries to look at the influences that affected that consciousness, its implicit philosophies: the unconscious of science. That is to say, historians of science look at the general rules of what constitutes knowledge within their field of study. But Foucault wants to go still deeper, to look at the *'positive unconscious* of knowledge: a level that eludes the consciousness of the scientist and yet is part of scientific discourse'.

> What was common to the natural history, the economics, and the grammar of the Classical period was certainly not present to the consciousness of the scientist . . . but unknown to themselves, the naturalists, economists, and grammarians employed the same rules to define the objects proper to their own study, to form their concepts, to build their theories. It is these rules of formation which were never formulated in their own right, but are to be found only in widely differing theories, concepts, and objects of study, that I have tried to reveal, by isolating, as their specific locus, a level that I have called, somewhat arbitrarily perhaps, archaeological. (OT xi)

It is unfortunate that we do not have the original French version of this text – the version in *Dits et écrits* is a retranslation of the English (see DE II, 7–13) – as the distinction between *connaissance* and *savoir* would appear to be central. Foucault distinguishes between the 'epistemological level of knowledge (or scientific consciousness) and the archaeological level of knowledge', and therefore explicitly distances himself from working in the field of epistemology. As I have suggested, his examination of the foundation of epistemology is, like Kant, ontology, but always a historical examination. Foucault is aware that this depersonalized analysis causes difficulty, specifically around the problem of the subject: 'Can one speak of science and its history (and therefore of its conditions of existence, its changes, the errors it has perpetrated, the sudden advances that have sent it off on a new course) without reference to the scientist himself . . .?' (OT xiii).[18] Foucault's aim is not to challenge the validity of intellectual biographies, or examinations at the usual level of the history of science, but to question if these are themselves sufficient for examining the 'systems of regularities that have a decisive role in the history of the sciences' (OT xiii–xiv).

How much are the subjects responsible for scientific discourse determined by conditions that 'dominate and even overwhelm them'? Foucault's aim, therefore, is to explore the discourse of science 'not from the point of view of the individuals who are speaking, nor from the point of view of the formal structures of what they are saying, but from the point of view of the rules that come into play in the very existence of such discourse'. What *conditions* did

Linnaeus, Petty or Arnauld have to fulfil? (OT xiv) Though Foucault was to move away from the vocabulary of his archaeological period, this problematic remains central to his concerns.

Concerning the second question and the relation to structuralism, we should note that Foucault was often thought of in this way, especially with regard to his works of the 1960s.[19] By the late 1960s he was distancing himself from the movement, but had earlier certainly used its language and, in a revealing interview given in Tunisia, had accepted the label, clarifying how he understood and used its tools (DE I, 580–4). But in the 1970 foreword to *The Order of Things*, he berates 'certain half-witted "commentators" [who] persist in labelling me a "structuralist". I have been unable to get it into their tiny minds that I have used none of the methods, concepts, or key terms that characterise structuralist analysis' (OT xiv). This is clearly protesting too much. As Neocleous notes, there are clear similarities between Foucault and the structuralists over the question of agency,[20] which links to a common anti-humanism. The ethnology of Lévi-Strauss and the psychoanalysis of Lacan are praised in *The Order of Things* for dissolving the human (M&C 385ff; OT 373ff; see also AS 22–3; AK 12–13); Foucault's debt to the work of Althusser, and their common heritage in Bachelard, Canguilhem and Heidegger showcase other links. Despite the fact that Foucault takes his anti-humanism from the same source many of these others do – Heidegger's *Letter on Humanism* and the wish to critique Sartre's appropriation of Heidegger – the links are clearly there. Similarly Foucault shares with the structuralists an appreciation of the work of Saussure, especially evident in the language used in *The Birth of the Clinic* – something he later admits to as a problem (AS 27; AK 16). Rather than accept his passage from structuralism to something else – sometimes termed poststructuralism – Foucault attempts to cover his tracks, revising *The Birth of the Clinic* in 1972, and purging it of structuralist language. James Miller suggests that the use of this *jargon* was largely cosmetic, as the 'buzzwords were easily jettisoned in 1972, without touching the book's central argument'.[21] There is another way of reading this however. The *argument* built on structuralist foundations remains untouched, and it is only the *language* of structuralism that was jettisoned.

Despite Foucault's repeated denials, his archaeological approach owes much to the French intellectual scene of the 1960s – although it differs in two central respects. The first is that while most structuralists marginalized history, preferring atemporal structures, Foucault was from the outset a historian (see DE III, 144–5; FR 56; AS 25; AK 15).[22] Second – and a point that will be returned to – while Foucault shared with the structuralists a predilection for spatial metaphors, he alone continually paired them with analyses of actual spaces.[23] His histories were not merely spatial in the language they used, or in the metaphors of knowledge they developed, but were also histories of spaces, and attendant to the spaces of history.

GENEALOGY

The events of 1968 seem to have had a major effect on Foucault. No longer did he concentrate on the workings of language, of discursive practices, but he returned to the examination of particular disciplines and their internal shifts, as he had in *Histoire de la folie*, and, to an extent, in *The Birth of the Clinic*. As noted above, Foucault only rarely uses the terms carefully elaborated in *The Archaeology of Knowledge* again. Hacking suggests that his 'obsession with words was too fragile too stand',[24] though my contention is that the theoretical apparatus elaborated simply fell into the background. The crucial text in examining the change is Foucault's inaugural lecture at the *Collège de France*, *The Order of Discourse*. In this text we find a burgeoning interest in the uses made of discursive practices, particularly their relation to non-discursive practices, rather than their internal workings. This was prefigured by some remarks toward the end of *The Archaeology of Knowledge* (see AS 212; AK 162). Foucault has become increasingly interested in political questions: 'history has constantly impressed upon us that discourse is no mere verbalisation of struggles and systems of domination, but is for what, and by what one struggles, the power [*pouvoir*] which one aims to seize' (OD 12). Foucault's work now looks increasingly at practices, and their necessary power relations: what he calls 'the social appropriation of discourse' (OD 45).

Foucault conceives of the historical *a priori* as a grid [*grille*] structuring possibilities at a given time. In *The Order of Discourse*, setting out his programme for future work, he suggests that, in our time, the

> regions where the grid is the most constricting [*resserrée*], where the danger spots multiply, are the regions of sexuality and of politics: as if discourse, far from being a transparent or neutral element where sexuality is disarmed and politics pacified, is one of those places where they exercise, in a privileged manner, some of their most formidable powers [*puissances*]. (OD 11)

Later in the same piece he gives the example of education, suggesting it is 'a political means of sustaining or modifying the appropriation of discourse, with the knowledge and the powers it carries with it . . . following the lines which are marked by distances, oppositions and social struggle' (OD 45–6).

Foucault looks at these questions of politics, sexuality and education in later works, suggesting that now he is making genealogical studies. With the adoption of the term 'genealogy' Foucault becomes more explicitly Nietzschean. Such an influence had always been acknowledged, but is now brought to the fore. In the 1961 preface to *Histoire de la folie* Foucault had likened his study to Nietzsche's *The Birth of Tragedy*; he gave a paper to a colloquium in 1964 entitled 'Nietzsche, Freud, Marx', where he clearly identified with the first of these thinkers (DE I, 564–79); and in 1967 he had suggested that his 'archaeology owes more to Nietzschean genealogy than to structuralism properly called' (DE I, 599; FL 31). In this period he had also been involved in the French publication of Nietzsche's *Complete Works* (see DE I, 549–52, 561–4). Nietzsche was central to Foucault's attempt to go beyond Hegel, Marx and (Kantian) humanism: 'It was Nietzsche, in any case, who burned for us, even before we were born, the intermingled promises of the dialectic and anthropology' (M&C 275; OT 263). This Nietzschean influence becomes especially pronounced in the 1971 key essay, 'Nietzsche, Genealogy, History' – one of Foucault's central theoretical pieces:[25]

> Genealogy is grey, meticulous, and patiently documentary. It operates on a field of entangled and confused parchments, that have been scratched over and recopied many times . . . Genealogy, consequently, requires patience and a knowledge of details, and it depends on a vast accumulation of source material. (DE II, 136; FR 76–7)

A number of points arise for discussion. The question of origins has been remarked upon before, in the discussion of Heidegger and his readings of art and Hölderlin. Returning to the original German of Nietzsche's texts, Foucault suggests that we need to be attentive to the number of different words Nietzsche used that are usually translated as 'origin' [*origine*]. The words Foucault singles out for treatment are *Ursprung*, *Herkunft* and *Entstehung* (DE II, 137ff; FR 77ff). Nietzsche, at least in his later works, carefully distinguishes between his use of *Ursprung* and the other two words. Foucault argues that *Herkunft* and *Entstehung* better capture the true objective of genealogy, and that translating them as 'origin' misses Nietzsche's point. He therefore suggests new translations: '*Herkunft* is the equivalent of stock or *descent* [*provenance*] . . . *Entstehung* designates *emergence*, the moment of arising' (DE II, 140–3; FR 80–3).[26] This distancing from the philosophy of origins – *Ursprungphilosophie* – was also shown in archaeology being of the archive not of the *arche*. As well as encouraging textual fidelity in our reading of Nietzsche, Foucault is also carefully distancing himself from the nostalgic, romantic excesses of Heidegger (see DE I, 372; FL 97).[27]

Crucially, Foucault also sees the domain of *Herkunft* as concerned with the body, and therefore picks up on Nietzsche's discussions in this area, developed, as shown in Chapter Two, by Heidegger.

The body is the inscribed surface of events (marked by language and dissolved by ideas), the locus of a dissociated self (adopting the illusion of a substantial unity), and a volume in perpetual disintegration. (DE II, 143; FR 83)

What is specifically Heideggerian about this is the abandonment of the simple equation of the body with an 'I', an 'ego' or a self. This is precisely where Heidegger was most critical of Nietzsche. Foucault concentrates on the question of the body without the subjectivism; instead there is an investigation of how subjection of the body forms the subject. Now whilst the body received some treatment in Foucault's earlier works – notably in *The Birth of the Clinic* – it is in *Discipline and Punish* and *The History of Sexuality* that this study becomes intensified. These discussions are examined in the second section of the following chapter. This interest in the body is also found in Nietzsche's historical sense which, as Foucault remarks, 'has more in common with medicine than philosophy . . . its task is to become a curative science' (DE II, 149; FR 90), a remark that is developed out of Nietzsche's understanding of history as a pharmacology. This orientation of history toward the present – a historical diagnosis to cure a current illness – is evidenced in Foucault's intention to write a history of the present, a point that will be discussed at length in the next section.

Although genealogy is sometimes seen as a replacement for archaeology, it is better to see the two as existing together, as two halves of a complementary approach. Archaeology looks at truth as 'a system of ordered procedures for the production, regulation, distribution, circulation, and operation of *énoncés*', whilst genealogy sees truth as 'linked in a circular relation with systems of power which produce and sustain it, and to effects of power which it induces and which extends it' (DE III, 160; FR 74).[28] This shows that, for Foucault, knowledge and power are linked and dependent on each other, but not that they are synonymous: 'the exercise of power perpetually creates knowledge and, conversely, knowledge constantly induces effects of power' (DE II, 752; P/K 52).[29] Just as Foucault's archaeological work was concerned with the ontological underpinning of ontic knowledge, he is now concerned with the relation this has to the question of power. Nietzsche's pronouncement that 'knowledge works as a tool of power: Hence it is plain that it increases with every increase of power' (WM 480) is clearly central. As Foucault recognizes in several places this emphasis on power is expressly Nietzschean. As he points out in an interview, 'it was Nietzsche who specified the power relation as the general focus . . . of philosophical discourse – whereas for Marx it was the productive relationship' (DE II, 753; P/K 53). But it is more complicated than that.

Nietzsche's tool of investigation is not power, but will to power. As I have shown in Chapter Two above, Heidegger is very critical of the voluntarism embedded in this idea: it remains Cartesian. As can be seen in Foucault's anti-humanism, his critique of the notion of the author, and other analyses, he wants none of this. Foucault's analyses of power, like his investigations of *savoir* rather than *connaissance*, escape subjectivity through their impersonal analysis. This relation between the knowledge/power dyad is examined in detail in Foucault's future works, though he realizes that this has been the case all along:

> When I think back now, I ask myself what else it was that I was talking about, in *Histoire de la Folie* or *The Birth of the Clinic*, but power? Yet I'm perfectly aware that I scarcely ever used the word and never had such a field of analyses at my disposal. (DE III, 146; FR 57)

Using this notion of power as a tool of analysis gives Foucault some key insights. However, it is important to note that Foucault's understanding of power is not the same as standard understandings.[30] Three points need to be made. First, power is often looked at in opposition to authority, with legitimacy as the distinction. For example, in Machiavelli the Prince seizes power, but needs to gain legitimate authority in order to perpetuate his rule.[31] Foucault suggests that we need to abandon a conception of power rooted in constitution and sovereignty, in juridical terms – the view of the right. As Foucault puts it in an oft-cited sentence: 'We need to cut off the king's head: in political theory that has still to be done' (DE III, 150; FR 63; see VS 117; WK 88–9). Similarly we must abandon the Marxist understanding of power, where it is posed 'only in terms of the state apparatus' (DE III, 146; FR 57).[32] Power must be understood as being exercised rather than possessed, it is a strategy rather than a property. This means power is often impersonal. Consequently power must be thought of as diffused throughout the social body rather than coming from above.

Foucault locates the change in the second of these two areas in the eighteenth century, which 'invented ... a synaptic regime of power, a regime of its exercise *within* the social body, rather than *from above* it' (DE II, 741; P/K 39). Walzer calls Foucault a 'power pluralist' because of his emphasis on the workings of power from diverse places, and at different levels.[33] The fact that power permeates society necessitates the use of a 'microanalysis' to examine its workings at the level of the quotidien, looking at *savoir de gens* – popular knowledge in the sense of particular, local, regional knowledge, rather than general, common-sense, knowledge (DE III, 164; P/K 82). However, Foucault has sometimes been criticized for concentrating too much on the microphysics of power, and neglecting the wider picture. His retort is that he accepts that the wider picture should be looked at, but argues that the microphysics has previously been neglected, and that he is attempting to redress the balance somewhat. He sees this micro-level as essential in any attempt at change: 'nothing in society will be changed if the mechanisms of power that function outside, below and alongside the State apparatuses, on a much more minute and everyday level, are not also changed' (DE II, 757–8; P/K 59–60).[34]

The third key point in understanding Foucault on power is shown by his use of the French word *pouvoir*. This is the word he uses to translate the German *Macht*, a word normally translated in French as *puissance*. In using the French word *pouvoir* – which as a verb means 'to be able' – Foucault attempts to capture the creative, productive sense of power, rather than merely the forceful, repressive sense.[35] He suggests that 'we must cease once and for all to describe the effects of power in negative terms: it "excludes", it "represses", it "censors", it "abstracts", it "masks", it "conceals". In fact power produces; it produces the real; it produces domains of objects and rituals of truth' (SP 227; DP 194). Rather than following the model of Reich, Foucault follows the model he finds in Nietzsche (FDS 17; P/K 91). Though in theory Foucault suggested power was productive as well as repressive, as Hunt suggests 'in practice he tended to reproduce a negative conception of discipline'.[36] This criticism is somewhat addressed in *The Use of Pleasure* and *The Care of the Self*, where the individual's self-constituting power is examined in detail.[37]

Foucault suggests that power is everywhere, not because it embraces everything, but because it comes from everywhere (VS 122; WK 93), and that power entails resistance – that resistance is a relation of power (VS 125; WK 95). Instead of resistance being understood as freedom, or emancipation from power, it is better thought of as empowerment. It is for this reason that Foucault talks of relationships of power, of tactics and strategies, of power as a game, with ordered rules and exchanges. Foucault's conception of power has been criticized for failing to allow any possibility for resistance,[38] a criticism that misunderstands him, or, more seriously, for not providing any normative frame that allows an answer to the question 'why resist?'[39] Concerning the first charge, we must recognize what Foucault means by power. Foucault's suggestion is that there are relations of power because the subjects are free: were they not free there would be no need to use power (DE IV, 720; FL 441). It is because it is power used – and not simple force or domination – that there must necessarily be some means of resistance.

The stress is not just on power, but on relations or strategies of power.

These are necessarily two way (at least) – resistance is part of the strategies of power:

> Should it be said that one is always 'inside' power, there is no 'escaping it'? ... this would be to misunderstand the strictly relational character of power relationships. Their existence depends on a multiplicity of points of resistance ... these points of resistance are present everywhere in the power network ... (VS 126; WK 95)

The existence of power *depends* on points of resistance, which are therefore necessarily everywhere there is power. This is why there is no single focus for resistance, just as there is not a single focus for power.

> But this does not mean that they [these resistances] are only a reaction or rebound ... they are the other term in relations of power; they are inscribed in the latter as an irreducible opposite. (VS 126–7; WK 96)

The freedom that is a necessary condition for relations of power is therefore the very thing that allows the possibility of resistance. Freedom is the ontological condition for ethics (DE IV, 712; FL 435). Because Foucault is talking of power and not domination; because by power he means relations or strategies of power; and because power requires the subjects to be free, the question is misconceived: if we understand what Foucault means by power then there cannot *not* be the potential for resistance.

If the second charge is allowed validity, it is hard to defend Foucault against it. Following Heidegger and Nietzsche, Foucault's understanding of power makes his analyses perspectivist rather than relativist, in that he attempts to see the bias, the power relations, inherent in interpretations, examining 'the place from which they look, the moment where they are' (DE II, 150; FR 90). Foucault recognizes that any interpretation predicates a norm by which it measures: even if the normal is defined in terms of what it is not, as a consequence.[40] Similarly, he realizes his own work is bound up within the constraints of his time and place (DE II, 720; FL 149). Why, however, we should aim to undermine and examine others' interpretations, and perhaps replace them with our own is not always clear. Foucault seemingly evades this question with the answer 'one makes war to win, not because it is just' (DE III, 503). But my sense is that what critics are looking for is something Foucault would not allow: some kind of moral positioning that would justify resistance, provide a rationale for it, and so forth. But Foucault, again following Nietzsche and Heidegger, would deny the very basis of this charge. Instead of providing a justification for resistance, Foucault is concerned with trying to find what allows resistance. One is a moral question, the other ontological.

The understanding of power that Foucault develops from his reading of Nietzsche and Heidegger also occasions a shift in his use of metaphor. Rather than the literary terms used in his earlier works, he shifts to a more militaristic tone. In his later works we can indeed hear 'the distant roar of battle' (SP 360; DP 308):

> I think that we decided to publish all these documents in order to draw some kind of a map [*plan*] of these diverse struggles, to reconstruct these confrontations and battles, to rediscover the play of those discourses, as weapons, as instruments of attack and defence in the relations of power and knowledge. (MPR 17)

Rhetorically, Foucault asks that 'if power is properly speaking the way in which relations of forces are deployed and given concrete expression ... should we not analyse it primarily in terms of *combat, conflict*, and *war*?' (FDS 16; P/K 90; see FDS *passim*). This leads him to his reversal of Clausewitz's famous dictum, suggesting that 'politics is war continued by other means' (FDS 16; P/K 90–1; see FDS 147; VS 123; WK 93).[41]

Foucault argues that it is important to look at relations of war, conflict and struggle, stressing that these are not merely metaphors but actually found in reality (DE III, 471). Indeed, he questions the lack of attention paid by Marxists – although he exempts Marx and Trotsky somewhat – to what constitutes struggle [*lutte*] when they talk of class struggle (DE III, 310–11; P/K 208; see also DE III, 206; FL 239–40). The emphasis, it would seem, is on 'class' rather than 'struggle'.[42] It will be shown in the rereading of *Discipline and Punish* how Foucault analyses the army and the figures of warfare as constitutive elements in the genealogy of modern punitive society. But, for the purpose here, it is important to note that his spatial metaphors often have a military tone in his more political later work. This is shown particularly in his interview with the geographers at the *Hérodote* journal, where he suggests that the metaphors which they claim are geographical are actually political, juridical, administrative and military. The military link is not surprising, concede his interlocutors, given that geography grew up in the shadow of the military (DE III, 32–4; P/K 68–70).[43]

In the extended treatment given to *Discipline and Punish* in the second section of the next chapter many of these issues around power will be contextualized. For the moment though, it is worth treating two key terms in Foucault's later work in more detail. These terms are technology and *dispositif*.

Foucault uses the word technology in a number of places, talking of technologies of power, of government and of the self. Occasionally he refers to them as 'arts' instead – both terms being renderings of the Greek *techne*. For example, in his discussion of the notion of 'discipline', he suggests that it should not be identified with an institution or with an apparatus; 'it is a type of power, a modality for its exercise, comprising a whole set of instruments, techniques, procedures, levels of application, targets; it is a "physics" or an "anatomy" of power, a technology' (SP 251; DP 215). Similarly in his work on governmentality he discusses the means of policing a society as a particular technology of power, a technology of government (see DE III, 635ff; FE 97ff).

A useful hint as to how Foucault understands this term is found in an interview when he was asked whether he considered architecture as a 'natural science' or a 'dubious science'. Foucault suggested that he is more interested in architecture as a *techne* – 'a practical rationality governed by a conscious goal'. He accepts that the disadvantage of the word *techne* is its relation to 'technology', but suggests that technology should not simply be thought of as technologies of wood, fire or electricity, but also of government (DE IV, 285; FR 255–6; see DE III, 515). He understands *techne* as a 'practice', as a *savoir-faire* (UP 73; UsP 62). Such an understanding is obviously related to that of the later Heidegger. As Heidegger says, 'τέχνη is the name not only for the activities and skills of the craftsman but also for the arts of the mind and the fine arts ... the word τέχνη is linked with the word επιστήμη. Both words are terms for knowing in the widest sense' (VA 16; BW 318). In Heidegger, however, most of his discussions of technology focus on what we would commonly understand by the term; in Foucault the term is used in its enriched sense.[44]

In the second and third volumes of *The History of Sexuality*, Foucault uses this notion in his understanding of the practices of the self in antiquity. In *The Use of Pleasure* he examines the three great arts of self-conduct, the three major technologies of the self – dietics, economics and erotics (US 275; UsP 251). In the second of these areas he considers Xenophon's *Oeconomicus*, a treatise on married life, looking at its rational practices – thought of as knowledges [*epistēmē* or arts/techniques [*technē*] (UP 169; UsP 152). In this, domestic art – or the government of a household – is looked at in the same way as the political or military art – as all three are involved in ruling others (UP 171; UsP 154). In the third volume, looking at the notion of *heautou epimeleisthai*, *cura sui* – the care of, or concern for, the self [*le souci de soi*] – Foucault sees these three arts as coming together in a wider 'art of existence – the *technē tou biou*' (SS 57–8; CS 43). Foucault suggests that this concern with the self is a development from the time when the human was pressed by needs:

The techniques and skills (*technai and epistēmai*) made it possible for him to escape from these pressures and to provide for himself in a better fashion. People learned to weave garments and build houses. Now as the work of the weaver is to the use of animal skins, and as the art of architecture is to caves for shelter, the love of boys is to intercourse with women. The latter, in early times, was necessary in order that the race [*espèce*] might not disappear. (SS 249; CS 216).

This needs to be compared to the suggestion in *The Will to Knowledge* that the nineteenth century saw a shift from the act of sodomy to the specification of the homosexual (VS 58–9; WK 42–3) – or more widely, the constitution of the self, or the subject. In these later works Foucault seems to tie the possibility of a technology of the self to a number of times and places. What becomes more important than historical development is a number of other factors – the space where it happens, the growth of urban society (RC 137), a surplus of leisure time, and therefore a concern for well-being rather than just survival.[45]

These technologies should not be analysed in isolation, but need to be located in the context in which they develop – what Foucault terms a *dispositif*. In Foucault's use this term defies translation – although 'construct', 'deployment', 'apparatus' and 'grid of intelligibility' are sometimes used.[46] Although Foucault uses the related term *disposition* in some of his earlier works – 'the grammatical arrangements [*dispositions*] of a language are the *a priori* of what can be expressed in it' (M&C 311; OT 297) – the term *dispositif* is first used in *Discipline and Punish*, and comes to the fore in *The Will to Knowledge*. What Foucault means by this term is clarified in a 1977 interview, when he described it as 'a thoroughly heterogeneous ensemble consisting of discourses, institutions, architectural forms, regulatory decisions, laws, administrative measures, scientific *énoncés*, philosophical, moral and philanthropic propositions'. What needs to be examined is the system of relations between these elements, the nature of their connections and their strategic functions (DE III, 298–9; P/K 194–5). The notion of the *episteme* developed in *The Order of Things* is now seen as 'a specifically *discursive dispositif*, whereas the *dispositif* in its general form is both discursive and non-discursive' (DE III, 301; P/K 197) – a theoretical reformulation paralleled in the shift from analysis of knowledge to the dyad power/knowledge.

Foucault's notion of *dispositif* is related to Heidegger's understanding of *Ge-stell*, which is usually translated as 'enframing'. In French the standard translation is *Arraisonnement*, though *Dispositif* has also been used.[47] Given the links between Foucault and Heidegger's understanding of technology and the roles they give to *dispositif* and *Ge-stell* it seems that Foucault is taking forward Heidegger's term. However, whilst Heidegger sees *Ge-stell* as arising only at a particular historical moment, through the calculative understanding of being, for Foucault, like the notion of the *episteme* it replaces, there have been many *dispositifs*. As Dean notes, 'technologies of government, techniques of the self and of living, spiritual exercises, systems of manners and habits, should be analysed not simply as instruments but as part of a frame (a *Ge-stell*, in Heidegger's sense)'. Dean, however, does not suggest that Foucault's conception of *dispositif* is precisely this frame.[48]

In *The Will to Knowledge* Foucault discusses the *dispositif* of sexuality (VS 99ff; WK 75ff). This sees sex as falling within this general *dispositif*, framed by practices and discourses such as biology, morality, government and mechanisms of confession. This understanding is deepened in the introduction to *The Use of Pleasure* – where Foucault suggests that knowledge, rules and norms, and individual conduct all form part of the experience of sexuality (UP 9–10; UsP 3–4).[49] It is also clearly evident in the texts surrounding the case of Herculine Barbin – where the biological theories of sexuality, the juridical conceptions of the individual and the modern forms of administrative control dictate the need for the hermaphrodite to have one 'true sex' (DE IV, 116–17) – and that of Pierre Rivière.[50] To examine this experience of sexuality, Foucault suggests we need to look at the 'correlation between fields of knowledge, types of normativity and forms of subjectivity in a particular culture' (UP 10; UsP 4). He suggests that he has shown how to examine the first two of these axes, with the analysis of discursive practices in his archaeological studies, and the analysis of relations and technologies of power in his genealogical works. What needs to be done now is to examine the technologies of the self that constitute the subject (UP 10–12; UsP 4–6). For this purpose, Foucault sees the models of archaeology and genealogy put to work together: 'this analysis of the desiring human is situated at the point where an archaeology of problematisations and a genealogy of practices of the self intersect' (UP 19; UsP 13).[51]

II: MAPPING THE PRESENT

Like Nietzsche in the *Untimely Meditations*, Foucault is opposed to some kinds of history, and demands the need for a historical sense. Likewise he is opposed to the tendency toward 'Egyptianism' – of dehistoricizing, or of tearing things from their true context. There are two potential situations. Either the historical sense is mastered by a 'suprahistorical point of view, metaphysics can bend it to its own purpose, and, by aligning it to the demands of objective science, it can impose its own "Egyptianism"', or, by refusing the certainty of absolutes, "the historical sense can evade metaphysics and become a privileged instrument of genealogy" (DE II, 146–7; FR 87). Genealogy was for Nietzsche a critical history, it was untimely, in the sense that it was 'acting counter to our time and thereby acting on our time and, let us hope, for the benefit of a time to come' (UB II, Preface). Heidegger's reading of Nietzsche on history, found in Division Two of *Being and Time*, made some fundamental points concerning the three modalities of history that Nietzsche discussed in the second *Untimely Meditation*. These points are central to understanding Foucault's reading of Nietzsche.

> In a sense, genealogy returns to the three modalities of history that Nietzsche recognised in 1874. It returns to them in spite of the objections that Nietzsche raised in the name of the affirmative and creative powers of life. But they are metamorphosed: the veneration of monuments becomes parody; the respect for ancient continuities becomes systematic dissociation; the critique of the injustices of the past by a truth held by humans in the present becomes the destruction of the human who maintains knowledge [*connaissance*] by the injustice proper to the will to knowledge [*savoir*]. (DE II, 156; FR 97)

Like Heidegger, Foucault sees the three modalities working together, and he follows Heidegger's shift in orientating the critical to the present, rather than the past. Nietzsche's critical history became for Heidegger a critique of the present, a critique which was historicized in Heidegger's later works. For Foucault it becomes a history of the present (SP 40; DP 31).[52]

Though Foucault describes his project in these terms in *Discipline and Punish*, it is clear that it applies to all his work. As he describes his early works: 'it is a question of presenting a critique of our own time, based upon retrospective analyses' (DE II, 183; FL 68).[53]

> I consider myself as a journalist, insofar as what interests me is the present [*l'actualité*] . . . Philosophy, until Nietzsche, had eternity for its *raison d'être*. The first philosopher-journalist was Nietzsche. He introduced the today [*l'aujourd'hui*] into the field of philosophy. Before, the philosopher knew time and eternity, but Nietzsche was obsessed by the present . . . If we want to be masters of our future we must pose fundamentally the question of the today. That is why, for me, philosophy is a type of radical journalism. (DE II, 434; see also DE III, 266; FL 222)

Such a critique, or history, of our own time, of the present, is exemplified in the advent of the death of the human in *The Order of Things*; the history of the modern subject pursued in *The History of Sexuality*; and in his engagement in debates over psychiatry, penal reform, homosexuality and various other issues. It also lends an explicitly political tone to his work. Some of the most direct links to present-day issues are found in his interviews and journalism,[54] whereas the analyses in his books tend to end around the middle of the nineteenth century. But as Foucault notes, the reason he goes back to earlier periods is the need to trace the genealogy of present concepts: 'genealogy means that I begin my analysis from a question posed in the present' (DE IV, 674; PPC 262). The attitude to the present is also the topic of Foucault's reflections on Kant's essay 'What is Enlightenment?'

In reading Kant, Foucault returns to the original German. The opening line of Kant's text reads: 'Enlightenment [*Aufklärung*] is the exit [*Ausgang*] of the human from their self-imposed immaturity [*Unmündigkeit*].'[55] It is important, contends Foucault, that Kant defines *Aufklärung* as 'an *Ausgang*, an "exit", a "way out"' (DE IV, 564; FR 34), a way out of the present to the future. This present is our immaturity, mentally, spiritually and physically, and *Aufklärung* will lead us into a new maturity, a modernity. This 'point of departure . . . the attitude to modernity' (DE IV, 568; FR 38) needs clarification. Foucault concedes that 'modernity is often spoken of as an epoch, or at least as a set of features characteristic of an epoch; situated on a calendar', but wonders 'whether we may not envisage modernity rather as an attitude than as a period of history . . . a bit, no doubt, like what the Greeks called an *êthos*' (DE IV, 568; FR 39). This *êthos* is conceived as 'a permanent critique of our historical being [*être*] . . . consisting in a critique of what we are saying, thinking and doing, through a historical ontology of ourselves' (DE IV, 571–4; FR 42–5; see DE IV, 618; FR 351).[56]

Foucault therefore suggests that Kant founds two great traditions in philosophy. One of these is the project found in the *Critiques*, where he looks for the conditions of true knowledge, and asks the question 'what is the human?' and the second is found in 'What is Enlightenment?' The former was criticized by Foucault in the secondary thesis and *The Order of Things*, but Foucault finds the second more interesting, characterizing it as 'an ontology of the present, an ontology of ourselves'. This is the tradition Foucault allies himself with (DE IV, 687–8; PPC 95), and these two ontologies clearly delineate the research he pursued in the last years of his life. This notion of historical ontology is, as I have suggested, related to Heidegger's project in his later works,[57] and ties to the notion of a history of the present. However, there is also clearly a shift from Foucault's earlier position, where he tended to conceive of periods, and epochs.[58] Kant uses the word *Unmündigkeit* for 'immaturity', the self-imposed state from which he claims Enlightenment provides an exit. This German noun is formed from the adjective *unmündig*, which literally means under-age, and its use is interesting because escaping from immaturity allows the time to achieve the status of being a self-constituting *age*. For

Foucault, the *Aufklärung* is the first period that names itself (DE IV, 681–2; PPC 89), and asks the fundamental question 'what is our present?' Interestingly, it appears that Foucault realizes that the notion of period is a tool of hindsight, as Couzens Hoy has put it: 'periodisation . . . is itself a modernist tool'.[59]

Reading Foucault in this way underlines the continuity that runs throughout his work. The notion of an ontology of the present is clearly linked to the general project of a history of limits. Speaking of the *êthos* he sees develop out of the Enlightenment, he conceives it as a *limit-attitude*:

> We have to move beyond the outside-inside alternative; we have to be at the frontiers. Criticism indeed consists of analysing and reflecting upon limits . . . The point, in brief, is to transform the critique conducted in the form of a necessary limitation into a practical critique that takes the form of a possible crossing [*franchissement* – clearing] . . . this criticism is not transcendental, and its goal is not that of making a metaphysics possible: it is genealogical in its design, and archaeological in its method. (DE IV, 574; FR 45–6)[60]

However, to read Foucault in this way is to continue the standard interpretation of him as a historian. In terms of the role of space, all it does is recognize what a 1967 interviewer called his 'predilection for spatial metaphors' (DE I, 599; FL 31). It was noted as a point of divergence from structuralism that Foucault also made analyses of actual spaces in his historical studies. As Flynn has remarked, 'Foucault's spatialised thinking extends far beyond his well-known use of spatial metaphors to include the use of lists, tables, geometrical configurations and illustrations.' However, Flynn's treatment only looks at two of Foucault's examples – Velázquez's 'Las Meninas' in *The Order of Things*, and Bentham's Panopticon in *Discipline and Punish*.[61] Foucault's spatial thinking, and his spatial histories, extend far beyond this.

In his recent *Justice, Nature and the Geography of Difference*, David Harvey takes issue with the current trend for producing 'cognitive maps' in politics, art and the humanities. He cites the recent books *Mapping the West European Left*, *Mapping Ideology* and *Locating Culture*, and suggests that this trend 'unfortunately evades the problem that mapping requires a map and that maps are typically totalising, usually two-dimensional, Cartesian, and very undialectical devices'.[62] Yet I think that Foucault's work can perhaps be subsumed under the designation not simply of writing a history of the present, but of *mapping* [repérage] *the present*.[63]

Foucault uses the word *repérage* in a number of places, some of which are noted in this and the following chapter. The term is especially used in *The Birth of the Clinic*. Similarly *The Archaeology of Knowledge* concerns itself with 'the mapping [*repérage*] of discursive formations' (AS 152; AK 116); its aim is to 'map [*repérer*] the space' which made earlier investigations possible (AS/AK jacket). *Repérage* is a military term, meaning location, landmark or point on a map. The related verb *repérer* means to locate or discover. In translations they are often rendered as 'mapping' and 'to map'. It is interesting that, in Foucault's early studies, this is the main military term used, and thereby prefigures his later metaphorical shift – providing another thread of continuity through his career.

It should be remembered that a map is for use, not to fully describe the terrain. Borges' oft-cited fable about the awkwardness of an exact map on the scale of 1:1 is worth remembering here.[64] Foucault's maps are not merely cognitive, but make use of the notions of site, space, place and location in both figurative and actual senses. Following Nietzsche and Heidegger, Foucault points out the important role that space plays in our history, and orientates this history toward the service of the present. In Chapter Two it was noted that Heidegger's understanding of the present, of presence, is a conflation of the two German words *Gegenwart* and *Anwesenheit* – temporal and spatial presence (see GA24, 305ff). (It is worth noting that in Binswanger's *Dream and Existence* Foucault translated Heidegger's *Dasein* as *présence*.) It was also argued above that the three dimensions of time, which as Heidegger showed relate to Nietzsche's three modes of history, come together in the *Augenblick* – the Moment. This gateway – the present – is where future and past collide. Just as the individual in the *Augenblick* must act, so too must history orientate itself toward the future with reference to the past: a *history of the present*.

The spatial links in *Thus Spoke Zarathustra*, the dual meaning of present, the word *Augenblick*, and the spatial site of the gateway, make it unsurprising that there is a role for space in this history. But the equal importance given to time and space in Heidegger's later works – thought as journeying and placing, as historical site, as the site of the moment, and the notion of time-space – make it *essential* that this history of the present must also be spatially aware: mapping the present. Indeed, Foucault once described himself as a 'cartographer' (DE II, 725), a designation that, despite Harvey's misgivings, seems particularly apt. Foucault's mappings are far from totalizing, perhaps best seen as sketchmaps, approximations toward, signposts. They highlight key features, outline contours, and provide an orientation. Far from being two dimensional, these maps work with both space and time, but are not Cartesian in their abstraction; rather, they work on the level of everyday action.

Foucault's work on space has received relatively little critical attention. Where it is analysed critics tend to either seize the Panopticon as the most apposite example or rely on Foucault's interviews and a 1967 lecture. The issues around the Panopticon receive sustained treatment in the next chapter, and need not detain us here. But the focus on a number of short pieces – 'Space, Knowledge, Power', 'Questions on Geography' and 'Of Other Spaces' – although understandable in that they are the most explicit discussions, discounts the places where Foucault makes his most useful analyses.[65] The best way to understand what Foucault is doing is to look at his studies in context, which will be done in the extended treatment given to *Histoire de la folie* and his study of modern discipline in the next chapter.[66]

In 1967 Foucault delivered a lecture to a group of architects, but only allowed the lecture notes to be published shortly before his death.[67] With the exception of the passage on the Panopticon, this piece has received more treatment than any of his other works on space. It is a fascinating piece but there is one central problem with it, or at least with its perception. This is that this piece is the closest Foucault ever comes to writing a history of space, or spaces, something he later suggested as a possible future project (DE III, 192; FL 228). Whilst this indeed would be a valuable study, in critical appropriations of Foucault this history of space is often given precedence over the spatial histories of his more major works. This is a point that will be returned to below.

However, Foucault's history of space is not without interest. Starting with the Middle Ages, Foucault suggests that at this time there was an 'ensemble of places [*lieux*]' – sacred and profane places; protected and open, exposed places; urban and rural places. He calls this medieval space – 'the space of localisation'. This understanding was disrupted by Galileo, who constituted an infinite and infinitely open space, thus dissolving the place of a thing by seeing it as only a point in its movement: 'starting with Galileo and the seventeenth century, extension was substituted for localisation'. In more recent times Foucault suggests that the understanding of space on the basis of extension has been replaced by the notion of site [*emplacement*]. 'The site is defined by relations of proximity [*voisonage*] between points or elements.' (DE IV, 753) The most concrete question that arises from this understanding of place [*place*] or site is that of demography:

> This problem of the human site [*l'emplacement humain*] is not simply that of knowing whether there will be enough room [*place*] for humans in the world – a problem that is after all quite important – but also that of knowing what relations of proximity, what type of storage, circulation, mapping [*repérage*], and classification of human elements should be adopted in a given situation in order to achieve a given end. We are in an epoch where space takes for us the form of relations among sites. (DE IV, 753–4)

Foucault's exposition here clearly puts him in the same field as Heidegger. Their understandings are not entirely identical, but there is clearly a degree of similarity. Like Heidegger, Foucault suggests that the modern era inaugurated an understanding of space in terms of extension – Heidegger attributes it to Descartes, Foucault to Galileo – and both suggest that a different understanding is now possible. In the chapters above it was argued that in Heidegger's later thinking there was an increased importance given to space, and that his understanding of space, or place, was resolutely non-Cartesian. This entailed space being understood not in terms of extension or mathematical co-ordinates, but in terms of lived experience, nearness and farness, locale and situation. In Foucault's work such an understanding is found in his most explicitly Heideggerian piece, the introduction to Binswanger's *Dream and Existence*:

> In lived experience [*l'expérience vécue*], at its original level, space is not presented as the geometric structure of simultaneity; this type of space, within which the natural sciences deploy the coherence of objective phenomena, is only constituted by way of a genesis of which the moments have been analysed by Oskar Becker . . . and by Husserl . . . Before being geometric or even geographic, space presents itself first and foremost as scene or landscape [*paysage*] . . . (DE I, 101)

Whereas Heidegger suggests that we need to move from 'space' to 'place', with a recognition that we can re-think the former through the latter, Foucault uses the terms *place*, *lieu*, *espace* and *emplacement* almost interchangeably – although the understanding of how the meanings attached to these terms have changed is implicit. His notion of lived space [*l'espace vécu*] (DE I, 102) is clearly Heideggerian. We should also consider that the French word *espace* has a wider range of meanings than 'space'. In English some of the other meanings might be translated as area, zone, or territory – or even place. With most of Foucault's histories looking at periods between the mid-seventeenth and nineteenth centuries, it is not surprising that he finds the spaces of these analyses to be those of the period of extension – classification, segmentation, order, and exclusion.

In this piece, however, he is looking at the spaces of our own era, and perhaps this is why the piece has been so popular with contemporary commentators. Here Foucault does understand space as the relation between sites. He suggests that we could look at 'the set of relations through which a given site can be defined . . . sites of transportation . . . sites of temporary relaxation . . . sites of rest', but centres his analysis on particular sites – ones that both link with and contradict other sites (DE III, 755). Foucault divides these sites along the lines of a division he suggested in *The Order of Things*:

> *Utopias* afford consolation: although they have no real place there is nevertheless a fantastic, untroubled region in which they are able to unfold; they

open up cities with vast avenues, superbly planted gardens, countries where life is easy, even though the road to them is chimerical. *Heterotopias* are disturbing, probably because they secretly undermine language, because they make it impossible to name this *and* that, because they shatter or tangle common names, because they destroy 'syntax' in advance, and not only the syntax with which we construct sentences but also that less apparent syntax which causes words and things (next to and opposite one another) to 'hold together'. (M&C 9; OT xviii)

Utopias are, literally, 'happy-places' or 'no-places'; heterotopias 'other-places'. In *The Order of Things* heterotopia had described Borges' Chinese Encyclopaedia; a similar understanding is found in Foucault's work on the Belgian painter René Magritte. Here too Foucault examines what might be called 'heterotopias', or, as James Harkess suggests, visual *non sequiturs*.[68] Where Kandinsky and Klee used abstraction to undermine representative realism, with colours, lines and shapes, Magritte used everyday objects – pipes, bowler hats, candles, shoes, paintings, windows and mirrors. Discussing Magritte's famous painting of a pipe with the words 'Ceci n'est pas une pipe' below it, Foucault suggests that the common place [*lieu commun*] has disappeared (DE I, 643; TNP 31). As a later comment makes clear, this is an elaborate pun. Magritte effaces the common place of language and art by creating a heterotopia of the everyday rather than a non-place (a utopia) of abstraction (DE I, 646; TNP 41), but, in doing so, he disrupts the commonplace, the everyday – bottles become carrots, paintings fuse with landscapes, mirrors reflect what they conceal, and shoes develop toes.[69]

In the lecture 'Of Other Spaces' Foucault more directly opposes utopias – 'sites with no real place [*lieu*]' – to heterotopias, which he now defines as places that do exist, as 'counter-sites, kinds of effectively enacted utopias' (DE IV, 755).[70] Foucault elaborates and discusses a number of different heterotopias – suggesting crisis heterotopias such as the boarding school or the honeymoon hotel; heterotopias of deviation such as rest homes, psychiatric hospitals and prisons; the cemetery; theatres, cinemas, gardens and carpets; museums and libraries – accumulations of time, and, in contrast, sites of fleeting time – travelling fairgrounds, vacation villages; and various others, including Muslim hammans, Scandinavian saunas, motel rooms, brothels, boats and colonies (DE IV, 756–62). All this is undoubtedly interesting, but it needs to be understood in context. If we examine Foucault's major works, we see that his histories are not merely ones in which space is yet another area analysed, but have space as a central part of the approach itself. In other words, rather than merely writing histories of space, Foucault is writing spatial histories. These spatial histories make use of many of the historical tools examined in the previous section of this chapter, but also use space itself as a critical tool of analysis.[71]

In one of the best general discussions of Foucault and space, Chris Philo suggests that 'the spatial relations discussed throughout Foucault's histories of social otherness can best be understood not as formal geometries, but as substantive geographies'. Philo argues that Foucault runs the risk of seeming to simply inject a 'geometric turn' into his histories, 'effectively elevating an abstract sense of space above a concrete sense of place', but suggests that the emphasis on specificities evades this difficulty. His examples draw on *Madness and Civilisation* and *Discipline and Punish*, arguing that they showcase what he terms a ' "truly" postmodern geography' (in opposition to Soja's reliance on a 'geometric imaginary').[72] In the majority of Foucault's studies, the understanding of the complex relationship between the real and the imaginary, the practical and the theoretical, between power and knowledge, is put to work, and this is true of space as well. It is this, rather than the emphasis on specificities that evades the difficulty. Indeed, like Heidegger before him, and Lefebvre around the same time, Foucault understands both physical and mental conceptions of space to be merely parts of a greater whole, abstractions from the more fundamental level of the lived experience. Even in *The Order of Things*, the historical study that seems most focused on knowledge alone, and removed from practical experience, Foucault suggests that the spatial 'metaphors' found within are often not of his own invention but ones he was 'studying as objects . . . spatial techniques, not metaphors' (DE IV, 284; FR 254). Another example is found in his analysis of architecture, where he examines its theoretical formulations, its practical applications, and the power relations it entails. Architecture is understood as a *techne*, and forms part of a *dispositif*. This needs to be remembered in our re-readings of Foucault's histories, in their recastings as spatial histories. If the guiding light of Foucault's historical researches is, following Nietzsche, the role of power, we would do well to bear the following in mind: 'Space is fundamental in any form of communal life; *space is fundamental in any exercise of power*' (DE IV, 282; FR 252; emphasis added).

CHAPTER 5

The Spaces of Power

Space is fundamental in any exercise of power. It is well known that power is central to Foucault's work, and that it is a fundamental focus of his historical studies. How then does space figure in these histories? In order to examine this, this final chapter re-reads two of Foucault's historical studies from the perspective of the suggestion that space is fundamental in any exercise of power. These two histories are read as spatial histories. In the first part I look at *Histoire de la folie*, known to the English speaking world as *Madness and Civilisation*. The spatial elements of this work – along with much interesting detail in other areas – become much clearer with a reading of the unabridged French text. This part therefore seeks to re-place *Madness and Civilisation*, showing what could be called Foucault's re-placing of the history of madness. In the second part I examine *Discipline and Punish* within the wider context of Foucault's work on medicine and the disciplinary society generally, in order to show that the emphasis on the prison, and particularly the Panopticon, is misleading, particularly on the issue of how space is used as a mechanism of power.

I: RE-PLACING MADNESS AND CIVILISATION

Colin Gordon's important call for the reading of the un-abridged French original of *Histoire de la folie*, rather than the English translation *Madness and Civilisation*, has provoked serious critical attention.[1] This is to be welcomed. Gordon argues that if the full French text is read several of the criticisms of Foucault's work will be seen to be misplaced. Some of the responses to his article have argued that the full text would rather reinforce the accusations of sloppy scholarship, reliance on literature and art instead of historical fact, and the extension of French examples to the European picture. My concern is not with these issues: several other people are better placed to debate such counts. But taking Gordon's mandate seriously, this section seeks to re-read *Histoire de la folie*, and in doing so, by being attentive to the role of space, re-place the reading of *Madness and Civilisation*.

For such an important text, both indispensable for an understanding of Foucault, and central to work since the late 1960s on mental illness, it is surprising that the oft-promised full translation has yet to appear. The original French edition, essentially Foucault's doctoral thesis, was published in 1961 as *Folie et déraison*, and an abridged version appeared in the non-academic *10/18* series three years later. Both editions went out of print, and in 1972 a second edition, with a new preface and two appendices, was published in Gallimard's *Bibliothèque des Sciences Humaines*; this text was then reprinted – without the appendices – in the cheaper *Tel* series. The English translation – unlike the German or the Italian – is of the abridged *10/18* version, with some additions from the 1961 original. Only about 45 per cent of the French original and its attendant notes, references and annexes is therefore available to the English reader, and, as Gordon has pointed out, this has led to a less than fair reading of Foucault's work. No French commentator could have got away with only reading the *10/18* version.[2] What the English reader has is a translation of a skilfully edited version of this text, but one that is intended for the general reader.

To understand Foucault's intent it is obviously necessary to work with the original, unedited, text. Reading this shows that not only have whole chapters been omitted from the translated version, but that sections from those chapters that have been retained are also missing.[3] Foucault's treatment of issues around space is immediately obvious even from the truncated version, but a detailed reading shows how deep this vein runs through his work.[4] As Gordon has argued, Foucault's book is often reduced to 'the compass of three or four striking tableaux: the medieval insane messing around in boats; the carceral monolith of the Great Internment; unreason treated as animality; the spurious emancipation of moral treatment'.[5] What this section seeks to do is to examine both those 'striking tableaux' and the less-often mentioned passages of *Histoire de la folie* that exhibit elements of a spatial history. Many of these passages greatly prefigure the work of the later Foucault, setting up conceptual apparatus used in *The Birth of the Clinic*, *The Order of Things* and *Discipline and Punish*.

LEPROSY, WATER AND MADNESS

The opening words of Foucault's book are well known: 'At the end of the Middle Ages, leprosy disappeared from the Western World. In the margins of the community, at the gates of cities, there stretched wastelands which sickness had ceased to haunt but had left sterile and long uninhabitable' (HF 13; MC 3). These words – as with the beginnings of so many of Foucault's books – provide both an evocative image and establish a backdrop to later events. The lazar houses became empty, but the values and images attached to the figure of the leper, notably the meaning of their exclusion, remained (HF 15–16; MC 6). These places of exclusion, and the formulas attached to them, would, Foucault argues, be reused two or three centuries later. The rigorous division between the lepers and the rest of the population – a division of social exclusion but spiritual reintegration – would be repeated for another marginal group (HF 16; MC 7). The group Foucault has in mind is, of course, the mad, and in the edited text the next image is of the appearance of the ship of fools. But in the original text, Foucault warns of getting ahead of the argument [*Mais n'anticipons pas*], and argues that before the mad take this position, 'a new leper is born, who takes the place of the first' (HF 16–17). These 'new lepers' are the venereally diseased, who inhabit a 'moral space of exclusion', one they would come to share with the mad (HF 18).

The use of the venereally diseased as a bridge is important, for it is only with them that the idea of moral exclusion is established. Like the lepers they are socially excluded, unlike them there is no spiritual integration.[6] This part of Foucault's book has received sustained criticism, particularly from H. C. Erik Midelfort. Midelfort argues that Foucault over-emphasizes the link between lazarettos and madhouses, and suggests that medieval hospitals and monasteries are more important precursors. He argues that Foucault sees the treatment of lepers as only negative – 'a monolithic image of rejection' – and cites recent studies that show that the real attitude was more nuanced, a mixture of 'fear and pity'. Midelfort also suggests that the middle link established is dropped in the edited text because 'perhaps Foucault no longer felt that venereal disease was strictly parallel to leprosy and madness'.[7] These points are difficult to sustain, as Foucault does look at the role of other precursors (HF 405–6), and the relative importance of these different institutions is moot. It should also be noted that Foucault's understanding of the attitude to leprosy is considerably more subtle than simple exclusion (see, for example, HF 16; MC 7). Midelfort's suggestion that the 1964 edits are revisions needs no response other than to suggest a reading of the new edition of 1972, where the main text is effectively unaltered.

The pages on the ship of fools are amongst the most discussed of Foucault's book, and once again, he sets up a vignette: 'Something new appears in the imaginary landscape of the Renaissance; soon it will occupy a privileged place there: it is the ship of fools, a strange "drunken boat" which glides along the calm rivers of the Rhine and the Flemish canals' (HF 18; MC 7). It is important to stress that Foucault notes the appearance of the ship on the *imaginary* landscape: the significance of the ship is as an image, one that appears in the painting of Bosch and the words of Brant, symbolic of the attitude to the mad. Foucault talks of other ships that appeared in literary compositions of the time, but then counters, 'but of all these fantastic [*romanesques*] or satirical vessels, the *Narrenschiff* is the only one which had a real existence, because they existed, these boats which brought their foolish cargo from one town to another' (HF 19; MC 8). Foucault's exact point is unclear, and he has been criticized here for elaborating an argument from sketchy documentary facts,[8] but he seems to be suggesting that the imaginary constructs have partners – if not exact – in the real. At the time, Foucault suggests, madmen simply had a wandering existence. They were driven outside the limits of towns, expelled, sometimes by boat, sometimes to wander in the open countryside.

Madmen were not invariably expelled – some were hospitalized – and there were sometimes towns where they gathered. These included the places of pilgrimage, shrines [*lieux de pèlerinage*], but also places like Nuremberg where the mad were simply thrown in prison (HF 20; MC 9–10). The village of Gheel is singled out for mention, a place of pilgrimage that developed into a place of exclusion, where 'interest in concern [*souci*] and in exclusion coincide: madmen were confined in the holy locus of a miracle [*l'espace sacré du miracle*]' (HF 21; MC 10).[9] Treatment of the mad is therefore shown to be erratic – sometimes tolerant, sometimes exclusionary, sometimes hospitable. There is no regimented model, no overall plan.[10] The literary model is one that emphasizes passage and displacement; what is similarly evident in practice is that the mad are often in transition – moving from town to town, to wastelands, to shrines. The ambiguity implicit in Foucault's now celebrated sentence – 'les fous alors avaient une existence facilement errante' (HF 19; MC 8) – may even help to showcase this irregular approach; although I would suggest that the most problematic word is the last, rather than the penultimate.[11] *Errant*, like the English word, has the sense both of wandering and of irregularity, as well as the more direct connotation of erring from the path of reason. The English and French both have their etymological roots in the Latin *errare* – to wander, to err. The sentence *could* be translated as 'At that time, the mad easily had an errant existence.'

Symbolically, if not actually, water and the passage of the ships across it play important roles.[12] Foucault characterizes the madman as a restless prisoner of the passage, of the transition, figuratively and actually caught between two places:

> the madman is entrusted to the river with a thousand arms, to the sea of a thousand routes, to this great uncertainty outside of everything. He is imprisoned in the middle of the most free, the most open of routes: bound fast at the infinite crossroads. He is the Passenger *par excellence* . . . (HF 22; MC11)

The land to which he is travelling is unknown, but as soon as he reaches it, so too is the land from which he came, 'he has his truth and his homeland only in that fruitless expanse between two countries that cannot belong to him'. Understanding all of this enables us to better make sense of Foucault's description of the madman's voyage 'across a half-real, half-imaginary geography'. The literary and attitudinal constructs loosely parallel the actual treatment. This treatment is one which inhabits the boundary between care and fear, 'the madman's *liminal* position on the horizon of the medieval concern [*souci*]'. It is therefore fitting that the mad are often confined within the city gates, a prisoner of the very threshold, kept at the point of passage, in the interior of the exterior, and vice versa (HF 22; MC 11).

CONFINEMENT AND CORRECTION

If the place of the mad was, in the medieval period, one continually open to question, a restless, transitional location, in the classical age it became fixed and immobile. 'It will never again be that fugitive and absolute limit. Behold it moored now, made fast among things and humans. Retained and maintained. No longer a ship but a hospital.' A restructuring of social space, to a hospital, where *confinement* replaces *embarkation* (HF 53; MC 35–6). Foucault argues that from the middle of the seventeenth century, madness is linked with the notion of confinement, and confinement is established as the natural abode [*lieu naturel*] of madness (HF 59; MC 39). This actual treatment of madness has parallels, Foucault suggests, in the binary divide between reason and unreason in René Descartes' *Meditations*.

In the *Meditations* Descartes tries to ascertain things that are true, things of which there can be no doubt. To this end, he decides to doubt everything, until he can be sure of something, and then from this position reconstruct the basis of knowledge. This is the method known as Cartesian doubt. Descartes suggests that there are three possibilities that might cause him to be misled: that he might be mad; that he might be dreaming, and that an 'evil genius' might be tricking him.[13] Having thought through these three possibilities, Descartes resolves that, whatever else, he cannot doubt that he is thinking, and, he argues, it follows from this that 'the statement "I am, I exist" is necessarily true every time it is uttered by me or conceived in my mind'.[14]

Foucault argues that although Descartes counts the possibility that he is mad as a potential area of doubt, he does not afford it the same significance that he does to the possibility that he is dreaming, or that he is being deceived: 'Descartes does not evade the danger of madness in the same way that he gets round the possibility of dreaming or of error' (HF 56), and, again, 'in the economy of doubt, there is a fundamental imbalance between madness on the one side, and dream and error on the other' (HF 57). Foucault sees in

Descartes' text a dismissal that is tantamount to exclusion. When Descartes asks 'how could one deny that these hands and that my whole body exist?', his only possibility, as he sees it, is that he could be 'insane', like those 'whose brains are so impaired by a stubborn vapour from a black bile that they continually insist . . . that they are gourds, or that they are made of glass'. Next comes the sentence that Foucault claims is so important: *'but they are all demented [amentes]*, and I would appear no less extravagant [*demens*] if I were to take their conduct as a model for myself'.[15]

This dismissal, for Foucault, is in contrast with the treatment Descartes gives to the other two possibilities – the deceit and the dream. Descartes believes that even if he is being deceived he is still thinking, for being misled into thinking that one is thinking is still thinking, and dreams can only be a reflection of things that exist, just as 'bizarre and unusual forms' created by painters are based on things that are true.[16] Indeed, for Foucault, this reading of Descartes would seem to suggest that the mad, 'the demented', are not only denied the thought, *the reason* – they are denied existence, if not entirely, certainly as equals.[17] This denial can be seen as legitimating the 'dividing practices' that came into play at a similar time to Descartes' text. *Meditations* was published in 1641, and Foucault sees the creation of the *Hôpital Général* in 1656 as a key development in the exclusion of the mad from society. 'Madness was excluded, leaving no trace, no scar on the surface of thought' (HF 156). Essentially, reason, in its situation in this text, and from then on, ruthlessly proclaims itself apart from madness or unreason; *a divide Foucault claims was not evident before*. For example, though the Greeks had a relationship to something they called ὕβρις, the Greek *logos* 'had no contrary' (DE I, 160; MC xiii). In other words, the poles of ὕβρις and *logos* co-existed, there was not the epistemological bifurcation of the either/or.

Foucault argues that the new houses of confinement were very often established in 'the same walls of the ancient lazar houses', and suggests that, just as 'the lazar house did not have a medical meaning; a good many other functions were active in the act of banishment which reopened these cursed places' (HF 64). A new social sensibility suddenly isolated a new group to take the place of the lepers, an act 'which by tracing the locus [*espace*] of confinement, conferred upon it its power of segregation and provided a new homeland for madness' (HF 67; MC 45–6). Understanding the Cartesian divide along with the division of confinement explains in part 'the mode in which madness was perceived [*perçue*], and experienced [*vécue*], by the classical age' (HF 67; MC 46). The fusion of imaginary and real attitudes – especially in the symbolic and actual use of space – is particularly evident here. The classical age sees the birth of an attitude, a sensibility which had 'drawn a line and raised a threshold' between reason and unreason (HF 90–1; MC 64). This is marked in the action of exclusion and in the thought of Descartes: the asylum replaced the lazar house both in the 'geography of haunted places' *and* in the 'landscape of the moral universe' (HF 84; MC 57).

The insane were often confined along with the poor [*les pauvres*], in a moral punishment of poverty. What is essential here, as was the case with the venereally diseased, is the ethical valorization. The poor are divided into the good and bad, and well before being seen as objects of knowledge or of pity, are treated as *moral subjects* (HF 70–3). A shift becomes apparent, madness is now an issue of social, rather than religious, concern. It is a problem for 'police', concerned with the order of individuals in the city. Foucault then contrasts the new situation with that which came before: 'They err [*erre*] . . . but it is no longer on the path of a strange pilgrimage: they disturb the ordering [*ordonnance*] of social space' (HF 74). Foucault locates a shift in the bourgeois conscience regarding the urban question, suggesting that by the seventeenth century there was a dream of an organized and moral city, which necessitated the negative organization of the walls of confinement, and prisons of moral order. Confinement is both a metaphysics of government and a politics of religion: 'police' is the civil equivalent of religion for the edification of cities (HF 87–90; MC 61–3). Madness 'began to rank among the problems of the city' (HF 90; MC 64).

This concern leads to *le monde correctionnaire*. *Correctionnaire* is a word that defies summary translation, as it covers such meanings as correction, proof-reading, marking, and punishment. What Foucault would call the disciplinary society in *Discipline and Punish* is clearly anticipated in the arguments here. The opening of the *Hôpital Général* is an epitome of a trend where 'internment played not only a negative role of exclusion, but also the positive role of organisation' (HF 96). It was a 'social mechanism' (HF 92) for the control of the city, for the establishment of a homogenous world (HF 97). The venereally diseased and the insane were held in the same place of enclosure, stigmatized and punished. 'By inventing, within the imaginary geometry of its morality, the space of internment, the classical epoch came to find at the same time a homeland [*patrie*] and a place of shared redemption from sins against flesh and errors against reason' (HF 100). This divide is one that Foucault thinks especially evident in our own time. He suggests that in all cultures and at all times there has been a system of constraint toward sex, but that we are remarkable for having such a strict divide between reason and unreason, health and sickness, and normal and abnormal (HF 103).

Within these places of confinement, the mad were treated in varying ways. Some had places in hospitals and almost had a medical status, whereas others were effectively in prison. These two institutions were often confused, partly because the mad were indiscriminately distributed between both (HF 127–9).

Internment and hospitalization were two ways of treating the insane, but – contra the standard reading of Foucault – there is not an abrupt transition from one to the other, but rather a 'chronological slippage', where the hospital became drawn toward the model of confinement, with assimilation following (HF 137–8). Within the division of thought, Foucault argues that there is similar confusion, in that the *homo natura* is posited as a given, prior to all experience of madness, but is, in fact, a creation, born out of an invention of opposition (HF 147). This is an initial glimpse of Foucault's arguments in later works, where he discusses the historicality of the *a priori*, and the invention of the same by the opposition to the other. The madman is now seen as responsible, ethically condemned, and is designated 'as the Other, as the Stranger, as the Excluded One' (HF 148–9).

OBSERVING AND CLASSIFYING

'There is there, before the gaze [*le regard*], someone who is indisputably mad, someone who is obviously mad' (HF 184). The rigorous division of the early years of the classical age is perpetuated by the use of two mechanisms: classification and observation.[18] A new distance is established between the mad, and the subject who pronounces them mad, which is no longer simply the Cartesian void of 'I am not them', but is a more elaborate divide (HF 199). Foucault suggests that the great concern of the classifiers of the eighteenth century was to transform the disorders of illness into something akin to the order of plants. The organization of botany could be used to classify pathology, the project of a garden of species belonged to the 'wisdom of divine forethought' (HF 206–7). Once again the organization of thought has a mirror in the organization of action, the organization of species [*espèces*] maps directly onto the organization of space [*espace*]; the social structures replicate the structures of knowledge [*savoir*] (HF 223), a theme Foucault later elaborates in *The Order of Things*.

The parallel with biology is also important in the transfer of elements of the ethical to the corporal. Cartesian dualism had established a strict divide between the body and the mind or soul, but a new shift to locating mental disorders in physical space allowed the treatment of madness as a disease of the body rather than of the soul. The body, specifically the brain, became an object of the medical gaze. Passion – a mode of illness – causes the circulation, the dispersion and the concentration of the spirits 'according to a spatial design which licences the trace of the object in the brain and its image in the soul . . . forming in the body a kind of geometric figure of passion' (HF 245; MC 87). A disease of the soul has, crucially, no place, and cannot be seen, observed, subjected to the normalizing gaze. Placing it in the observable brain enabled a whole host of new approaches. The corporal space is as ethical as it is organic; the seat of the corporal soul is the brain (HF 270–1). Foucault uses as a particular example hysteria, which was located within the space of the body: 'in the coherence of its organic values and its moral values' (HF 302; MC 143).[19]

Foucault looks at the work of Thomas Sydenham, whose *Observationes medicae* was published in 1676. Sydenham's reputation is based on his notion that observation was a more useful medical tool than speculation. But Foucault refuses to see this as a scientific, neutral advance.

> This 'interior body' which Sydenham tried to penetrate with 'the eyes of the mind' was not the objective body available to the dull gaze of a neutralised observation; it was the site where a certain manner of imagining the body and of deciphering its internal movements combined with a certain manner of investing it with moral values. (HF 308; MC 150)

Madness is slowly becoming 'treatable', or at least open to medical perception. But this shift is only possible with an attendant shift toward the subject responsible, defining a moral space of responsibility. In this space established, of physical and moral dimensions, 'madness will never again be able to speak the language of unreason . . . it will be entirely enclosed in a pathology' (HF 358–9; MC 196–7).

At the same time, the attitude to the houses of confinement also began to change. Rather than people being afraid of confinement itself, or those confined within, they began to be afraid of its effects, of the disease spreading from these prisons and madhouses – 'a fear formulated in medical terms but animated, basically, by a moral myth' (HF 375; MC 202). Continuing the parallel with the lazarettos, Foucault claims that the fear was no longer of the place of exclusion, but of leprosy itself confronting the town: 'a terrible ulcer on the body politic'.[20] 'All those forms of unreason which had replaced leprosy in the geography of evil, and which had been banished into the remotest social distance, now became a visible leprosy and offered their running sores to the promiscuity of humans.' The evil, with its attendant fear of contagion, which the classical age had attempted to confine, was transgressing the carefully established boundaries between reason and madness, and threatening the barrier between health and illness – 'a mélange combining the dread of unreason and the old spectres of disease' (HF 377–8; MC 205).

The result of this new fear is the introduction of a new series of structures of organization in the places of confinement: 'a new exclusion in the interior of the old' (HF 406). Foucault suggests that the introduction of a medical figure – *homo medicus* – into the world of confinement is not as an *arbiter* between crime and madness, evil and illness, but as a *guardian* to protect others from the emanating danger (HF 378; MC 205). The aim was to purify these spaces through organization. This resulted in the separation of the mad from the others confined in the same loci, and this happened on both the theoretical and practical level, slowly, through 'imperceptible slippage within structures', or by 'moments [*instants*] of violent crisis'. The mad were gradually isolated, and the monotony, the homogeneity, of insanity was divided into rudimentary species: Foucault suggests that 'no medical advance, no humanitarian approach was responsible'. Rather, it was a direct result of confinement (HF 418; MC 224). The separation of the mad from other prisoners, the ill or the poor was a result of a number of changes. It is suggested that 'an abyss yawns in the middle of confinement; a void which isolates madness ... the presence of the mad appears as an injustice; but *for others*' (HF 422; MC 228). Poverty, for example, is now seen as an economic phenomenon, the poor are now treated in two separate aspects: as a problem of poverty and as a population. To confine was looked at as a gross error and an economic mistake (HF 428–30; MC 229–32).

Instead of being imprisoned within its homogeneity, madness was now freed, 'free for a perception which individualised it, free for the recognition of its unique features and for all the operations that would finally give it its status as an object' (HF 440; MC 234). The old space of internment, now reduced and limited, and a medical space formed elsewhere become confused; the twin mechanisms of classification and observation become entwined. Foucault suggests that 'another structure is established between madness and those who recognise it, survey it and judge it, a new connection, neutralised, apparently purified from all complicity, which is the order of the objective gaze [*le regard*]' (HF 446). This objectifying, individualizing gaze marks a contrast between 'the old space of exclusion, homogeneous, uniform, rigorously limited', and the fragmented, polymorphous, social space of assistance, segmented 'in accordance with the psychological and moral forms of devotion' (HF 447).

Within this entirely restructured social space, madness still takes its place. Foucault's example is that of Brissot, who drew up the plan of a perfect house of correction, 'in accordance with a geometric rigor which is at the same time architectural and moral. Each fragment of space took the symbolic values of a socially meticulous hell' (HF 448–9). But this exclusion of the mad now took on another meaning, 'it no longer marked the great caesura between reason and unreason, on the ultimate limits of society; but within the group itself it was laid out like a line between sentiments and duties – between pity and horror, between assistance and security' (HF 453). The practice of confinement and the mechanisms of observation and classification concur. What is important is that this transformation of the house of confinement into an asylum is not achieved by the progressive introduction of medicine, but through an internal restructuring of space (HF 457).

THE BIRTH OF MORAL IMPRISONMENT

Sadism, a phenomenon that bears the name of an individual man, was born of confinement, and it is therefore no accident that 'Sade's entire *œuvre* is dominated by the imagery of the Fortress, the Cell, the Cellar, the Convent, the inaccessible Island which thus form, as it were, the natural habitat of unreason'. Nor is it an accident 'that all the fantastic literature of madness and horror, which is contemporary with Sade's *œuvre*, takes place, preferentially, in the strongholds of confinement . . . in the very places where unreason had been reduced to silence' (HF 381–2; MC 210). Foucault suggests that the architecture of confinement, the enclosed natures of the places of imprisonment, affected Sade in such a way as to direct his creative output, the state of his mind. The power of environment, locale, over mind was one of the insights of the late eighteenth and early nineteenth centuries. It was suggested that the mad would respond in different ways to differing external stimuli: their abode was clearly central.

Such indeed was the view of Samuel Tuke: 'It does not require much acquaintance with the character of lunatics, to perceive in how great a degree, the prevention of abuses, and the compatibility of comfort with security, must depend on the construction of their abodes.'[21] The York Retreat, founded by Tuke's father William, was based on just such a calculation: 'A place in which the unhappy might obtain a refuge – a quiet haven in which the shattered bark might find a means of reparation or of safety.'[22] Foucault argues that the Retreat still functions as an instrument of segregation, but it was a segregation of moral and religious dimensions, one that sought to create a milieu similar to that of the Quaker community. Madness was not cured but controlled, mainly by placing the individual in a situation where they were in moral debate with themselves, 'in a perpetual anxiety, ceaselessly threatened by Law and Transgression [*Faute*]' (HF 502–3; MC 243–5).

The power of space, and concomitantly, the importance of the spaces of power, was recognized by those involved in the early nineteenth century in the design of asylums. Samuel Tuke's *Practical Hints* are symptomatic. Tuke suggests four aims for architectural design: the separation of male and female patients; the separation of patients by state of mind; a design that allowed easy and constant surveillance; and a design that allowed the patients a voluntary change of place and scenery, compatible with security.[23] Within the actual geography of the Retreat, there was also the precedent of moving people around the Retreat, to other rooms or buildings depending on their behaviour and social class.[24] The use of architecture and surroundings is clearly central, a point noted in Erving Goffman's thoughts on total institutions (published the same year as *Histoire de la folie*): 'Their encompassing or total character is symbolised by the barrier to social intercourse with the outside and to departure that is often built right into the physical plant, such as locked doors, high walls, barbed wire, cliffs, water, forests, or moors.'[25] Whilst Tuke hoped to remove the visible barriers, the internal space was carefully controlled, and indeed, the very name Retreat signals its distance from the outside community.

Within the Retreat, overt physical constraints were removed, so as to lend an air of freedom to the surroundings. Rooms were structured so that the apparent autonomy of the patients was greater than the actual – false handles on certain doors, with some spaces forbidden; custodial features were minimized, such as the muffling of bolts, and the use of cast iron frames around windows to remove the need for bars.[26] Although the design was based on William Tuke's original idea of an 'architecture of compassion',[27] Foucault sees a more sinister intent. The ostensible freedom of the individual actually placed them within a system of self-restraint, with the potential threat of guilt (HF 507; MC 250). The notion of judgement becomes paramount, with the individual objectified for scrutiny by the other, both through the mechanism of work and that of observation [*le regard*] (HF 505; MC 247). For Foucault what this initiates is a system of 'moral imprisonment', with the individual disciplining himself and subject to the judgement of the normalizing gaze, 'more genuinely confined than he could have been in a dungeon and chains, a prisoner of nothing but himself' (HF 516; MC 261). The observation, the clinical gaze, becomes a tool in the hands of a new personage in the Asylum, the keeper [*la surveillant*], who intervenes in the lives of the mad without recourse to instruments of constraint, but who simply operates with the use of observation and language. Crucially the keeper introduces a presence 'from the other side', representing both the authority that confines and the reason that judges (HF 508; MC 251).

The name of Tuke is often coupled with that of Philippe Pinel, who wrote on the situation of the mad, and famously released them from their chains in Bicêtre. At least, so goes the story. As Gordon has pointed out, for Foucault the important thing about this tale is not its historical veracity – something that rightly has been questioned – but its impact as a founding gesture.[28] This impact is not something that can be doubted: the apocryphal tale is taken as a fundamental shift to a more humane treatment of the insane. Foucault is therefore interested in how this story affects the theoretical discourse at the time. Like Tuke, Pinel's intervention is one that replaces physical with moral constraint. As Foucault suggests, 'the asylum is a religious domain without religion, a domain of pure morality, of ethical uniformity'. Whereas before the house of confinement was a 'foreign country', limited and separated like the lazar house, as an asylum it now represents 'the great continuity of social morality' (HF 513; MC 257). The previously uniform space of exclusion was medically fragmented into a polymorphous garden of species, but in moral terms this shift introduced a 'homogeneous rule', extended to all those who would tend to escape from it. 'In one and the same movement, the asylum becomes, in Pinel's hands, an instrument of moral uniformity and of social denunciation' (HF 514; MC 258).

Foucault suggests that although both Pinel and Tuke effected a moral transformation with their patients, the situations are not entirely congruent. At the Retreat, religious segregation was used for the purposes of moral purification. For Pinel, the operation ensured a continuity of ethics between the world of madness and the world of reason. This act of social segregation allowed the bourgeois morality of the outside to posit itself as an effective norm, and therefore permitted it to be imposed upon all forms of insanity as an absolute law (HF 515; MC 258). Pinel's importance also lies in the nosography of disease that he formulated. Although he was not the first author to attempt a classification of mental derangements,[29] his *Nosographie philosophique* and *Traité médico-philosophique*, both published in the years of the Revolution, were enormously influential. The changes in treatment of various illnesses 'did not only signify a reorganisation of nosological space, but, beneath the medical concepts, the presence and the operation of a new structure of experience' (HF 547). The system of classifications therefore reflects the effort to impose system and order upon the variations of vital phenomena,[30] but also often has parallels in the physical situation of the patients, with different diseases located in different locations, as with Brissot.[31]

The other aspect of the twofold mechanism of the classical age, observation, is also an important part of Pinel's work. Once more, he is contrasted with the Retreat. There, although the mad were observed, and knew they were being observed, madness had only an indirect apprehension of itself, it lacked an immediate grasp of its own character. With Pinel, on the contrary, Foucault suggests that 'observation operated only within the space defined by madness, without surface or exterior limits. Madness would see itself, would be seen by itself – pure spectacle and absolute subject' (HF 517; MC 262). Pinel suggested that he relied 'entirely on observation',[32] a practical (and medical) device that allowed a moral and normalizing dimension to intrude: 'This theme is very important for the psychiatry of the nineteenth century: madness imprisons the human in objectivity' (HF 542).

This objectivity, this moral divide, produces a new dialectic, one that is forever renewed, between the Same and the Other. The shift is one such that 'the madman is no longer the *insane* in the divided space of classical unreason; he is the *mental patient [aliéné]* of the modern form of illness' (HF 546–7). But whilst some would see this as the dispassionate advance of pure medicine, Foucault argues that the doctor takes a 'preponderant place within the asylum' by essence of his position, rather than his training. His presence converts the old house of confinement into a medical space, but his intervention is not made by virtue of a medical skill, but by the power of morality: 'It is not as a scientist [*savant*] that *homo medicus* has authority in the asylum, but as a *sage* . . . as a juridical and moral guarantee, not in the name of science' (HF 523–4). What is key though is that the doctors think that they can make judgements by virtue of their scientific knowledge. Foucault therefore suggests that despite the restructuring of space on both the level of the real and the imaginary, the divide remains. Instead of the simply physical division, there is 'that gigantic moral imprisonment which we are in the habit of calling, doubtless by antiphrasis, the liberation of the insane by Pinel and Tuke' (HF 530; MC 278).

Before the explicit formulation of much of his critical apparatus, Foucault's *Histoire de la folie* showcased many details of a spatially aware historical approach. This history of madness looks at the way space has been used in relation to the mad, tracing the patterns of exclusion, ordering, moralization and confinement that were brought to bear on their situation, altering their perception. Foucault shows an awareness of the way in which conceptions of space – theoretical, medical, moral, and philosophical – often relate to the exercise of power over the mad.

II: NOT THROUGH BENTHAM'S EYES

The same point concerning the importance of space to the exercise of power can be made for the disciplinary project. Since its publication in 1975, *Discipline and Punish* has been read as a historical investigation of the prison, especially within French history.[33] The book begins by contrasting the explosive torture of the regicide Damiens with the regime of the House of young prisoners – 'a public execution [*un supplice*] and a time-table' (SP 14; DP 7).[34] But much of the book is not about the punishment of criminals. Indeed, the majority of the text does not speak of the prison, but the standard reading of it certainly emphasizes those parts that do. Just as Colin Gordon has argued that *Histoire de la folie* is often reduced to 'three or four striking tableaux',[35] we could argue that the same is done to *Discipline and Punish* – the torture of Damiens and the House of young prisoners, the Panopticon, and the Carceral Archipelago.

As the following reading makes clear, the research presented in *Discipline and Punish* is part of a much wider project – one that occupied Foucault for much of his life. This is a research project that picks up on themes initially explored in *Histoire de la folie*, is developed in *The Birth of the Clinic* and dominates the research of the 1970s. This project is what I will call the policing of society. The concept of police is one to which Foucault returns again and again in his major works. However, the comments in these works are frequently made in passing and it is not always clear in what way he is using the concept. Support for his use of the concept has to be gleaned from remarks in lectures, essays and conference papers, as well as from the wider discussion of the term in Europe in the seventeenth to nineteenth centuries.

Foucault suggests that, from the beginning of the seventeenth century, there appeared a number of treatises concerning the government of territory. At their core these texts argued that for a state to be well organized it should extend over its entire territory a system of policing as tight and efficient as that found in cities. By police it is clear that Foucault means more than a uniformed force for the prevention and detection of crime. Rather, the concept is one which is concerned with a far more general set of regulations embodying a *type* of rationality to ensure good government.[36] This meant that the term extended far beyond the juridical: it was involved in education, welfare, assuring urban supplies and the correct standards necessary for handicrafts and commerce, the pricing of daily necessities, maintaining hygiene and health, fostering good working relations, and extended to the ways in which the city should be provided with street lighting, bridges, adornment and splendour. The police would therefore oversee a range of activities – religion, morality, health, supplies, roads, highways and town buildings, public safety, the liberal arts, trade, factories, manservants and factory workers, and the poor (DE IV, 272–4; FR 241–2; DE IV, 153–60; PPC 77–83).[37] 'Police is the ensemble of mechanisms serving to ensure order, the properly channelled growth of wealth and the conditions of preservation of health "in general"' (DE III, 17; FR 277).

When Foucault discusses Louis Turquet de Mayenne's *La Monarchie aristo-démocratique* (1611) he notes that there are four boards of police – two concerned with people in the positive and negative aspects of life, and two concerned with things, the first looking at commodities and manufactured goods and the second overseeing space and territory: private property, manorial rights, roads, rivers and public buildings (DE IV, 154–5; PPC 77–8). Similarly the discussion of von Justi's manual *Elements of Police* notes that it begins with a study of territory (DE IV, 158–9; PPC 81–2). Foucault notes that this theme is frequently referred to in texts of this period: 'architecture and urbanism occupy a place of considerable importance'. This is a development from works of the sixteenth century (DE IV, 270–1; FR 239–40). Foucault is interested in cameralism and *Polizeiwissenschaft* because of this notion of police, which, because it is concerned in very general ways with principles of order, security and discipline, can be used to understand the notion of power. What is of interest here is how the understanding of the control of space is central to police. Such a theme is developed in many of Foucault's studies of this time, and understanding how the themes of police and space interlink sheds light on Foucault's conception of power, which he suggests has space as a central component.

In tandem with this it is worth discussing the subtitle of the book: the birth of the prison. *Discipline and Punish* is clearly about issues concerned with the penal, but also about something much wider. Early in the book Foucault makes it clear that his project is to write the 'history of the modern soul' (SP 30; DP 23), and a few pages later he is even more explicit: 'The history of this "micro-physics" of punitive power would then be a genealogy or an element in a genealogy of the modern "soul"' (SP 38; DP 29). Foucault then suggests that the 'soul is the prison of the body', and that he 'would like to write the history of *this* prison, with all the political investments of the body that it gathers in its closed architecture' (SP 38–9; DP 30–1; emphasis added). *This* prison, not *the* prison. The shift from the definite article to the particular appears to have been lost on most commentators. Quite clearly Foucault is explaining that the birth of the prison is about the birth of the *soul*.[38]

Recasting *Discipline and Punish* within this wider context opens up a number of themes for discussion. First, the most viable model for the disciplined society is not the prison, but the army. Second, shifting the emphasis away from the prison allows us to better understand Foucault's remarks about schools, monasteries, hospitals and factories. These too are instruments in the birth of the modern soul and in the policing of society. Third, if the soul is the prison of the body, and the body is not simply understood in the singular but as the social body, we gain insights into Foucault's remarks about the control of the population – *bodies in plural*. Fourth, we can note in passing how Foucault sees the links between the human, the human sciences and the notion of the subject – an analysis that builds on the work of *The Order of Things* and is developed in *The History of Sexuality*. Fifth, implicit in the preceding, and important for the overall emphasis of this book, we can be attentive to questions of space in the disciplined society without solely restricting ourselves to the Panopticon.

It is this last issue with which this reading most seriously wishes to take issue. Jeremy Bentham's Panopticon is treated in a striking passage, and Foucault did help in its rediscovery, but it takes up only a few pages of the text. Many have taken it not only as the most apposite example of the new method of surveillance-led control, but also as the model for many of the others. If *Madness and Civilisation* has been reduced to three or four tableaux, *Discipline and Punish* is often simplified to just one. Pasquale Pasquino suggests this to Foucault in a 1978 interview with him. Foucault replies:

> In reference to the reduction of my analyses to that simplistic figure which is the metaphor of the Panopticon . . . let us compare what they attribute to me with what I have said; and here it is easy to show that the analyses of power which I have made cannot at all be reduced to this figure . . . (DE III, 628; FL 257)

Instead of a reading which pays due attention to the place the Panopticon plays within the overall argument, all too often the world Foucault describes is seen through Bentham's eyes.[39] There is much more than that here.

A TORTUROUS SEDIMENT

Before I look at the wider genealogy it is worth re-reading *Discipline and Punish* with attention to the question of punishment. This is because noting the basic error that is made in many readings helps to contextualize the other research. Foucault's understanding of *supplice* is both judicial and political – it is one of a number of rituals by which power is manifested (SP 58–9; DP 47–8). Its manifestation of military might is important in its role as public spectacle: 'A whole military machine surrounded the *supplice*: cavalry of the watch, archers, guardsmen, soldiers' (SP 61; DP 50). The ceremonies of *supplice* are visual displays of power, the marks of the sovereign are left in prominent places: 'Pillories, gallows and scaffolds were erected in public squares or by the roadside; sometimes the corpses of the executed persons [*des suppliciés*] were displayed for several days near the scenes of their crimes. Not only must people know [*sachent*], they must see [*voient*] with their own eyes' (SP 70; DP 58).

Penal reformers – Foucault quotes de Mably – wished for a form of punishment that touched the soul rather than the body (SP 24; DP 16). Rather than simply destroy the body of the condemned, a gentle way in punishment could be found, one that took on several non-juridical elements, so as to make the punishment not solely legal: 'We punish, but this is a way of saying that we wish to obtain a cure' (SP 30; DP 22). 'There must be no more spectacular, but useless [*inutiles*] penalties' (SP 128; DP 109) – punishment must be ordered, organized and thoughtful. Just as the garden of species had proved a model for the understanding of the mad, it could also be used for a taxonomy of crimes: 'One sought to constitute a Linnaeus of crimes and punishments . . .' (SP 118; DP 99).

Regarding the new phase of punishment discussed by Beccaria, Bentham and Brissot, Foucault talks of four possible types of punishment. The first he finds expressed in the affirmation: 'You have broken the social pact, you no longer belong to the social body, you have put yourself outside of the space of legality; we expel you from the social space where that legality functioned' (DE II, 590). This is the punishment of exile, banishment and deportation. The second is also a species of exclusion, but its mechanism is not of material deportation, of transfer outside the social body, but isolation in the midst of moral space, of public opinion. Punishment at the level of scandal, shame, humiliation. The transgression [*faute*] is made public, the individual is held up for public condemnation. The third is that of forced labour, of reparation for social injury, making amends in a way useful for the State or the society, a compensation. The fourth is the penalty of talion, making the punishment correspond to the crime – killing those who kill, taking the goods of those who steal (DE II, 589–90).

In the reformers' dream the object of punishment is 'no longer the body, with the ritual play of excessive pains, spectacular brandings [*marques éclatantes*] in the ritual of *supplices*; it is the mind or rather a play of representations and signs circulating discreetly but necessarily and evidently in the minds of all' (SP 120; DP 101). Punishment needs to be constantly visible, a learning curve for the population as a whole,

> a school rather than a festival; an ever-open book rather than a ceremony ... The spectators must be able to consult at each moment the permanent lexicon of crime and punishment. Let us conceive of places of punishment as a Garden of the Laws that families would visit on Sundays. (SP 131–2; DP 111)

> This, then, is how one must imagine the punitive city. At the crossroads, in the gardens, at the side of roads being repaired or bridges built, in workshops open to all, in the depths of mines that may be visited, will be hundreds of tiny theatres of punishment ... The great terrifying ritual of the *supplices* gives way, day after day, street after street, to this serious theatre, with its multifarious and persuasive scenes. (SP 133; DP 113)

However – and this is a point that is sometimes missed – this didn't actually happen, at least not for long. Foucault argues that deportation disappeared fairly quickly, mechanisms of scandal were never arrived at in practice, forced labour was generally a symbolic punishment and equivalence was thought of as archaic. Instead another mode of punishment comes to the fore – one that Brissot and Beccaria had barely mentioned – imprisonment, which arose suddenly at the beginning of the nineteenth century as an institution (DE II, 591–2). There are therefore *three* moments to the change examined in *Discipline and Punish*. The first is the one based on the old monarchical law – a punishment directed at the body. 'The other two both refer to a preventive, utilitarian, corrective conception of a right to punish that belongs to society as a whole; but they are very different from one another at the level of the mechanisms they envisage' (SP 154; DP 130). The problem arises in looking at what kind of punishment could strike the soul without touching the body: 'What would a non-corporal punishment be?' Even prison causes some physical pain or privation. Foucault therefore suggests that modern forms of punishment retain 'a "torturous" sediment [*un fond «suppliciant»*]' (SP 23; DP 16).

The third moment in this history of punishment 'put to work procedures for the dressage of bodies' (SP 155; DP 131) – it used the mind to affect the body, and vice versa. This is what Foucault means by suggesting that the soul is the prison of the body. To show these three moments, he sets up a series of triads:

> The sovereign and his force, the social body, the administrative apparatus. Mark, sign, trace . . . The tortured body, the soul with its manipulated representations, the body subjected to training . . . three series of elements that characterise the three mechanisms . . . three technologies of power. (SP 155; DP 131)[40]

The key question in *Discipline and Punish* is not so much why the sovereign and his force was replaced, but why the third was adopted in preference to the second. Why did the administrative apparatus replace the social body, why did the enclosed place of reform get chosen over the punitive city, 'why did the physical exercise of punishment (which is not *supplice*) replace, with the prison that is its institutional support, the social play of the signs of punishment and the chattering [*bavarde*] festival that circulated them?' (SP 154–5; DP 130–1)

In his answer to these questions Foucault suggests that four themes should be borne in mind. Punishment should be thought of both as 'a complex social function' and 'a political tactic', the technology of power should be made 'the very principle both of the humanisation of the penal system and of the knowledge of the human', and we should 'try to discover whether this entry of the soul onto the scene of penal justice . . . is not the effect of a transformation of the way in which the body itself is invested in power relations' (SP 31–2; DP 23–4). This last claim is particularly worth pursuing. How does a spatialized history help us to understand the changes in power/body relations – especially in non-penal institutions?

THE ARMY, SCHOOLS, MONASTERIES, FACTORIES

Foucault's discussion of the army, schools, monasteries and factories serves a dual purpose. First they provide many of the techniques later adopted in the modern prison; second they show how bodies were trained in a variety of ways, leading to the development of the modern soul. In the emphasis on the prison these examples are often passed by, though as Neocleous notes 'if there is one institution that Foucault uses as his model it is the military rather than the prison'.[41] The example of the military, and the use of military metaphors, is certainly key to Foucault's work. His emphasis on strategies, tactics and battle shows this, as does his remark in conversation with the geographers of *Hérodote* that many of his spatial metaphors are taken from military discourse (DE III, 32–4; P/K 68–70). It is noteworthy that the first two chapters of the section entitled 'Discipline' both heavily rely on the military model, and hardly mention criminal law. In looking at the roots of disciplinary methods, Foucault suggests that many had long been in existence, and in a note he states that though his examples in these two chapters are drawn from the military, medicine, education and industry – note the lack of the penal – he could equally have taken them from colonization, slavery and child rearing (SP 166n1; DP 314n1).

Foucault's understanding of discipline is that it begins at the same time that 'an art of the human body was born ... discipline is a political anatomy of detail'. This is why it needs to be interrogated with a 'micro-physics' of power (SP 162–3; DP 137–9). The use of detail, of minute regulations, the exacting gaze of the inspections, the continual supervision in schools, barracks, hospitals and workshops provide the political dream of 'docile bodies'. 'From such trifles', suggests Foucault, 'the human of modern humanism was born' (SP 165–6; DP 140–1). What is important about these new mechanisms of power is that they introduce the notion of the norm. This norm – although probably a retrospective invention defined as much by what it is not as by what it is – allows 'the shading of individual differences' (SP 216; DP 184; see FDS 225) – a potential polarization.[42] Behaviour and ability can be regulated according to an established standard. This is especially found in the examination, which 'combines the techniques of an observing hierarchy and those of a normalising judgement', and is found in both schools and hospitals (SP 217–19; DP 185–7).

Foucault suggests four arts of discipline: distribution within space; the control of activity – timetables, rhythms, dressage; the use of exercises; the articulation and combination of forces. The first is the most important for the purpose here – indeed as Foucault states, 'discipline is above all an analysis of space' (DE III, 515). Foucault subdivides this into four techniques. *Enclosure* [*clôture*] is the first of these, 'the protected place of disciplinary monotony'. Obvious examples include the confinement of paupers and beggars, but Foucault also talks of boarding schools, based on the monastic model, barracks and certain factories. But he suggests that enclosure alone is not sufficient, and a further subdivision, or *partitioning* [*quadrillage*] is needed – 'each individual has his own place; and each place its individual . . . discipline organises an analytical space'. Its model is 'an old architectural and religious method', the monastic cell – discipline is cellular.[43] The partitions in dormitories serve this purpose (see VS 37; WK 27–8). These subdivided places are designated with particular purposes – Foucault calls these *functional sites*. This allows places to be coded, or recoded and used for new purposes, such as the lazarettos reused as venereal hospitals and madhouses in *Histoire de la folie*, but also for the spatial distribution of diseases in hospitals, especially military and naval ones. Finally these enclosed, partitioned, and coded sites are placed in a classification, a *rank*. Foucault gives examples of the class, drawing out its parallels with the mechanisms of the army.

These spaces are both real – they suggest the disposition of buildings, rooms and furniture – and ideal – they enable characterizations, assessments, hierarchies. They function as '*tableaux vivantes*', much as the project of the garden of species had organized the mad, and the nosology of disease had the clinic, they capture humans in real and imaginary classifications – 'the table was both a technique of power and a procedure of knowledge'. A pairing of real and imaginary spaces – 'tactics, the spatial ordering of men; taxonomy, the disciplinary space of natural beings; the economic table, the regulated movement of wealth' (SP 166–75; DP 141–9; see FDS 215, 223–4).

Foucault also looks at the ideal model of the military camp:

> The old, traditional square plan was considerably refined in innumerable new projects [*schémas*]. The geometry of the paths, the number and distribution of the tents, the orientation of their entrances, the disposition of files and ranks were exactly defined; the network of gazes that supervised one another was laid down . . . The camp is the diagram of a power that acts by means of general visibility.

As Foucault points out, the model of the camp or its underlying principle was found in urban development, working-class housing estates, hospitals, asylums, prisons, schools. A shift has been made from the architecture of visual excess – palaces or churches – or that designed to observe the outside – fortresses – to that which allows internal control (SP 201–2; DP 171–2; DE III, 192; FL 228). It is also worth noting that although these models have primarily an internal function, occasionally they exercise 'a role of external surveillance, developing around themselves a whole margin of lateral controls', in the way that schools train children and supervise parents (SP 246; DP 211). Similarly the areas surrounding institutions of this sort are obviously shaped by them – garrison towns, the environs of prisons, ports, and so forth.[44]

It is important to note that procedures for the control of space in one realm were often used in others. For example, the links between the spatial organization of architecture and the organization of bodies is clearly found in Foucault's description of the medal struck to commemorate Louis XIV's first military review in 1666 (SP plate 2; DP plate 1):

> In the background is a piece of classical architecture. The columns of the palace extend those formed by the ranks of men and the erect rifles, just as the paving no doubt extends the lines of the exercise . . . The order of the architecture . . . imposes its rules and its geometry on the disciplined men on the ground. The columns of power. (SP 221; DP 188)

Foucault also explicitly links the mechanisms used for tabulating the results of examinations – examinations that enabled both the individualizing of specific features and a calculation of differences within a population – with those of the examination itself: 'small techniques of notation, of registration, of constituting files, of arranging facts in columns and tables' (SP 223; DP 190).

It is somewhat of a mystery as to why the standard reception of Foucault has ignored so much of this text. This is especially so for those who wish to look at his work on space. The military camp, the naval hospital, the monastic cell are all examples of spatial analyses – albeit less striking than the Panopticon.[45]

THE SPACES OF MEDICINE

It was suggested above that Foucault's work in *Discipline and Punish* needs to be examined in the context of the wider research project he was engaged in during the 1960s and 1970s. As with so many of his major concerns, this wider project picked up on themes discussed in *Histoire de la folie*. The research was continued in *The Birth of the Clinic*, and was pursued in Collège de France courses and occasional essays and lectures elsewhere. Much of this work is not translated into English and has only recently become available in French. Foucault begins the first chapter of *The Birth of the Clinic* with a passage that serves as a succinct summary of how his histories are spatialized and how space is historicized. He suggests that, for us, now, the human body defines the space of origin and distribution of disease, a familiar geometry, an anatomical atlas. But, he counters, 'this order of the solid, visible body is only one way in which one spatialises disease. Without doubt neither the first, nor the most fundamental. There have been, and will be, other distributions of illness'. Some of these other distributions will not necessarily rely on Euclidean anatomy, on classical geometry. The model that seems the norm to us is a 'historical, temporary datum' (NC 1; BC 3).

In the eighteenth century medicine organized diseases on the basis of species – the *Nosologie* of Sauvages, the *Nosographie* of Pinel – and treated localization in the organism as a subsidiary problem (NC 2–3; BC 4–5). The disease is defined by its *place* in a family, secondarily by its *seat* in an organism: 'the organs are the concrete supports of the disease; they never constitute its indispensable conditions' (NC 9; BC 10). Foucault suggests that this location in a family and a body are the primary and secondary forms of spatialization. The tertiary spatialization is 'all the gestures by which, in a given society, a disease is circumscribed, medically invested, isolated, divided up into closed, privileged regions, or distributed throughout cure centres, arranged in the most favourable way'. It is the place of political struggles, economic constraints, and social confrontations. It is here that the changes that led to a reformulation of medical knowledge occurred (NC 14–15; BC 16). We have here space of imaginary classifications, space of corporal reality, and space of social order.

The ordered garden of species can only work in theory, as social reality complicates the picture: 'Like civilisation, the hospital is an artificial locus [*lieu*] in which the transplanted disease runs the risk of losing its essential identity.' The individuated disease comes into contact with a number of other diseases, the hospital is an 'unkempt garden where the species cross-breed', and there is also the problem that doctors call prison or hospital fever. No hospital disease is a pure disease; therefore the family is the natural and desired locus of disease (NC 15–16; BC 17). In the classifier's abstraction, we can see an echo of that practised by Cartesian geometry: 'For the classifiers, the fundamental act of medical knowledge was the establishment of a location [*repérage*]: a symptom was situated within a disease, a disease in a specific *ensemble*, and this *ensemble* in a general plan of the pathological world' (NC 29; BC 29).

After the Revolution, however, the clinic – the teaching hospital and clinical medicine – takes precedence over the family. This emergence – in its overall arrangement [*disposition*] – is due to a number of changes, many of which are spatial. There is a change in the understanding of corporal space, from two-dimensional *tissue* to the mass of the organ, with its 'internal surface'; a shift from a botany of symptoms to a grammar of signs; and symptoms are now located in the space of the body, rather than grouped into a single logical figure. A shift in the spaces of medicine; but space is still a central part of the analysis. The doctor's question changes from 'what is the matter with you?' to 'where does it hurt?' (NC xiv; BC xviii).

Two key points are found in the new understanding of disease: the notion of the gaze [*le regard*] and the importance of the physical body – especially open to examination in death. Foucault quotes Bichat's suggestion to his pupils – 'Open up a few corpses: you will dissipate at once the darkness that observation alone could not dissipate' (NC 149; BC 146) – suggesting that this allows a greater knowledge of the disease: 'From the point of view of death, disease has a land, a mappable [*repérable*] territory, a subterranean, but secure place where its kinships and its consequences are formed; local values define its forms' (NC 151; BC 149). Foucault suggests that our epoch is one 'that marks the suzerainty of the gaze' (NC 2; BC 4). Of course, the analysis of the living body has to presuppose much that cannot be seen:

> Disease exists *in space* before it exists *for sight*. The disappearance of the two great *a priori* classes of nosology, opened up for medicine an entirely spatial field of investigation, determined throughout by these local values. It is curious to observe that this absolute spatialisation of medical experience is due not to the definitive integration of normal and pathological *anatomy*, but to the first effort to define a *physiology* of the morbid phenomenon (NC 192; BC 188).

Therefore, in *The Birth of the Clinic*, Foucault shows how spatial analyses help to map out the beginning of the modern *episteme*: 'Since 1816, the doctor's eye has been able to confront a sick organism. The historical and concrete *a priori* of the modern medical gaze was finally constituted' (NC 197; BC 192).

But *The Birth of the Clinic* is somewhat light in its analysis of social space. In *The Archaeology of Knowledge* Foucault recognizes this deficiency, suggesting that 'we must also describe the institutional *sites* [*emplacements*] from which the doctor makes his discourse, and from which this discourse derives its legitimate source and point of application (its specific objects and instruments of verification)'. The hospital is 'a place of constant, coded, systematic observation ... constituting a quantifiable field of frequencies'; private practice offers 'a field of less certain, lacunary, and far less numerable observations, but which sometimes facilitates observations that are more far-reaching in their effects, with a better knowledge of the background and environment'; and there are the research sites of the laboratory, 'an autonomous place, long distinct from the hospital', and the library or 'documentary field'. Foucault goes on to suggest that the relative importance and impact of these sites has changed. (AS 69–71; AK 51–2).

Foucault's research in this area was the topic of his 1973–4 seminar at the *Collège de France*, which studied 'the history of the institution and the architecture of the hospital in the eighteenth century' (RC 69). The results of this research were published in a volume entitled *Généalogie des équipements de normalisation* in 1976, and reissued as *Les Machines à guérir* [*Curing Machines*] in 1979.[46] Foucault's introduction to this work – 'The Politics of Health in the Eighteenth Century' – and the three conference papers given to the Institute of Social Medicine in Rio de Janeiro in October 1974 help to patch together his thoughts in this area. The research looks at the development of hospitalization and its mechanisms in the eighteenth and early nineteenth century, and at the establishment of plans to make a study of habitat and all that surrounds it: waste collection, means of transport, and public resources which allow the functioning of everyday life, particularly in the urban environment (DE III, 208).

Foucault suggests that social medicine is developed in France along with the expansion of urban structures. There are various interesting analyses. One suggests that the birth of cemeteries, on the edges of towns, with individual graves, is not due to Christianity and a respect for the dead but a politico-medico concern for the living and the contagion that the old graves brought. A similar move was made with abattoirs. There is also a greater control of movement – not just of people, but of things and elements, principally water and air. This includes a look at the development of sewers, where the underground [*le sous-sol*] was controlled by the authorities, even when the space above was privately owned (DE III, 219–21). Medicine undertakes the 'control of urban space in general ... The city with its principal spatial variables appears as a medicalisable object' (DE III, 22; FR 282). A variant on the French model is found in Germany, with the development of the concept of *Medizinischepolizei*, the medical police, which appeared in 1764 (DE III, 212), and in England, where the principal aim is the health of the work force. Foucault suggests that in this period 'urban topographies' were undertaken, which can outline the principles of an urban policy. This is in contrast to topographies of regions, which can only recommend corrections and compensations to matters such as climate and geology that are outside of human control (DE III, 22; FR 282).

Foucault also discusses the 'spatial adaptation of the hospital, and in particular its adaptation to the urban space in which it is located'. This works on two levels: the situation of the hospital within the larger community – should it be large and encompassing, perhaps outside the town, where the risk of contagion is limited, or should there be a number of smaller hospitals spread throughout the community – and the internal space of the hospital itself, where the hospital is turned into a 'curing machine' (DE III, 26; FR 286–7). Before the eighteenth century the hospital was essentially an institution for the assistance of the poor, an institution of separation and exclusion, the place where one went to die (DE III, 511). The model for the 'medicalization' of the hospital was not the civil hospital, but the naval hospital, such as those in London, Marseilles and La Rochelle. Some of the mechanisms developed out of the treatment of epidemics and the use of quarantine, some from the new means of discipline found in the army (DE III, 513–14). It is obvious that the models Foucault uses in his earlier work to show the development of medicine – the army, monasteries, slavery, schools, the Roman legion – are also those that shape the prison (DE III, 515).[47]

Foucault suggests that the 'question of the hospital at the end of the eighteenth century was fundamentally a question of space'. This is evidenced in a number of areas. Examples include the locale of the hospital, where its situation had to conform to the sanitary controls of the town – the dangerous miasmas, contaminated air, and dirty water; the individuation of patient space, with the single beds, as opposed to the *lit dortoir* in which six slept, and the screens [*draps*] placed around the beds; and the constitution of a modifiable environment, with changeable temperature and air cooling. All of these showed the attempt to make the hospital not simply the place of the cure but also an instrument of the cure itself: 'the space of the hospital is medicalised in its purpose and its effects' (DE III, 518–19). And, like the mechanisms of discipline in wider society, the new hospital technology allows both the individual and the population to become objects of knowledge and medical intervention. The medicine of the eighteenth century, by its use of space, is simultaneously a medicine of the individual and the population (DE III, 521).

THE PANOPTICON AND PANOPTICISM

It is surprising that the spatial analyses of the military, schools, monasteries and hospitals are neglected, but even more so that the chapter where Foucault introduces the Panopticon is given a partial reading. At the beginning of the chapter two methods of dealing with diseases, leprosy and the plague, are contrasted. These had earlier been examined in the second of the Rio medicine lectures (DE III, 517–18). Foucault suggests that whilst 'the leper gave rise to rituals of exclusion ... the plague gave rise to disciplinary diagrams' (SP 231; DP 198).[48] These disciplinary diagrams [*schémas disciplinaires*] are shown in a plague town, where there is a strict spatial partitioning, careful surveillance, detailed inspection and order. This way of dealing with disease is not 'a massive, binary division between one set of people and another', it is rather one that involves 'multiple separations, individualising distributions, an organisation in depth of surveillance and control, an intensification and a ramification of power' (SP 231; DP 198).[49] Foucault goes on to link these two models with their political/social counterparts:

> the leper and his separation; the plague and its segmentations. The first is marked; the second analysed and distributed. The exile of the leper and the arrest of the plague do not bring with them the same political dream. The first is that of a pure community, the second that of a disciplined society. (SP 231–2; DP 198)

The military model of organized discipline replaces the religious model of exclusion (DE III, 218).

As Foucault points out, the leper is the symbolic figure; the real figures were often beggars, madmen and criminals; the plague similarly stands as a symbol of how 'all forms of confusion and disorder' were dealt with from the late eighteenth century (SP 232; DP 199). The opposition of the leper and the plague, as opposed to that of torture and the timetable, is less frequently used or commented on in a Foucauldian study.[50] What is important about the use of these examples is that Foucault suggests that the former use of power, the exclusion, has the organizational grid of the treatment of the plague victim superimposed on top of it, providing a model for the growth of the disciplined surveillance society – 'treat "lepers" as "plague victims", project the subtle segmentations of discipline onto the confused space of internment' (SP 232; DP 199). Instead of the exclusion *without control* of banishment, what Bender has called 'liminal boundedness . . . a reign of randomness and licence with the precinct of confinement',[51] the space of exclusion is now rigidly regimented and controlled. 'All the mechanisms of power which, even today, are disposed around the abnormal individual, to brand him and to alter him, are composed of those two forms from which they distinctly derive. Bentham's *Panopticon* is the architectural figure of this composition' (SP 233; DP 199–200).

Before I discuss the Panopticon itself it is worth dwelling on the mechanism of the plague town. Foucault suggests in a number of places that in the early nineteenth century there was a shift towards what he calls bio-politics, where the methods of dealing with populations within territories are modified in certain ways. These include the building up of profiles, increasing knowledge through monitoring and surveillance, and control through discipline. There is a move towards prevention and regulation, within sites of exclusion clearly, but, by extension, this control is expanded to take in the whole society. Foucault's understanding of populations as 'bodies in plural' perhaps, as Eckermann remarks, provides a defence against the charge of critics like Rorty and Taylor that Foucault's project is 'apolitical', as it would seem that conceiving of bodies *en masse* is an inherently political exercise.[52] In this period, governments deal not just with a territory and the individuals or a 'people' within, but with an 'economic and political problem' – population (VS 35–6; WK 25).

It is into this understanding that we must insert the Panopticon. What is important in Foucault's analysis is that there are two poles in the new mode of power. One is the mode of discipline, perhaps in enclosed institutions; the other is the understanding of bio-power, of control of populations.[53] These controls are facilitated by police or governmentality. As Foucault notes, the Panopticon 'is a form of architecture, of course, but it is above all a form of government. It is a way for mind to exercise power over mind' (DE II, 437). Rather than see the rise of disciplinary mechanisms as the result of the birth of the prison, we should look at the emergence of the prison from the rise in general discipline and policing.

In this section's call for an end to seeing Foucault's text through Bentham's eyes the important role of Bentham himself could easily be neglected.[54] I have suggested that we need to be attentive to the place in the text where the Panopticon appears – as the architectural figure of the convergence of the mechanisms for dealing with lepers and plague victims; as a product of a number of disciplinary themes. The Panopticon is an exceptional example, certainly, of the uses of power and space, but it is the culmination of a variety of technologies of power rather than their beginning. And yet Foucault designates the disciplinary society under the general rubric of panopticism. To understand this we need to be attentive to what Foucault actually says. Why does Foucault suggest that 'Bentham is more important for our society than Kant or Hegel' (DE II, 594), that 'our society is much more Benthamite than Beccarian' (DE II, 729), and that Bentham is the 'Christopher Columbus of politics' (DE III, 466; see SP 240)?

Such comments make sense if we cease thinking of the Panopticon simply as a prison. Foucault notes its polyvalency – reforming prisoners, treating patients, instructing schoolchildren, confining the insane, supervising workers, putting beggars and idlers to work – and suggests that Bentham takes the penitentiary house as his prime example because it 'has many different functions to fulfil – safe custody, confinement, solitude, forced labour and instruction' (SP 239, 240n; DP 205–6).[55] Foucault tellingly makes the remark that in Bentham's scheme, 'police, the French invention which immediately fascinated all European governments, is the twin of the Panopticon' (DE II, 729). Indeed, Bentham himself saw the Panopticon as having two branches: the prisoner branch and the pauper branch.[56] The prison is one piece of this general panopticism – this new form of police, of government. 'It is there, in the general panopticism of society that one must place the birth of the prison' (DE II, 438).

I would therefore contend that in looking at the role of Bentham in *Discipline and Punish*, we need to look at panopticism, rather than the Panopticon. The former, although it bears a Benthamite designation, is much older than the 1791 text. Panopticism provides a way of 'dispensing with the need for the Prince. Panopticism is the general principle of a new "political anatomy" whose object and end are not the relations of sovereignty but the relations of discipline' (SP 243; DP 208).[57] Foucault suggests that there are two images of discipline – the discipline-blockade, and the discipline-mechanism. The first of these is the enclosed institution, on the edges of society, turned inwards, the second is a functional device [*dispositif*] that makes the exercise of power more effective and enables subtle coercion of the society; a schema of exceptional discipline, and a generalized surveillance. The latter of these Foucault designates 'panopticism' (SP 244; DP 209), the former is surely exemplified by the Panopticon.

We can best understand the birth of the prison from the general rise of what is designated panopticism, rather than the reverse. Foucault makes the obvious point that the prison was not born within these codes, that it had existed for centuries before it became part of a penal system, but that its basic principle – the 'deprivation of liberty' – became the penalty *par excellence* in the new society which so valued its freedoms (SP 267–8; DP 231–2).[58] Given that it is the culmination of trends found in military and scholastic discourse, it is indeed not surprising

> that the cellular prison, with its regular chronologies, forced labour, its authorities of surveillance and registration, its experts in normality, who continue and multiply the functions of the judge, should have become the modern instrument of penality . . . that prisons resemble factories, schools, barracks, hospitals, which all resemble prisons. (SP 264; DP 227–8)

In these terms, suggests Foucault, the prison is 'a rather strict barracks, a school without leniency, a dark workshop, but not qualitatively different' (SP 269; DP 233). Rather than other institutions being a diluted form of the prison, the prison is the general trend in its most extreme form, with no gaps, no limits: 'it carries to their greatest intensity all the procedures to be found in the other disciplinary *dispositifs*' (SP 273; DP 236).

We can now respond to the charge that Bentham's *Panopticon* is not a good description of 'real life' in nineteenth-century prisons. Foucault suggests that if he had wanted to describe 'real life' in the prisons, he would not have gone back to Bentham (DE IV, 28–9; FE 81). Bentham's work is important as a theoretician's schema, because 'he describes, in the utopia of a general system, particular mechanisms that really exist' (DE III, 207; FL 240):

The fact that it [the Panopticon] should have given rise, even in our own time, to so many variations, projected or realised, is evidence of the imaginary intensity that it has possessed for almost two hundred years. But the Panopticon must not be understood as a dream building: it is the diagram of a mechanism of power reduced to its ideal form; its functioning, abstracted from any obstacle, resistance or friction, must be represented as a pure architectural and optical system: it is in fact a figure of political technology that may and must be detached from any specific use (SP 239; DP 205).[59]

In his 1972–3 *Collège de France* course résumé, Foucault provided a succinct summary of the themes in this research project. Understanding how the parts of the research fit together enables a wider reading of this than simply one that looks at the mechanisms of punishment and the establishment of the prison:

A new *optics*, first: an organ of surveillance generalised and constant; all must be observed, seen, transmitted: organisation of a police; institution of a system of archives (with individual files), establishment of a *panopticism*.
 A new *mechanics*: isolation and regrouping of individuals; localisation of bodies; optimal utilisation of forces; control and improvement of productivity; in short, the putting into place of a complete *discipline* of life, time and energies.
 A new *physiology*: definition of norms, exclusion and rejection of those who do not conform, mechanisms for their restoration by corrective interventions which are in an ambiguous manner therapeutic and punitive.
 Panopticism, discipline and normalisation schematically characterise this new hold [*prise*] of power over the body, which was put in place in the 19th Century. And the psychological subject which appears at this moment ... is only the reverse side [*l'envers*] of this process of subjectification [*assujettissement*]. The psychological subject is born at the point of conjunction of power and the body: it is an effect of a certain 'political physics'. (RC 49–50)

What *Discipline and Punish* shows is how the *supplice* of the eighteenth century is replaced by the disciplinary *dispositif* of the nineteenth century: a *dispositif* that encompasses technologies of power that produce a docile body, a knowable 'soul', and a subjectification of the individual (SP 308, 345; DP 264, 295). Being attentive to the meaning of the book's subtitle leads to two main realizations: first that the birth of the actual prison is enmeshed within the birth of the figurative prison, within the genealogy of the modern subject, an insight that better explains the change in penal practice; and second it allows us to see this genealogy as the main scope of the book. This genealogy of the modern soul and of the policing of urban space – two themes that are closely linked – is not simply pursued in *Discipline and Punish*, but is also the subject matter of other research. It is also further pursued in *The History of Sexuality* series. Realizing all of this enables us to better understand the larger project – to be attentive to the role of Bentham certainly – but not to see the world and the text solely through his eyes.

Conclusion

Recent work asserting the importance of space to social theory has largely been concerned with making a case for detailed treatment of questions of spatiality. Space is the topic of examination, and the tools of critical theory, historical materialism, Foucauldian genealogy or whatever are brought to bear on it. This has led to some interesting analyses of the spaces of our contemporary world and of globalization, histories of space of variable quality, and incessant commentaries on Los Angeles. Against this contemporary focus – but very much in keeping with its underlying project – I have argued that space should not be simply an object of analysis but part of the conceptual armoury we have for analysis itself. This is the difference between a spatial history and a history of space. I believe this would be a far more challenging reassertion of the importance of space than the many practical analyses that have dominated recent research.

In Foucault's spatial histories we can clearly see the way in which space is fundamental to any exercise of power. Given that Foucault uses power relations to investigate society, rather than the Marxist productive relationship, and that power relations are in and through space, we can see that *questions of space are inherently political*. Important though questions of rent, land use and similar are, this politics of space is not simply a political economy of space. Production is an element within the larger terrain of power relations. However, I would go further than this: *politics is inherently spatial*. This last point is indebted to Heidegger's rethinking of the πόλις in his lectures on Hölderlin and Parmenides. The distancing of the political from the *polemical* and arguing that the πόλις is, at root, a place, is potentially a major contribution to political theory. Lefebvre suggests 'there is a politics of space because space is political'.[1] Following Heidegger, we might suggest that 'there is a politics of space because *politics is spatial*'.

This book has shown that the relation between Heidegger and Foucault is indeed one that repays close attention. Against the current of scholarship which suggests Nietzsche is Foucault's primary precursor I have argued – following Foucault's late enigmatic comment – that Heidegger was for him the 'essential philosopher', and that where Nietzsche is important it is Nietzsche through a Heideggerian lens. Heidegger's influence on twentieth-century French thought – from Sartre, Merleau-Ponty and Lefebvre to Lacan, Althusser and Derrida, among many others – is well known. In Foucault we can see yet another example. Whilst Foucault – unlike many of the others – does not directly speak *of* Heidegger, he often speaks in a thoroughly Heideggerian way. Not all elements of Foucault's work are Heideggerian, and in places – usually without explicitly stating this is the case – he is engaged in critique. But very striking affinities can be found.

In his *Thirdspace*, Edward Soja suggests that there remains to be written a study that looks at the role of space in some of the key thinkers of the Western tradition. He mentions Foucault and Heidegger – amongst many others – but suggests that 'what would severely hinder such an archaeology, however, is *the almost complete absence of a secondary literature that explicitly and perceptively addresses the problematic relation between historicality and spatiality* presumed to be embedded in these sources'.[2] If we are to critically explore the importance of space and its role within a historical study we must ensure that the tools we use function adequately. In working on Foucault and space it quickly became apparent that there was a dearth of adequate material. Key questions remained unanswered, fundamental texts were left obscure, and intellectual genealogies were inadequately explored. This book has sought answers to some of these questions, to examine these texts, and to trace these genealogies.

In terms of Foucault's own work I have argued that Foucault's historical studies are spatial through and through, and that this is the fundamental legacy of his work to those interested in the question of space – rather than the two figures to which so much study has been given: the Panopticon and heterotopias. Understanding how space is fundamental to the use of power and to historical research into the exercise of power allows us to recast Foucault's work not just as a history of the present but as a mapping of the present. This orientation of a historical study to the present, rather than the past, is a theme I find common to Nietzsche, Heidegger and Foucault – and is framed by their responses to the Kantian question 'how are synthetic *a priori* judgements possible?' Taking Nietzsche's response 'why is belief in such judgements *necessary?*' as a guiding principle within his genealogical approach, and seeing how Heidegger's response to Kant is crucial to understanding the shift between the published and the unpublished divisions of *Being and Time* (the *Kehre*) and to the development of *historical ontology*, I have recast Foucault's historical approach as a historical ontology. Like Heidegger – and in, for example, *The Birth of Tragedy*, Nietzsche – this is a history framed as a history of the present. Noting how Foucault's *connaissance/savoir* distinction parallels Heidegger's ontic/ontological difference allows us to see both the continuity between archaeology and genealogy and between two of the twentieth century's foremost thinkers.

This link, crucial though it is, is but one area of many where I suggest Heidegger is important in understanding what Foucault is doing. Other important issues – *dispositif*, technologies and the question of power/knowledge – become clearer from a Heideggerian perspective. Perhaps most importantly though, the crucial work that Nietzsche began in sketch form, and that Heidegger elaborated in careful studies throughout his career, paves the way for Foucault's treatment of questions of space and time together in his spatial histories. The modernist marginalization of space and prioritization of time is abandoned with a carefully developed analysis of how they function together. As the final chapter has demonstrated, they are best seen at work in Foucault in their practical application. Work reasserting the importance of space to social and political theory must *not* be at the expense of a critical interrogation of history itself, and it must not ignore the specific situation of the thinkers marshalled to its cause. In thinking the relation of space to history it should spatialize history and not simply historicize space. Above all, it must be philosophically and theoretically sound. In seeking to avoid these pitfalls, this book contributes to that broad aim.

Notes

Introduction

1. Jacques Derrida, 'Être juste avec Freud', in Michel Delorme (ed.), *Penser la folie: Essais sur Michel Foucault*, Paris: Galilée, 1992, p. 180n, suggests that 'this blank silence ... the spacing of these omissions ... is anything but the empty and inoperative sign of an absence'. This is a useful corrective to Derrida's earlier claim that 'Heidegger was almost never named by Foucault, who in any case never confronted him and, if one may say so, never explained himself on his relationship to him'. See Jacques Derrida, 'Introduction: Desistance', in Philippe Lacoue-Labarthe, *Typography: Mimesis, philosophy, politics*, edited by Christopher Fynsk, Cambridge, MA: Harvard University Press, 1989.
2. On the influence of Bachelard and Canguilhem, see Dominique Lecourt, *Marxism and Epistemology: Bachelard, Canguilhem, Foucault*, translated by Ben Brewster, London: NLB, 1975; and Gary Gutting, *Michel Foucault's Archaeology of Scientific Reason*, Cambridge: Cambridge University Press, 1989. The former offers some useful interpretations of Bachelard and Canguilhem, but is less helpful on their influence on Foucault; the latter is far more useful. As James Miller, *The Passion of Michel Foucault*, London: Harper Collins, 1993, p. 59, notes, Althusser's enduring legacy to Foucault may have been to push him in the direction of Bachelard and Canguilhem. See Louis Althusser, 'A Letter to the Translator', in *For Marx*, translated by Ben Brewster, London: Verso, 1969, and for a discussion, Etienne Balibar, From Bachelard to Althusser: The Concept of the Epistemological Break, *Economy and Society*, Vol. 7, No. 3, August 1978. Though I do not wish to marginalize the influence of Bachelard and Canguilhem on Foucault, I think it can be overstated and, in any case, Heidegger is central to Bachelard, Nietzsche important to Canguilhem. Foucault discusses their work in Piéger sa propre culture (DE II, 382), some interviews (see, for example, DE IV, 431–57; PPC 17–46), the introduction to *The Archaeology of Knowledge* and the introduction to Georges Canguilhem, *The Normal and the Pathological*, translated by Carolyn R. Fawcett, Dordrecht: D. Reidel, 1978 (DE III, 429–42). See Gaston Bachelard, *The Poetics of Space*, translated by Maria Jolas, New York: Orion Press, 1964.
3. Their study conceives of four stages in Foucault: Heideggerian; Archaeological/Quasi-Structuralist; Genealogical; Ethical. See Hubert Dreyfus and Paul Rabinow, *Michel Foucault: Beyond structuralism and hermeneutics*, Brighton: Harvester, 1982. Foucault commented that Dreyfus and Rabinow were the

first to suggest the influence: 'Of course it was quite true, but no one in France has ever perceived it' (DE IV, 780; TS 12). Since their joint venture – which itself 'was born out of a disagreement amongst friends' (p. vii) – it seems Dreyfus and Rabinow differ on their understanding of the links between the two thinkers. See Dreyfus, Beyond Hermeneutics: Interpretation in Late Heidegger and Recent Foucault, in Gary Shapiro and Alan Sica (eds), *Hermeneutics: Questions and proposals*, Amherst: University of Massachusetts Press, 1984; and On the Ordering of Things: Being and Power in Heidegger and Foucault, in Timothy J. Armstrong (ed.) *Michel Foucault Philosopher*, Hemel Hempstead: Harvester Wheatsheaf, 1992, which suggests that the links are large, and that power plays for Foucault a role similar to Being for Heidegger; while Rabinow tries to distance them, partly due to the political issues around Heidegger. See his Modern and Counter-modern: Ethos and Epoch in Heidegger and Foucault, in Gary Gutting (ed.) *The Cambridge Companion to Foucault*, Cambridge: Cambridge University Press, 1994. Dreyfus undoubtedly knows Heidegger better than Rabinow does, and the latter is perhaps guilty of a selective reading of Foucault. More useful – in its general pronouncement that there are affinities between Foucault and the later Heidegger, if not in its detail – is Allan Megill, *Prophets of Extremity: Nietzsche, Heidegger, Foucault, Derrida*, Berkeley: University of California Press, 1985. See also Hinrich Fink-Eitel, Zwischen Nietzsche und Heidegger: Michel Foucaults 'Sexualität und Wahrheit' im Spiegel neuerer Sekundärliteratur, *Philosophisches Jahrbuch*, Vol. 97, No. 2, 1990; William V. Spanos, *Heidegger and Criticism: Retrieving the cultural politics of destruction*, Minneapolis: University of Minnesota Press, 1993, Chapter 5; Neil Levy, The Prehistory of Archaeology: Heidegger and the Early Foucault, *Journal of the British Society for Phenomenology*, Vol. 27, No. 2, May 1996; and Michael Schwartz, Critical Reproblemization: Foucault and the Task of Modern Philosophy, *Radical Philosophy*, No. 91, Sept/Oct 1998. Despite the promise of its title, Tom Rockmore, *Heidegger and French Philosophy: Humanism, antihumanism and being*, London: Routledge, 1995, never really explains his comment on p. 57 that 'Foucault's relation to Heidegger's thought is important for an understanding of his own theory'.

4. Charles E. Scott, *The Question of Ethics: Nietzsche, Foucault, Heidegger*, Bloomington: Indiana University Press, 1990, p. 216, n1.

5. Thomas Dumm, *Michel Foucault and the Politics of Freedom*, Thousand Oaks: Sage, 1996, p. 25, n3. Gilles Deleuze, *Foucault*, translated by Séan Hand, London: Athlone Press, 1988, p. 113, suggests that Foucault could understand Heidegger 'only by way of Nietzsche and alongside Nietzsche (and not the other way round)'. Interestingly, some of those that make the most explicit links are those who wish to criticize Foucault for his Heideggerianism, in the wake of the Nazi revelations. See for example, Keith Windshuttle, *The Killing of History*, Paddington NSW: Macleay Press, 1996. This is discussed by Didier Eribon, *Michel Foucault et ses contemporains*, Paris: Fayard, 1994, pp. 93–100.

6. This also sets up a critical distance from Habermas's reading, which suggests that 'Nietzsche's motif of a critique of reason reached Foucault not via Heidegger, but through Bataille'. Jürgen Habermas, *The Philosophical Discourse of Modernity*, translated by Frederick Lawrence, Cambridge: Polity Press, 1987, p. 239. It has also been suggested in a couple of places that Max Weber is the

link. See John O'Neill, The Disciplinary Society: From Weber to Foucault, *The British Journal of Sociology*, Vol. XXXVII, No. 1, March 1986, p. 43; and David Owen, *Maturity and Modernity: Nietzsche, Weber, Foucault and the ambivalence of reason*, London: Routledge, 1994. Occasionally commentators discuss Heidegger in relation to Foucault, only to conclude that there is no important link. See, for example, J. G. Merquior, *Foucault*, Berkeley: University of California Press, 1985, p. 143.

7. David Macey, *The Lives of Michel Foucault*, London: Hutchinson, 1993, p. 34; Didier Eribon, *Michel Foucault*, translated by Betsy Wing, London: Faber & Faber, 1993, p. 30.
8. It is worth noting that Foucault read Heidegger again in 1963 (DE I, 25) and that he clearly knew Heidegger's *Nietzsche* by 1966 (DE I, 551); that he was taught by Jean Beaufret, the recipient of Heidegger's *Letter on Humanism*, and a noted Heideggerian; and worked on the translation of Ludwig Binswanger's *Dream and Existence*, a work informed by Heideggerian *Daseinanalyse*, meeting with Binswanger and discussing Heidegger in the process. See Eribon, *Michel Foucault*, pp. 30–1.
9. Miller, *The Passion of Michel Foucault*, pp. 138, 418, n48; 50; 159.
10. Derrida, 'Être juste avec Freud', p. 180.
11. Some of these issues have been explored by Will McNeill, Care for the Self: Originary Ethics in Heidegger and Foucault, *Philosophy Today*, Vol. 42, No. 1, Spring 1998.
12. See, for example, Edward W. Soja, *Postmodern Geographies: The Reassertion of Space in Critical Social Theory*, London: Verso, 1989; *Thirdspace: Journeys to Los Angeles and Other Real-and-Imagined Places*, Oxford: Blackwell, 1996; Derek Gregory, *Geographical Imaginations*, Oxford: Blackwell, 1994; Nigel Thrift, *Spatial Formations*, London: Sage, 1996; Scott Lash and John Urry, *Economies of Signs and Space*, London: Sage, 1994; David Harvey, *The Condition of Postmodernity*, Oxford: Blackwell, 1989; Rob Shields, *Places on the Margin*, London: Routledge, 1991; Trevor Barnes and Derek Gregory (eds), *Reading Human Geography: The poetics and politics of inquiry*, London: Arnold, 1997; Michael Keith and Steve Pile (eds), *Place and the Politics of Identity*, London: Routledge, 1993; Helen Liggett and David C. Perry (eds), *Spatial Practices*, Thousand Oaks: Sage, 1995; Marcus Doel, *Poststructuralist Geographies: The Diabolical Art of Spatial Science*, Edinburgh: Edinburgh University Press, 1999. More successful – though not without their own problems – have been works by Edward S. Casey, *Getting Back into Place: Toward a renewed understanding of the place-world*, Bloomington: Indiana University Press, 1993; *The Fate of Place: A philosophical history*, Berkeley: University Presses of California, 1997; and Jeff Malpas, *Place and Experience: A philosophical topography*, Cambridge: Cambridge University Press, 1999.
13. On this criticism, see Henri Lefebvre, *La production de l'espace*, Paris: Anthropos, 1974, p. 10; translated by Donald Nicolson-Smith as *The Production of Space*, Oxford: Blackwell, 1991, pp. 3–4; Doreen Massey, Politics and Space/Time, *New Left Review*, No. 192, Nov./Dec. 1992, p. 66. Lefebvre suggests that Foucault fails to explain what he means by space, a claim that will be disputed throughout this book.
14. This is, for example, a common criticism of Soja. See, for example, Eleonore

Kofman and Elizabeth Lebas, Lost in Transposition – Time, Space and the City, in Henri Lefebvre, *Writings on Cities*, translated and edited by Eleonore Kofman and Elizabeth Lebas, Oxford: Blackwell, 1996; Lynn Stewart, Bodies, Visions and Spatial Politics: a Review Essay of Henri Lefebvre's *The Production of Space*, in *Environment and Planning D: Society and Space*, Vol. 13, 1995; and Stuart Elden, Politics, Philosophy, Geography: Henri Lefebvre in Anglo-American Scholarship, *Antipode: A radical journal of geography*, Vol. 33. No. 5, November 2001.
15. See, for example, Jeffrey Minson, *Genealogies of Morals: Nietzsche, Foucault, Donzelot and the eccentricity of ethics*, Basingstoke: Macmillan, 1985; Owen, *Maturity and Modernity*.
16. Colin Gordon, *Histoire de la folie*: an Unknown Book by Michel Foucault, *History of the Human Sciences*, Vol. 3, No. 1, 1990.
17. One of the best examples of this is Stephen Kern, *The Culture of Time and Space 1880–1918*, Cambridge, MASS: Harvard University Press, 1983.

Chapter One: Space and History in Being and Time

1. See Theodore Kisiel, Heidegger's *Gesamtausgabe*: An International Scandal of Scholarship, *Philosophy Today*, Vol. 39, No. 1, Spring 1995.
2. Theodore Kisiel, *The Genesis of Heidegger's Being and Time*, Berkeley: University of California Press, 1993.
3. Kisiel, *The Genesis of Heidegger's Being and Time*, p. 360.
4. David Farrell Krell, *Intimations of Mortality: Time, Truth, and Finitude in Heidegger's Thinking of Being*, Pennsylvania: Pennsylvania State University Press, 1986, p. 5.
5. See Stephen Mulhall, *Heidegger and Being and Time*, London: Routledge, 1996, p. 4; George Steiner, *Heidegger*, London: Fontana, third edition, 1992, p. 80. Derrida claims that 'from *The Introduction to Metaphysics* onward, Heidegger renounces the project of and the word ontology'. See Jacques Derrida, *Of Grammatology*, translated by Gayatri Chakravorty Spivak, Baltimore: Johns Hopkins University Press, 1976, p. 22. But not only does Heidegger not drop the word (see GA48, 279ff; N IV, 150ff, GA15; HS for example), it is clear that what is later called the history of being is of course precisely an examination of these, and similar, conditions. Similar arguments to those of Derrida are made by William J. Richardson, *Heidegger: Through phenomenology to thought*, The Hague: Martinus Nijhoff, third edition, 1974, p. 15. For a discussion, see Ralph Powell, The Late Heidegger's Omission of the Ontic-Ontological Structure of Dasein, in John Sallis (ed.) *Heidegger and the Path of Thinking*, Pittsburgh: Duquesne University Press, 1970. See too, the remark made in *History of the Concept of Time*: 'There is no ontology *alongside* a phenomenology. Rather, *scientific ontology is nothing but phenomenology*' (GA20, 98). Note also that Heidegger defines essence [*Wesen*] as '(1) *quidditas* – the "what" – κοινόν; (2) enabling – condition of possibility; (3) ground of enabling' (GA9, 73n. a).
6. See GA24, 313–16; and Allan Megill, *Prophets of Extremity: Nietzsche, Heideg-*

ger, Foucault, Derrida, Berkeley: University of California Press, 1985, p. 163. More generally on science see GA41, 66–108.
7. See, for example, Hubert Dreyfus' comments in Bryan Magee, *The Great Philosophers*, London: BBC Books, 1987, pp. 269–71, and his *Being-in-the-World*, Cambridge, MASS: MIT Press, 1991, p. 127.
8. The phrase 'historical *a priori*' is also used by Edmund Husserl in his late work, particularly *Die Krisis der europäischen Wissenschaften und die tranzendentale Phänomenologie: Eine Einleitung in die Phänomenologische Philosophie*, in *Husserliana: Gesammelte Werke*, edited by Walter Biemel, The Hague: Martinus Nijhoff, 1950, Vol. VI. Arguably this is Husserl's response to the criticisms of the ahistorical nature of his earlier work.
9. See Kisiel, *The Genesis of Heidegger's Being and Time*, p. 326.
10. On this, see Jorge Luis Borges, Funes the Memorious, translated by Anthony Kerrigan, in *Fictions*, London: Calder Publications, 1991, especially p. 104: 'to think is to forget a difference, to generalise, to abstract'.
11. For a detailed discussion of this, see Peter Berkowitz, Nietzsche's Ethics of History, *The Review of Politics*, Vol. 56 No. 1, Winter 1994; and Paul Redding, Child of the English Genealogists: Nietzsche's Affiliation with the Critical Historical Mode of the Enlightenment, in Paul Patton (ed.), *Nietzsche, Feminism and Political Theory*, London: Routledge, 1993.
12. Though see the point made by Jacques Taminiaux, *Heidegger and the Project of Fundamental Ontology*, translated by Michael Gendre, Albany: State University of New York Press, 1991, p. 187.
13. See Michael Inwood, *Heidegger*, Oxford: Oxford University Press, 1997.
14. For a discussion of this, see Charles Guignon, History and Commitment in the Early Heidegger, in Hubert L. Dreyfus and Harrison Hall (eds), *Heidegger: A Critical Reader*, Oxford: Blackwell, 1992; and David Couzens Hoy, History, Historicity and Historiography in Being and Time, in Michael Murray (ed.), *Heidegger and Modern Philosophy*, New Haven: Yale University Press, 1978.
15. Charles R. Bambach, *Heidegger, Dilthey, and the Crisis of Historicism*, Ithaca: Cornell University Press, 1995, p. 201.
16. See Bambach, *Heidegger, Dilthey*, pp. 203, 205.
17. See Kisiel, *The Genesis of Heidegger's Being and Time*, p. 254.
18. 'Moment', or 'moment of vision', is the translation of *Augenblick* Macquarrie and Robinson give in *Being and Time*, Stambaugh uses 'moment', suggesting 'moment of vision' has mystical connotations (p. xvi). Hofstader uses 'instant' in *The Basic Problems of Phenomenology*. Though 'instant' has much to recommend it, and is probably, on balance, the closest English equivalent that does not resort to a phrase or a neologism, I have stuck to 'moment' throughout. This point is discussed in much more detail in Chapter Two below. For a wide-ranging discussion see William McNeill, *The Glance of the Eye: Heidegger, Aristotle and the Ends of Theory*, Albany: State University of New York Press, 1999.
19. Rüdiger Safranski, *Martin Heidegger: Between good and evil*, translated by Ewald Osers, Cambridge, MA: Harvard University Press, 1998, pp. 173ff, provides an overview of this concept, discussing its beginning in Kierkegaard and Nietzsche, and its use by a range of writers – Carl Schmitt, Ernst Jünger and Ernst Bloch amongst them.

20. Following Kisiel's detective work with the manuscripts in *The Genesis of Heidegger's Being and Time*, it is clear that the existential language that permeates *Being and Time* was a very late addition to the drafting. Heidegger's marginal notes to *Being and Time* (see GA2, 12n, 436n) and certainly the *Letter on Humanism* (GA9) demonstrate how keen he was to distance himself from the movement.
21. In a number of places Heidegger criticizes the standard understands of time, for example: 'Yet does time consist of hours, minutes, and seconds? Or are there not merely measures in which *we* entrap it, something we do because, as inhabitants of the earth, we move upon this planet in a particular relation to the sun' (GA29/30, 147).
22. Werner Marx has convincingly argued that Heidegger's attitude to space in *Being and Time* is linked to this reading of Aristotle. He suggests that Aristotle's time as a point on a line is viewed from the view of space, being partly dependent on space (see CT 18). Marx argues that 'Heidegger will try to understand space as dependent on time and, later, as of equal rank with time, whereby of course the essence of time is comprehended in non-Aristotelian fashion.' The later Heideggerian notion of 'time-space' is very different from the Aristotelian 'now-here'. See his *Heidegger and the Tradition*, translated by Theodore Kisiel and Murray Greene, Evanston: Northwestern University Press, 1971, pp. 27–9.
23. Similarly he is critical of Kant's understanding of time for the same reason. Kant founds ontology on time, not understood as original temporality, but as the traditional and ordinary understanding of time. See GA25, 341ff, 426. This is a central theme of Heidegger's Kant interpretation, discussed later in this chapter.
24. Heidegger's marginal notes to *Being and Time* suggest that he sees 'what is past' as 'what preceded beforehand and now still remains' (GA2, 378n).
25. See Megill, *Prophets of Extremity*, p. 124; Kisiel, *The Genesis of Heidegger's Being and Time*, p. 346; Alain Boutot, *Heidegger*, Paris: Presses Universitaires de France, 1989, p. 56; Marx, *Heidegger and the Tradition*, p. 133; Frederick A. Olafson, Being, Truth and Presence in Heidegger's Thought, *Inquiry*, Vol. 41 No. 1, 1998.
26. Dreyfus, *Being-in-the-World*. This is the reason why Dreyfus' text only looks at the first division of *Being and Time* in detail.
27. On the restrictive scope of Heidegger's early thoughts on history, see Calvin O. Schrag, Phenomenology, Ontology and History in the Philosophy of Heidegger, in Joseph J. Kockelmans (ed.), *Phenomenology: The Philosophy of Edmund Husserl and Its Interpretation*, New York: Anchor Books, 1967.
28. See Jean-Paul Sartre, *L'être et le néant: Essai d'ontologie phénoménologique*, Paris: Gallimard, 1943; translated by Hazel E. Barnes as *Being and Nothingness: An essay on phenomenological ontology*, London: Routledge, 1958. We should note the late Heidegger's discussion of this: 'In French, Dasein is translated as *être-là*, for example by Sartre. But with this, everything that was gained as a new position in *Being and Time* is lost. Are human beings there, like a chair? . . . Dasein does not mean being there and being here [*Dort- und Hiersein*]' (GA15, 206; HS 126).
29. This showcases the problems faced by Edward W. Soja, when he suggests that 'all excursions into Thirdspace begin with this ontological restructuring, with

the presupposition that being-in-the-world, Heidegger's *Dasein*, Sartre's *être-là*, is existentially definable as being simultaneously historical, social, and spatial'. See *Thirdspace: Journeys to Los Angeles and other real-and-imagined places*, Oxford: Blackwell, 1996, p. 73. Soja's slightly more detailed treatment is found in his earlier *Postmodern Geographies: The reassertion of space in critical social theory*, London: Verso, 1989, pp. 133–7, but here too he shows his lack of knowledge of Heidegger, relying largely on Joseph Fell, *Heidegger and Sartre: An essay on being and place*, New York: Columbia University Press, 1979, taking Sartre as a better interpreter of Heidegger than Heidegger, and neglecting or misrepresenting several key issues.
30. Jacques Derrida has pointed out the problems of Heidegger's founding Dasein's spatiality on the basis of spirit rather than on corporeality in his *Of Spirit: Heidegger and the question*, Chicago: The University of Chicago Press, 1989, p. 25.
31. For a discussion of some of the issues that arise from this, see Dreyfus, *Being-in-the-World*, pp. 130ff. Important discussions of space in Heidegger are found in Maria Villela-Petit, Heidegger's Conception of Space, in Christopher Macann (ed.), *Martin Heidegger: Critical assessments*, London: Routledge, Four Volumes, 1992, Volume I; Edward S. Casey, *The Fate of Place: A philosophical history*, Berkeley: University Presses of California, 1997; and Didier Franck, *Heidegger et le problème de l'espace*, Paris: Les Éditions de Minuit, 1986. Franck's is the most extensive treatment on Heidegger and space, although he perhaps overlooks the differences between the early and later Heidegger, and neglects much of the material available in the *Gesamtausgabe*. Casey's chapter on Heidegger raises a number of important issues, but also has a number of problems. He makes no real distinction between Heidegger's use of *Platz* and *Ort*, makes only passing reference to political questions, neglects some key texts, subscribes to a problematic notion of the 'turn', and tends to conflate the notion of 'place' as a metaphor (the topology of being, see Q IV, 433) with the analysis of place. Perhaps most unfortunately, he uses Heidegger's 'space is split up into places' (GA2, 104) as a motto for his entire work, which Heidegger later refutes (GA2, 104n). See, particularly, p. 340.
32. In the last of these lecture courses, *The Basic Concepts of Metaphysics*, there is a detailed discussion of how bees relate to space. See GA29/30, 353–62.
33. In *Being and Time* Heidegger suggests that 'bare space is still veiled over. Space has been split up into places (*Plätze*)' (GA2, 104). In his marginal notes he writes 'No, rather a proprietary and not split up unity of places!' (GA2, 104n). This is a peculiar claim, and one that is not at all clear, especially as there is no date given for the marginalia. As Chapter Two will show, it is when Heidegger thinks through the notion of τόπος as *Ort* rather than *Platz* that he begins to elucidate this concept in detail. And, as discussed in Chapter Three, in the lectures 'Building Dwelling Thinking' and 'Art and Space', Heidegger rethinks the space/place relation.
34. This is discussed in much more detail in Stuart Elden, 'The Place of Geometry: Heidegger's Mathematical Excursus on Aristotle', *The Heythrop Journal*, Vol. 42, No. 3, July 2001.
35. For a discussion of δύναμις in Aristotle see GA33, particularly 58–61.
36. Aristotle, *Physics*, Oxford: Clarendon Press, 1936; translated by Robin Waterfield, Oxford: Oxford University Press, 1996, 212a7.

37. Kisiel, *The Genesis of Heidegger's Being and Time*, pp. 313, 423. Kisiel argues that the dominant question of progressive drafts always has the other two lurking in the background. Although it cannot be pursued here, we might note that the figures of Husserl and Dilthey play important roles in the published version of *Being and Time*.
38. Reported in Bernd Magnus, Foreword to the English Translation, in Karl Löwith, *Nietzsche's Philosophy of the Eternal Recurrence of the Same*, translated by J. Harvey Lomax, Berkeley: University of California Press, 1997, p. xvii, n5. See also GA3, Preface to the Second Edition. As Heidegger notes, 'we are for Kant against Kantianism. And we are for Kant only in order to give him the possibility to live with us anew in a lively confrontation' (GA25, 279–80). Most of the scholarship on *Kant and the Problem of Metaphysics* has been by Heidegger scholars; Kant scholars tend to ignore it. See Frank Schalow, *The Renewal of the Heidegger-Kant Dialogue: Action, thought and responsibility*, Albany: State University of New York Press, 1992; Charles M. Sherover, *Heidegger, Kant and Time*, Lanham: University Press of America, 1988; W. H. Werkmeister, *Martin Heidegger on the Way*, edited by Richard T. Hull, Amsterdam: Rodopi, 1996; Frank Schalow, The Kantian Schema of Heidegger's Late Marburg Period, in Theodore Kisiel and John van Buren (eds), *Reading Heidegger From the Start: Essays in his earliest thought*, Albany: State University of New York Press, 1994. A more critical appraisal is found in Chapter IV of Marjorie Greene, *Martin Heidegger*, London: Bowes & Bowes, 1957.
39. See Daniel O. Dahlstrom, Heidegger's Kant Courses at Marburg, in Kisiel and van Buren (eds), *Reading Heidegger From the Start*. This is hinted at in GA2, 10–11.
40. Immanuel Kant, *Kritik der reinen Vernunft*, Hamburg: Felix Meiner, 1956; *Critique of Pure Reason*, edited by Vasilis Politis, London: J. M. Dent, 1993, Bxvi. This disagreement with neo-Kantianism is the subject of the Davos Disputation between Ernst Cassirer and Martin Heidegger (GA3, 274–96); the movement is outlined in On the History of the Philosophical Chair since 1866 (GA3, 304–11).
41. Kant, *Kritik der reinen Vernunft*; *Critique of Pure Reason*, A50/B74.
42. See Dahlstrom, Heidegger's Kant Courses at Marburg, p. 297.
43. Heidegger recognizes that as 'ontology has for its fundamental discipline the analytic of the Dasein . . . ontology cannot be established in a purely ontological manner. Its possibility is referred back to a being, that is, to something ontical – the Dasein. Ontology has an ontical foundation' (GA24, 26). See also the letter to Karl Löwith, 20 August 1927, cited in John van Buren, *The Young Heidegger: Rumor of the hidden king*, Bloomington: Indiana University Press, 1995, p. 242.
44. See also JGB 4, where Nietzsche suggests that the falsest judgements (which include the synthetic *a priori*) are however necessary, as without them humans could not live. It seems clear though that Nietzsche realizes that more – historical – investigation is needed.
45. Paul Natorp, *Die logischen Grundlagen der exakten Wissenschaften*, Leipzig: Verlag Teubner, 1910, pp. 276ff, cited in GA25, 78. See Dahlstrom, Heidegger's Kant Courses at Marburg, p. 301.

46. An earlier discussion is found in GA21, 298–305.
47. Immanuel Kant, *Grundlegung zur Metaphysik der Sitten*, in *Werke*, edited by Ernst Cassirer, Berlin: Bruno Cassirer, Eleven Volumes, 1912–22, Vol. IV, p. 286; translated by Paul Carus and James W. Ellington as *Groundwork for the Metaphysic of Morals*, in Stephen M. Cahn (ed.), *Classics of Western Philosophy*, Indianapolis: Hackett, Third edition, 1990, p. 1010.
48. See Theodore Kisiel, The Language of the Event: The Event of Language, in Sallis (ed.), *Heidegger and the Path of Thinking*, pp. 87ff.
49. This point is extended to space in Yoko Arisaka, Heidegger's Theory of Space: A Critique of Dreyfus, *Inquiry*, Vol. 38 No. 4, 1995, p. 458.
50. Kant, *Kritik der reinen Vernunft*; *Critique of Pure Reason*, A34/B50.
51. See Villela-Petit, Heidegger's Conception of Space, p. 120.
52. A similar claim is made in GA41, 16: 'that we name time first, saying *Zeitraum* and not *Raumzeit*, should show that in this question time plays a special role. This does not mean, however, that space is derived from time or in second place to it.'
53. See Richardson, *Heidegger*, pp. 117–18. For an attempt to rethink *Being and Time* through space, see Robert Frodeman, Being and Space: A Re-reading of Existential Spatiality in *Being and Time*, *Journal of the British Society for Phenomenology*, Vol. 23, No. 1, January 1992.
54. 'The unitary essence of boredom in the sense of the unitary structure of the two moments must therefore be sought in time after all. Not merely in time in general and universally, however, not only in time as we know it, but in the manner and way in which we stand with respect to the time that is familiar, in the manner and way in which this time stands into our Dasein and in which our Dasein itself is temporal. *Boredom springs from the temporality of Dasein*' (GA29/30, 191).
55. Villela-Petit, Heidegger's Conception of Space, p. 127, does however suggest that these analyses should have been made from the point of view of spatiality, citing Pierre Kaufmann, *L'Experience emotionnelle de l'espace*, Paris: Vrin, 1967.
56. Mulhall, *Heidegger and Being and Time*, pp. 52–4. Kisiel, *The Genesis of Heidegger's Being and Time*, pp. 360–1.
57. As Heidegger admits late in life, 'the body phenomenon is the most difficult problem' (GA15, 236; HS 146).
58. Villela-Petit, Heidegger's Conception of Space, p. 117.
59. Martin Heidegger, letter to Rudolf Bultmann, 31 December 1927, quoted in Kisiel, *The Genesis of Heidegger's Being and Time*, p. 452.
60. Kisiel, *The Genesis of Heidegger's Being and Time*, pp. 452–3. Kisiel's conspicuous absences are Eckhart, Paul, Schleiermacher and Jaspers.
61. See Rainer A. Bast and Heinrich P. Delfosse, *Handbuch zum Textstudium von Martin Heideggers 'Sein und Zeit'*. Vol. 1: *Stellenindizes; Philologisch-Kritischer Apparat*, Stuttgart-Bad Cannstatt: frommann-holzboog, 1979, where Nietzsche does not feature in the bibliographic references. However, Krell has suggested that, 'however rarely cited in *Being and Time*, Nietzsche may well be the regnant genius of that work'. See *Intimations of Mortality*, p. 128; and Taminiaux, *Heidegger and the Project of Fundamental Ontology*, Chapter Six.
62. Heidegger certainly read Hölderlin early in his life, but whether he was at that stage inspirational in his philosophy is debatable.

63. Though right at the end of the 1973 seminar in Zähringen Heidegger says 'the thinking that is demanded here is what I call tautological thinking. This is the originary sense of phenomenology' (Q IV, 487). See also My Way to Phenomenology (ZSD/TB).

64. Following Kisiel's work, it is possible to suggest that this was the initial direction Heidegger was pursuing, and that *Being and Time* was a side move undertaken and then abandoned. The initial project, as outlined in the Aristotle book introduction, certainly suggests as much: 'For philosophical research, the de-structive confrontation [*Auseinandersetzung*] with its history is not merely an annex for the purposes of illustrating how things were earlier . . . De-struction is rather the proper path upon which the present must encounter itself in its own basic movements' (PIA 20-1). In distinction to the suggestion at the end of the introduction to *Being and Time*, which stated that Part Two would contain 'a phenomenological de-struction of the history of ontology with the problematic of temporality as our clue' (GA2, 39), towards the end of the actually published book, Heidegger talks of the 'historiographical de-struction of the history of philosophy' to follow (GA2, 392). Given that Part Two was never published it is impossible to know what Heidegger would have achieved in it. See also van Buren, *The Young Heidegger*.

Chapter Two: In the Shadow of Nazism: Reading Hölderlin and Nietzsche

1. The *Kehre* is one of the most disputed areas of Heidegger scholarship. David Farrell Krell provides a useful summary of the key issues in Chapter 6 of his *Intimations of Mortality: Time, Truth, and Finitude in Heidegger's Thinking of Being*, Pennsylvania: Pennsylvania State University Press, 1986. He suggests three contexts for the *Kehre*: an impending *turn* in Western history concerning the technological era; the *turn* from *Being and Time* to *Time and Being* – i.e. the shift from the analysis of Dasein in particular to being in general that should have been found in the third division of *Being and Time* but that Heidegger was unable to think clearly at that time; a biographical *turn* introduced by Heidegger scholars to understand the development of his thought. Krell is critical of the developmentalist aspects associated with the third of these, but concedes that Heidegger's path of thought is far from one dimensional or unidirectional. My reading of this issue is that Heidegger's work after the first two divisions of *Being and Time* is precisely to articulate the *turn* to *Time and Being*, but that this path of thought takes far longer than expected, and necessitates a rethinking of key notions. The historical de-struction of the tradition – envisioned before but not performed in *Being and Time* (see the final note to Chapter One above) – takes place not simply through Aristotle, Descartes and Kant, but also through the pre-Socratics, Hölderlin and Nietzsche. Such a path of thought requires a rethinking of key issues such as space and place; the role of history in the study of being; and the notion of the political. As Krell notes, Heidegger remarked in 1953/54 that in *Being and Time* 'perhaps I ventured too far too soon' (GA12, 93; WL 7). Krell suggests that the work afterwards is 'a catching up that actually moves backward' (p. 111). Such a

reading gels with Kisiel's genealogy of *Being and Time*, and with Heidegger's remark that 'the thinking of the *Kehre* results from the fact that I stayed with the matter-for-thought [of] *Being and Time*, i.e. by inquiring into that perspective which already in *Being and Time* (p. 39) was designated as "Time and Being"'. See Letter to Richardson, in William J. Richardson, *Heidegger: Through phenomenology to thought*, The Hague: Martinus Nijhoff, 1963, p. xvi/xvii. Bruce V. Foltz, *Inhabiting the Earth: Heidegger, environmental ethics, and the metaphysics of nature*, New Jersey: Humanities Press, 1995, p. 33, n2 argues that the *Kehre* is not at issue in the topics he discusses. However later in the same note he suggests that the shift in Heidegger's treatment of nature is due to his reading of Hölderlin. As shall be shown, this is one of the key issues at stake here. A very valuable discussion is found in Laurence Paul Hemming, Speaking Out of Turn: Martin Heidegger and *die Kehre*, *International Journal of Philosophical Studies*, Vol. 6 No. 3, 1998.

2. Quoted by Heinrich W. Petzet, Preface to Martin Heidegger and Erhart Kästner, *Briefwechsel*, Frankfurt am Main: Insel, 1986, p. 10.

3. The basic documents are available in HC, which also includes a number of critical pieces. Also useful is the selection of articles in the Symposium on Heidegger and Nazism, edited by Arnold I. Davidson, *Critical Inquiry*, No. 15, Winter 1989. The recent furore was initiated by Victor Farías, *Heidegger and Nazism*, translated by Paul Burrell and Gabriel R. Ricci, Philadelphia: Temple University Press, 1989; although the most respected source of the case against is Hugo Ott, *Martin Heidegger: A political life*, translated by Allan Blunden, London: HarperCollins, 1993. A study that attempts to relate the politics to the philosophy is Richard Wolin, *The Politics of Being: The political thought of Martin Heidegger*, New York: Columbia University Press, 1990. More successful, and nigh-on essential, is Jacques Derrida, *Of Spirit: Heidegger and the question*, Chicago: The University of Chicago Press, 1989. Peter Osborne, Tactics, Ethics or Temporality? Heidegger's Politics Reviewed, *Radical Philosophy*, No. 70, March/April 1995, provides a balanced survey of the available literature. Useful on the intellectual context generally are Jeffrey Herf, *Reactionary Modernism: Technology, culture and politics in Weimar and the Third Reich*, Cambridge: Cambridge University Press, 1984; Michael E. Zimmermann, *Heidegger's Confrontation with Modernity: Technology, politics, art*, Bloomington: Indiana University Press, 1990; and Hans Sluga, *Heidegger's Crisis: Philosophy and politics in Nazi Germany*, Cambridge MA: Harvard University Press, 1993. Several other recent publications on Heidegger also provide thoughts on the subject, and indeed it has become almost a requirement to do so, but often little of interest is added.

4. This approach is greatly shaped by the work of Dominique Janicaud, *The Shadow of That Thought: Heidegger and the question of politics*, translated by Michael Gendre, Evanston IL: Northwestern University Press, 1996. See also Pierre Bourdieu, *The Political Ontology of Martin Heidegger*, translated by Peter Collier, Cambridge: Polity Press, 1988; and Julian Young, *Heidegger, Philosophy, Nazism*, Cambridge: Cambridge University Press, 1997. A useful representation of this case is Derrida's Heidegger: The Philosopher's Hell, a text that was included in the first edition of the Wolin collection as an unauthorized translation, which has been removed from later editions. This interview now

appears in Jacques Derrida, *Points . . . Interviews, 1974–1994*, edited by Elizabeth Weir, translated by Peggy Kamuf and others, Stanford: Stanford University Press, 1995, retranslated, and with a detailed explanation of *why* Derrida objected to its original English publication. In the interview, Derrida argues that Heidegger's thought cannot simply be reduced to 'that of some Nazi ideologue', and that 'for more than half a century, no rigorous philosopher has been able to avoid an "explanation" with [*explication avec*] Heidegger' (p. 182). The French word *explication*, together with its verbal form *expliquer*, has a number of potential translations in English, among them explanation, discussion, argument and analysis, but can also, particularly in a later context in this same interview (p. 183) mean the more direct 'having it out with' or 'confrontation'. It bears comparison with Heidegger's repeated use of the word *Auseinandersetzung*.

5. See Alfred Baeumler, *Nietzsche: Der Philosoph und Politiker*, Leipzig: Reclam, 1931; and his Nietzsche and National Socialism, in George Mosse (ed.) *Nazi Culture*, London: W. H. Allen, 1966. Georges Bataille's Nietzsche and the Fascists, in *Visions of Excess: Selected writings 1927–39*, edited by Allan Stoekl, Minneapolis: University of Minnesota Press, 1993, and his *On Nietzsche*, translated by Bruce Boone, New York, Paragon House, 1992 provide a contemporary response. See also Henri Lefebvre, *Nietzsche*, Paris: Éditions Sociales Internationales, 1939; *Hegel, Marx, Nietzsche ou le royaume des ombres*, Paris: Casterman, 1975.

6. Otto Pöggeler, Den Führer führen? Heidegger und kein Ende, *Philosophische Rundschau*, Bd. 32, 1985.

7. This reading of the German word was suggested, in a slightly different context, by Derrida's *Of Spirit*, pp. 42ff.

8. In this context see Heidegger's interview Only a God Can Save Us, HC 104, where he claims that the parenthetical remark was present in the original manuscript but not read as he 'was convinced that [his] audience were understanding [him] correctly'. See also Jürgen Habermas, Martin Heidegger: On the Publication of the Lectures of 1935, in HC.

9. See also the approach taken to the questions of the thing in GA41, to truth in GA45, and the 1951 suggestion that 'we cannot think without thinking historically' (GA15, 427).

10. Walter Biemel, *Martin Heidegger*, translated by J. L. Mehta, London: Routledge & Kegan Paul, 1977, p. 28, provides a useful note to this: 'The customary separation of systematic and historical modes of inquiry became untenable, for the systematic method of inquiry can be grasped only in the context of history, being itself always historically conditioned.'

11. Heidegger points out elsewhere that *wesan*, derived from *Sein*, to be, means to dwell, to sojourn (GA40, 76; IM 72).

12. See Jacques Derrida, *Ousia* and *Gramme*: Note on a Note from *Being and Time*, in *Margins of Philosophy*, translated by Alan Bass, Hemel Hempstead: Harvester Wheatsheaf, 1982, p. 33, n6; and on Heidegger and translation more generally, the essays in Section VIII of John Sallis (ed.) *Reading Heidegger: Commemorations*, Bloomington: Indiana University Press, 1993; and Marc Froment-Meurice, *That is to Say: Heidegger's poetics*, translated by Jan Plug, Stanford: Stanford University Press, 1998.

13. In GA54, 174; 209–10 Heidegger discusses τόπος in slightly more detail, and suggests that it should be translated as 'place' [*Ort*] not 'space'. See GA9, 318–19.
14. See Plato, *Timaeus and Critias*, translated by Desmond Lee, Harmondsworth: Penguin, 1971.
15. For a critical discussion of Heidegger's reading, see Jacques Derrida, *Khōra*, Paris: Éditions Galilée, 1993. Joseph Fell argues that Heidegger's '*Kehre* is the "turn" of space (dissimulated place) "into" place, which it originally and always is', in *Heidegger and Sartre: An essay on being and place*, New York: Columbia University Press, 1979, p. 204. On space and place in Greece generally, and the change from religious, qualitative, differentiated space to homogenous geometric space, see Chapter Three of Jean Pierre Vernant, *Mythe et pensée chez les Grecs*, Paris: François Maspero, second edition, 1969.
16. Sophocles, *The Three Theban Plays: Antigone, Oedipus the King, Oedipus at Colonus*, translated by Robert Fagles, New York: Quality Paperback Book Club, 1994, p. 77.
17. The standard text is Beda Allemann, *Hölderlin und Heidegger*, Zürich: Atlantic Verlag, 1954; though this is somewhat dated and cannot, of course, take into account the *Gesamtausgabe*. For a useful discussion of some of the other issues at stake see Werner Marx, *Is There a Measure on Earth? Foundations for a nonmetaphysical ethics*, translated by Thomas J. Nenon and Reginald Lilly, Chicago: University of Chicago Press, 1987; George Kovacs, *The Question of God in Heidegger's Phenomenology*, Evanston IL: Northwestern University Press, 1990; Christopher Fynsk, *Heidegger: Thought and historicity*, Ithaca: Cornell University Press, 1986; the essays in the special editions of *Research in Phenomenology*, Volume XIX, 1989; and *Philosophy Today*, Vol. 37 No. 4, Winter 1993; André Schuwer, Nature and the Holy: On Heidegger's Interpretation of Hölderlin's Hymn 'Wie wenn am Feiertage', in John Sallis (ed.), *Radical Phenomenology: Essays in honor of Martin Heidegger*, Atlantic Highlands: Humanities Press, 1978; and Krysztof Ziarek, Semiosis of Listening: The Other in Heidegger's Writings on Hölderlin and Celan's 'The Meridian', *Research in Phenomenology*, Volume XXIV, 1994. On Hölderlin as understood in mainstream literary scholarship, see Ronald Peacock, *Hölderlin*, London: Methuen & Co, 1973 [1938]; and David Constantine, *Hölderlin*, Oxford: Clarendon Press, 1988.
18. For some of the reasons for this see Ott, *Martin Heidegger*, p. 14.
19. Heidegger, Only a God Can Save Us, p. 102. See also Karl Löwith, My Last Meeting with Heidegger in Rome, 1936, in HC.
20. Ott, *Martin Heidegger*, pp. 133–4. Löwith's postcard to Jaspers is quoted from the personal papers of the latter in the German Literary Archive in Marbach.
21. Ott, *Martin Heidegger*, p. 305.
22. On the role of time in Heidegger's reading of Hölderlin, see the dispute between Richard Rorty and Michael Murray. Rorty, in Overcoming the Tradition: Heidegger and Dewey, in Michael Murray (ed.), *Heidegger and Modern Philosophy*, New Haven: University Press, 1978, p. 251, argues that 'there is no indication that Heidegger thinks that poetry has a history. Less crudely put, there is no indication that Heidegger thinks that the historicity of being can be seen in poetry'. Murray's response, in Heidegger's Hermeneutic

Reading of Hölderlin: The Signs of Time, in *The Eighteenth Century*, Vol. 21 No. 1, 1980, convincingly shows this to be an error.
23. Heidegger is later critical of this notion of *Erlebnis* as still within the Cartesian *cogito ergo sum* it aims to refute (GA45, 149; GA65, *passim*). He had recognized the inadequacy early on, but continued to use the term because of its essential nature. See GA56/57, 66.
24. On this part of the course see Arthur Grugan, Heidegger on Hölderlin's *Der Rhein*: Some External Considerations, *Philosophy Today*, Vol. 39 No. 1, Spring 1995.
25. On place and locale in Hölderlin more generally, though without reference to Heidegger, see David J. Constantine, *The Significance of Locality in the Poetry of Friedrich Hölderlin*, London: The Modern Humanities Research Association, 1979. Constantine suggests that place need not interest a poet, that many make no use of it, but it was important for Hölderlin, especially in his later work. He argues that Hölderlin celebrates rather than describes the places in his poetry.
26. See Friedrich Hölderlin, *Selected Verse*, translated by Michael Hamburger, Harmondsworth: Penguin, 1961, p. 246n for a note on the status of this poem.
27. J. M. Bernstein, *The Fate of Art: Aesthetic alienation from Kant to Derrida and Adorno*, Cambridge: Polity Press, 1992, p. 115.
28. J. Hillis Miller, *Topographies*, Stanford: Stanford University Press, 1995, p. 242 suggests that by the time of Building Dwelling Thinking, 'Heidegger's thinking about space or enspacing has changed little, if at all, [from *Being and Time*] except in dropping the emphasis on falling'. I would suggest that there is a fundamental change, the occlusion of which mars Miller's otherwise important discussion.
29. On this, see Schuwer, Nature and the Holy.
30. For a discussion on the topic of blood, soil and earth, see Karsten Harries, Heidegger as Political Thinker, in Murray (ed.), *Heidegger and Modern Philosophy*. The conclusion (p. 324) is that Heidegger 'came to see that his hope had been in vain and misguided, that the Nazi's *Blut und Boden* had little in common with Hölderlin's *Erde*. This recognition forced Heidegger to reinterpret the nature of their leadership'. It does not necessarily follow that Heidegger's use of earth and soil in his analyses is a move following Nazism, but it is certainly a dangerous political manoeuvre. The concept of earth – important in On the Origin of the Work of Art and later essays – develops from the work on Hölderlin. See Hans-Georg Gadamer, *Philosophical Hermeneutics*, edited and translated by David E. Linge, Berkeley: University of California Press, 1976, p. 217. Theodor W. Adorno, *The Jargon of Authenticity* [*Eigentlichkeit*], translated by Knut Tarnowski and Frederic Will, London: Routledge & Kegan Paul, 1973, p. 85, sees Hölderlin as the 'secret model' for the jargon of authenticity.
31. See for example, Heidegger's own address of May 26th 1933 on Albert Leo Schlageter in Political Texts, 1933–34, HC 40–2. On this issue see also GA39, 72–3.
32. See the 'Letter on Humanism' for a more detailed discussion of the reason for this (GA9, 314; BW 218).
33. In the discussion of 'The Rhine' Heidegger suggests that no Dasein is purely

poetic, thinking or acting, but that we must think them together (GA39, 184–5). For a discussion of these issues see Janicaud, *The Shadow of That Thought*, pp. 99–100. Some important themes are also discussed in Jacques Derrida, Heidegger's Ear: Philopolemology (*Geschlecht* IV), in Sallis (ed.), *Reading Heidegger*.
34. Allan Megill, *Prophets of Extremity: Nietzsche, Heidegger, Foucault, Derrida*, Berkeley: University of California Press, 1985, p. 172. See GA9, 337–8; BW 241 for Heidegger's explicit distancing from the patriotic and nationalist overtones to *Heimat*.
35. E. G. Kolbenheyer, *Vorträge, Aufsätze*, Darmstadt: Reden, 1966, cited in GA39, 27.
36. See Otto Pöggeler, Heidegger's Political Self-Understanding, HC 203.
37. Heidegger, Only a God Can Save Us, p. 101.
38. On *Auseinandersetzung*, see David Farrell Krell, Analysis, N I, 230–1; and Will McNeill, Traces of Discordance: Heidegger-Nietzsche, in Peter R. Sedgwick (ed.), *Nietzsche: A Critical Reader*, Oxford: Blackwell, 1996.
39. Quoted in Jacques Derrida, Geschlecht II: Heidegger's Hand, in John Sallis (ed.), *Deconstruction and Philosophy*, Chicago: The University of Chicago Press, 1987, p. 165.
40. For more detail about the political implications of this and later courses on Hölderlin see, particularly, Miguel de Beistegui, *Heidegger and the Political: Dystopias*, London: Routledge, 1998; James F. Ward, *Heidegger's Political Thinking*, Amherst: University of Massachusetts Press, 1995; and Tom Rockmore, *On Heidegger's Nazism and Philosophy*, London: Harvester Wheatsheaf, 1992.
41. See Dominique Janicaud, The 'Overcoming' of Metaphysics in the Hölderlin Lectures, in Sallis (ed.), *Reading Heidegger*. Although Janicaud provides much useful detail, and is correct to see a shift between the first lecture course and the later two regarding the attitude to metaphysics (a shift from an attempt at a replacement to an overcoming) he neglects the differences between the attitudes to space and time, claiming that the project of a poetic dwelling is common to both.
42. In the 1927 course *The Basic Problems of Phenomenology*, Heidegger makes a very similar point about time. See GA24, 361.
43. Janicaud, The 'Overcoming' of Metaphysics in the Hölderlin Lectures, p. 384.
44. Megill, *Prophets of Extremity*, p. 118.
45. Jacques Derrida, *Spurs: Nietzsche's Styles/Éperons: Les Styles de Nietzsche*, translated by Barbara Harlow, Chicago: University of Chicago Press, 1979, p. 72/73.
46. Heidegger, Letter to the Rector of Freiburg University, HC 65. See also Only a God Can Save Us, HC 101–3. For a supportive comment, see Thinking the Apocalypse: A Letter from Maurice Blanchot to Catherine David, in Davidson (ed.), Symposium on Heidegger and Nazism, p. 476, n2.
47. Derrida, *Of Spirit*, p. 73.
48. English translation from *The Holy Bible*, 1 Corinthians, Chapter 15, Verses 51–2, p. 1157. See Jean Graybeal, *Language and 'The Feminine' in Nietzsche and Heidegger*, Bloomington: Indiana University Press, 1990, p. 169, n28; and Gary Shapiro, In the Shadows of Philosophy: Nietzsche and the Question of

Vision, in David Michael Levin (ed.), *Modernity and the Hegemony of Vision*, London: University of California Press, 1993.
49. Friedrich Nietzsche, *Ainsi parlait Zarathustra*, traduction révisée de Geneviève Bianquis, Paris: Flammarion, 1969.
50. 'Thus decision straddles the threshold of the Nietzschean gateway called "moment" or "flash of an eye", *Augenblick*'. David Farrell Krell, Introduction to the Paperback Edition, N I, xv. See also Donna Gene Hayes, Nietzsche's Eternal Recurrence: A Prelude to Heidegger, *Journal of Existentialism*, Vol. VI, No. 22, Winter 1965/66; Charles Guignon, History and Commitment in the Early Heidegger, in Hubert L. Dreyfus and Harrison Hall (eds), *Heidegger: A Critical Reader*, Oxford: Blackwell, 1992.
51. For Nietzsche on time, see Joan Stambaugh, *The Problem of Time in Nietzsche*, London: Associated University Presses, 1987; David Wood, Nietzsche's Transvaluation of Time, in David Farrell Krell and David Wood (eds), *Exceedingly Nietzsche: Aspects of contemporary Nietzsche interpretation*, London: Routledge, 1988; and, more generally, Elizabeth Deeds Ermarth, *Sequel to History: Postmodernism and the crisis of representational time*, Princeton: Princeton University Press, 1992.
52. For the difficulties of translating the word, one of the several important words in *Thus Spoke Zarathustra* that plays on the use of *ünter* and *über*, see Kaufmann's note on p. 115. Kaufmann's 'go under' is, as he admits, not perfect, but it is surely better than the French *le declin*, decline.
53. It is worth noting that John Sallis, *Crossings: Nietzsche and the space of tragedy*, Chicago: The University of Chicago Press, 1991, makes no reference to this.
54. Translator's note to GT 8, p. 63.
55. Richard Wagner, The Art-Work of the Future, in *The Art-Work of the Future and Other Works*, translated by W. Ashton Ellis, Lincoln and London: University of Nebraska Press, 1993, pp. 184–5.
56. Bryan Magee, *Aspects of Wagner*, London: Alan Ross, 1968, pp. 97–8. See also Geoffrey Skelton, *Wagner at Bayreuth*, London: White Lion, 1976, pp. 33–4.
57. Magee, *Aspects of Wagner*, p. 99.
58. We should note here Heidegger's discussion of two sections of *The Wanderer and his Shadow* (WS 218; 278) in GA48, 14–15.
59. During the Zollikon seminar, Medard Boss reminds Heidegger of Sartre's criticism that *Being and Time* contained only six lines on the body. The response is simply that it was the hardest problem to solve, and that he did not know how to say any more. See Martin Heidegger, *Zollikoner Seminar: Protokolle – Gespräche – Briefe*, edited by Medard Boss, Frankfurt am Main: Vittorio Klostermann, 1987, p. 292. In these seminars – given between 1959 and 1969 – Heidegger provides detailed analysis of the nature of the body, and long discussions of other key parts of his work, including the issues of space, place and time. For a discussion see William J. Richardson, Heidegger among the Doctors, in Sallis (ed.), *Reading Heidegger*; and Charles E. Scott, Heidegger and Psychoanalysis: The Seminars in Zollikon, *Heidegger Studies*, Vol. 6, 1990.
60. Nietzsche occasionally links physiology with history. See GD 9, 44.
61. One of the more useful, and critical, contributions to this debate is Krell's Introduction to the Paperback Edition, NI.

62. The main lecture course where Heidegger finds the results of an ontic science (in this case biology) important for his ontological project is GA29/30.
63. See Maurice Merleau-Ponty, *La phénoménologie de perception*, Paris: Gallimard, 1945.
64. This particular formulation – though not the general attitude – is not found in the original transcripts of the course. It looks like a clarification added in 1961.
65. See also Q IV, 410.
66. The third lecture course on Nietzsche, delivered in 1939, two years after the second, is where this perspective first becomes apparent.
67. For some of the difficulties inherent in reading this work, see George Kovacs, An Invitation to Think through and with Heidegger's *Beiträge zur Philosophie*, *Heidegger Studies*, Vol. 12, 1996.
68. See GA44, 404; N II, 186. Heidegger clarifies the points of divergence from Hegel regarding history in The Onto-Theological Constitution of Metaphysics in ID, and Grundsätze des Denkens, in GA79.
69. David Farrell Krell, *Daimon Life: Heidegger and Life Philosophy*, Bloomington: Indiana University Press, 1992, p. 109.
70. Hubert Dreyfus, *Being-in-the-World*, Cambridge, MA: MIT Press, 1991, p. 259. See pp. 278ff and *passim*. See Thomas S. Kuhn, *The Structure of Scientific Revolutions*, Chicago: University of Chicago Press, third edition, 1996. Of Heidegger's work, see GA41 and Science and Reflection in VA; QCT. Dreyfus suggests that certain readings of Nietzsche, such as that of Alexander Nehamas, *Nietzsche: Life as literature*, Cambridge MA: Harvard University Press, 1985, also find this understanding there.
71. The *Letter on Humanism* – addressed to a Frenchman, Jean Beaufret (see Q III, 129–30) – was particularly important in France, as it helped a generation (including Foucault and Derrida) to read Heidegger yet distance themselves from Sartre. For a commentary on this, see Jean Beaufret, Heidegger Seen From France, in Edward G. Ballard and Charles E. Scott (eds), *Martin Heidegger in Europe and America*, The Hague: Martinus Nijhoff, 1973. In Germany the situation was somewhat different, see Jürgen Habermas, Jürgen Habermas on the Legacy of Jean-Paul Sartre: Conducted by Richard Wolin, *Political Theory*, Vol. 20 No. 3, August 1992.
72. Hannah Arendt, Martin Heidegger at Eighty, in Murray (ed.) *Heidegger and Modern Philosophy*, p. 302, n3. On Arendt's relationship with Heidegger, which contextualizes this remark, see Elżbieta Ettinger, *Hannah Arendt Martin Heidegger*, New Haven: Yale University Press, 1995; and more generally see Dana R. Villa, *Arendt and Heidegger: The fate of the political*, Princeton: Princeton University Press, 1996.

Chapter Three: Art, Technology, Place and the Political

1. Bibliographical information taken from David Farrell Krell's introduction to this piece in BW 140–2, and Heidegger's own note in GA5, 344; PLT xxiii–iv.
2. Jacques Taminiaux, through a close reading of the three versions of the lecture, situates the *Kehre* within this period. It seems unlikely, however, that the *Kehre*

is a *result* of the meditation on art. See The Origin of 'The Origin of the Work of Art', in John Sallis (ed.), *Reading Heidegger: Commemorations*, Bloomington: Indiana University Press, 1993. A useful discussion of this essay and its relation to other works is found in Harold Alderman, The Work of Art and Other Things, in Edward G. Ballard and Charles E. Scott (eds), *Martin Heidegger in Europe and America*, The Hague: Martinus Nijhoff, 1973.

3. The main exception is found in the first lecture course on Nietzsche, in a discussion of Wagner (GA43, 100–7, N I, 85–90). However a discussion later in this course was not included in the 1961 published edition (GA43, 151–2, 157–9). See also GA10, 70–2; PR 47–8; Memorial Address in G; DT. On this, see Béatrice Han, Au-delà de la métaphysique et de la subjectivité: Musique et *Stimmung, Les Études philosophiques*, No. 4, 1997.

4. Meyer Schapiro, The Still Life as Personal Object: A Note on Heidegger and Van Gogh, in Marianne L. Simmel (ed.), *The Reach of Mind: Essays in memory of Kurt Goldstein*, New York: Springer Publishing Company, 1968, p. 205. This debate is one of the themes in the last essay of Jacques Derrida, *The Truth in Painting*, translated by Geoff Bennington and Rachel Bowlby, Chicago: The University of Chicago Press, 1987, pp. 255ff. The argument is reported and summarized in J. M. Bernstein, *The Fate of Art: Aesthetic alienation from Kant to Derrida and Adorno*, Cambridge: Polity Press, 1992, p. 140.

5. Bernstein, *The Fate of Art*, p. 142. Derrida suggests that the location *is* important, as Schapiro's essay appeared in a volume dedicated to Kurt Goldstein, who had first introduced Schapiro to Heidegger's work (see Schapiro, The Still Life as Personal Object, p. 203, n1). Goldstein fled Nazi Germany for a number of reasons which, Derrida suggests, may not have been entirely foreign to the 'pathos of the "call of the earth", of the *Feldweg* or the *Holzwege*'. Derrida agrees with Schapiro that 'nothing in the painting proves that they are peasant shoes', but concludes that there is no evidence to swing the case either way. Supporting Heidegger, he suggests the rural, earthy ideology of the soil Heidegger is accused of projecting would not have been alien to Van Gogh. See *The Truth in Painting*, pp. 272–3, 345, 362, 367. Foltz again, this time implicitly, defends Heidegger, using the idea of earth as a link to deep ecology. Bruce V. Foltz, *Inhabiting the Earth: Heidegger, Environmental ethics, and the metaphysics of nature*, New Jersey: Humanities Press, 1995.

6. R. J. Hall, Heidegger and the Space of Art, *Journal of Existentialism*, Vol. VIII No. 29, Fall 1967, uses this passage as a springboard into an interesting, though limited, discussion of some of the themes that will be picked up later in this piece.

7. Cited by Michael Hamburger, Introduction in Friedrich Hölderlin, *Selected Verse*, translated by Michael Hamburger, Harmondsworth: Penguin, 1961, p. xxi.

8. Andrej Warminski, *Reading in Interpretation: Hölderlin, Hegel, Heidegger*, Minneapolis: University of Minnesota Press, 1987, p. 67. Foltz, *Inhabiting the Earth*, p. x, does not consider that the return to the rural is an example of nostalgia, and uses this as an opportunity to berate 'recent French philosophers' for not having much 'to say about the natural environment or about the world outside of large cities in general'.

9. See Schöpferische Landschaft: Warum bleiben wir in der Provinz? and Der Feldweg in GA13; Why do I Stay in the Provinces? and The Pathway in Thomas Sheehan (ed.), *Martin Heidegger: The man and the thinker*, Chicago: Precedent Publishing, 1981.
10. J. Hillis Miller, *Topographies*, Stanford: Stanford University Press, 1995, p. 253, notes that Building Dwelling Thinking fails to address the fact that the housing shortage which gives the essay its impetus and contemporaneity is primarily urban and the result of the bombing of German cities by the Allies. Heidegger suggests that 'the proper plight of dwelling is indeed older than the world wars with their destruction' (VA 156; BW 363). There is therefore a double lacuna: political and platial.
11. See also GA5, 8; BW 149; Science and Reflection in VA; QCT. John Sallis, *Echoes: After Heidegger*, Bloomington: Indiana University Press, 1990, pp. 195–9.
12. See, for example, GA29/30, 36ff; Logos (Heraclitus, Fragment B50) in VA/EGT; Letter on Humanism, GA9, 184ff; On the Being and Conception of Φύσις in Aristotle's *Physics* B, 1 in GA9.
13. Whilst this is true in the published works of the time, Theodore Kisiel has convincingly argued that in his 1924 course *Basic Concepts of Aristotelian Philosophy* (to appear as GA18, as yet unpublished), Heidegger puts forward a view of the political as founded upon speech [λόγος], based on his detailed reading of Aristotle's *Rhetoric*. The ζῷον πολιτικόν is the ζῷον ἔχον λόγον, the emphasis is on our mode of being with others [*als Sein im Miteinandersein*]. See Theodore Kisiel, *The Genesis of Heidegger's Being and Time*, Berkeley: University of California Press, 1993, pp. 294–5; and for a much more developed account, Situating Rhetorical Politics in Heidegger's Protopractical Ontology (1923–1925: The French Occupy the Ruhr), *Existentia*, Vol. IX, 1999, especially p. 16. This makes a little clearer the somewhat throwaway comment in the following semester's course: 'Insofar as the ἄνθρωπος is the ζῷον πολιτικόν, πρᾶξις is to be understood as a mode of being with others; and insofar as this is the τέλος, φρόνησις is of the character of the πολιτική. Hence what is decisive for φρόνησις is πρᾶξις. This gives rise to an essential distinction between φρόνησις and ἐπιστήμη, one which concerns their *genesis*' (GA19, 140). I am grateful to Theodore Kisiel and Allen Scult for instructive discussions regarding the unpublished Aristotle course.
14. Heidegger takes issue with the standard translations of the title of this dialogue in GA54. This is discussed later in this section. It is notable that in a letter to Elizabeth Blochmann, dated 19 December 1932, Heidegger suggests she read Plato's Letter VII, which explains his political involvement in Syracuse. See Martin Heidegger, *Correspondance avec Karl Jaspers*, texte établi par Walter Biemel et Hans Saner, traduite de l'allemand par Claude-Nicolas Grimbert, suivi de *Correspondance avec Elizabeth Blochmann*, traduite de l'allemand par Pascal David, Paris: Gallimard, 1996, pp. 271–2. See Plato, Letter VII, in *The Collected Dialogues of Plato Including the Letters*, edited by Edith Hamilton and Huntingdon Cairns, Princeton University Press, 1961.
15. The same translation is found in GA22, 99.
16. On the motive of *Führung* in the Rectorship Address, see Philippe Lacoue-Labarthe, Transcendence Ends in Politics, in *Typography: Mimesis, philosophy,*

politics, edited by Christopher Fynsk, Cambridge, MA: Harvard University Press, 1989.
17. Pöggeler, Heidegger's Political Self-Understanding, HC 212. See Ernst Jünger, *Werke*, Stuttgart: Ernst Klett, ten volumes, 1960. *Der Arbeiter* is in Volume 6, a useful summary essay, Die Totale Mobilmachung, is in Volume 5; translated by Joel Golb and Richard Wolin, as Total Mobilisation in HC. J. P. Stern, *Ernst Jünger: A writer of our time*, Cambridge: Bowes & Bowes, 1953, p. 11 suggests in Jünger's usage, *Arbeiter* means 'Technocrat'. This is useful because of the reference it makes to the role of technology in the new society of workers.
18. Wolin, in HC 121.
19. For a commentary, see Jean-Michel Palmier, *Les Écrits politiques de Heidegger*, Paris: L'Herne, 1968, pp. 160–4.
20. Michel Haar notes in passing that the Greek does not contain δεινόν or δεινότατον, but the plural δεινά and the comparative δεινότερον. See *Heidegger et l'essence de l'homme*, Grenoble: Jérôme Millon, 1990, pp. 209–10. This remark is found in Haar's useful, if brief, discussion of Heidegger's reading of this choral ode.
21. The Greek word παντα is one of the central terms discussed in Martin Heidegger and Eugen Fink, Heraklit, in GA15; HS. See John Sallis and Kenneth Maly (eds), *Heraclitean Fragments: A companion volume to the Heidegger/Fink seminar on Heraclitus*, Alabama: University of Alabama Press, 1980.
22. See the untitled foreword to *Holzwege* (GA5): 'Wood is an old name for forest. In the wood are paths, most of which suddenly become impassable and end in an overgrown copse. They are called woodpaths. They all lead their own way but in the same forest. It often appears that one is the same as the other. Yet it only appears so. Woodmen and forest rangers know the paths. They know what it means to be on a woodpath.'
23. Kisiel, *The Genesis of Heidegger's Being and Time*, p. 3. See Heidegger's handwritten pages reproduced at the beginning of GA1.
24. Sophocles, *The Three Theban Plays: Antigone, Oedipus the King, Oedipus at Colonus*, translated by Robert Fagles, New York: Quality Paperback Book Club, 1994, p. 77. Heidegger's own translation of the full choral ode is found as 'Chorlied aus der Antigone des Sophokles' in GA13.
25. This stress on place rather than space does not mean that I adhere to the reading of Miguel de Beistegui, *Heidegger and the Political: Dystopias*, London: Routledge, 1998. Although generally a very useful discussion of Heidegger's reading of the πόλις, de Beistegui suggests that the difference between space and place is that between the ontic and the ontological, that 'the difference between space and place lies in the fact that the place refers to the very possibility from out of which anything like a constituted social, economic and political space might arise' (p. 143). Rather, as is clear throughout Heidegger's career, place is that which is a more originary, lived, understanding; space (founded on extension) an abstraction. See also 'Der Kunst und der Raum', in GA13. Another useful general reading of Heidegger's discussion of the πόλις is found in James F. Ward, *Heidegger's Political Thinking*, Amherst: University of Massachusetts Press, 1995.
26. See Aristotle, *The Politics*, translated by T. A. Sinclair, revised and represented

by Trevor S. Sanders, Harmondsworth: Penguin, 1981, 1253a. Sanders' note (p. 59, n14) is that πολιτικόν ζῷον should be seen as 'who lives/whose nature is to live in a *polis*'.
27. See GA54, 100–1 for a discussion of why 'animal' is a poor translation of ζῷον. For the wider context, see GA29/30 and David Farrell Krell, *Daimon Life: Heidegger and life philosophy*, Bloomington: Indiana University Press, 1992.
28. Plato, *Republic*, translated by Robin Waterfield, Oxford: Oxford University Press, 1993, 473c.
29. To the earlier discussion, GA34, 100, cited above, compare also GA43, 204; N I, 166, which is closer to that found in the Hölderlin lecture. It would appear therefore that by 1935–6 – with *An Introduction to Metaphysics* and the first Nietzsche course, that the retreat(ment) has begun. That said, Jacques Taminiaux, *Heidegger and the Project of Fundamental Ontology*, translated by Michael Gendre, Albany: State University of New York Press, 1991, pp. 134–5, sees things somewhat differently. He suggests that there is no indication that Heidegger abandoned the Platonism of the Rectoral Address. A similar argument is made by Philippe Lacoue-Labarthe, *La fiction du politique: Heidegger, l'art et la politique*, Paris: Christian Bourgois, 1987. In distinction I would suggest that the Platonism may remain, but Heidegger's interpretation of it changes, as does his use of the word πόλις, leading to his retreat from the political, at least in its modern sense.
30. On this course, see Manfred S. Frings, Parmenides: Heidegger's 1942–43 Lecture Course Held at Freiburg University, *Journal of the British Society for Phenomenology*, Vol. 19, No. 1, January 1988. A more detailed reading of this course's discussion of the πόλις and its relation to truth and justice is found in Michael Dillon, *Politics of Security: Towards a political philosophy of continental thought*, London: Routledge, 1996, Chapter Three.
31. See Plato, *Republic* (especially Waterfield's note on p. xi); Platon, *Der Staat*, translated and edited by Karl Vretske, Stuttgart: Reclam, 1958.
32. This is a theme found throughout Heidegger's work. As well as the whole of GA54, see, for example, 'Vom Wesen der Wahrheit'; 'On the Essence of Truth' in GA9, and GA34.
33. We might note that in their 1966/67 seminar, Heidegger lets Fink's translation of πόλις in Heraclitus' Fragment 114 as *Stadt* go without note. See GA15, 47; HS 25.
34. See Fred Dallmayr, *The Other Heidegger*, Ithaca: Cornell University Press, 1993, pp. 9, 50; Ernst Vollrath, The 'Rational' and the 'Political': An Essay in the Semantics of Politics, *Philosophy and Social Criticism*, Vol. 13, No. 1, 1987; Philippe Lacoue-Labarthe and Jean-Luc Nancy, in *Retreating the Political*, edited by Simon Sparks, London: Routledge, 1997.
35. Carl Schmitt, *The Concept of the Political*, translated by George Schwab, Chicago: The University of Chicago Press, 1996, p. 19. On the friend/enemy distinction see pp. 27–37. For a discussion, see Jacques Derrida, *Politics of Friendship*, translated by George Collins, London: Verso, 1997.
36. Indeed, Schmitt recognizes as much, distinguishing between the public enemy [πολέμιος) and the private one [ἐχθρός], a distinction he claims finds support in Plato's *Republic*. See *The Concept of the Political*, pp. 28–9. For an account of the role war plays in the Schmittian friend/enemy distinction, see Mark

Neocleous, Perpetual War, or, 'War and War Again': Schmitt, Foucault, Fascism, *Philosophy and Social Criticism*, Vol. 22, No. 2, March 1996.

37. Martin Heidegger to Carl Schmitt, 22 August 1933, English/German version, in *Telos*, No. 72, 1987, p. 132.
38. See for example, Chantal Mouffe, *The Return of the Political*, London: Verso, 1993.
39. This allusion is to the work of Lacoue-Labarthe and Nancy, *Retreating the Political*, influenced as it is by Heidegger. On the two (at least) meanings of *retreating*, see pp. 112, 138–9. For a discussion, see Nancy Fraser, The French Derrideans: Politicising Deconstruction or Deconstructing the Political, in *Unruly Practices: Power, discourse and gender in contemporary social theory*, Cambridge: Polity Press, 1989; and Simon Critchley, *The Ethics of Deconstruction: Derrida and Levinas*, Oxford: Blackwell, 1992, pp. 200ff. It is unfortunate that Ernst Cassirer, *The Myth of the State*, New Haven: Yale University Press, 1946, treats Heidegger only very sketchily, and, because of the unavailability of materials at the time, is unable to discuss this retreat.
40. David Farrell Krell, *Intimations of Mortality: Time, Truth, and Finitude in Heidegger's Thinking of Being*, Pennsylvania: Pennsylvania State University Press, 1986, p. 96.
41. Bernstein has criticized Heidegger's attitude to equipment (he specifically means in *Being and Time* and *The Origin of the Work of Art*), by claiming that we relate to hydroelectric dams or assembly line robots in a different way to how we relate to hammers and shoes: 'the essence of equipment has changed'. This essay of Heidegger's seems to provide the corrective needed. See *The Fate of Art*, p. 133.
42. Harold Alderman, 'Heidegger's Critique of Science and Technology', in Michael Murray (ed.), *Heidegger and Modern Philosophy*, New Haven: Yale University Press, 1978, pp. 46–7, provides a useful example. Alderman quotes an advertising slogan: 'Nature creates ore deposits. Anaconda creates mines', and comments 'the advertisement further states that ores are not much good until someone uses them; with this use they become natural resources. Thus we have from within contemporary technology a partial recognition of its own nature'.
43. See also Heidegger's letter to Herbert Marcuse, of 20 January 1948: 'To the serious legitimate charges that you express "about a regime that murdered millions of Jews, that made terror into an everyday phenomenon, and that turned everything that pertains to the ideas of spirit, freedom, and truth into its bloody opposite", I can merely add that if instead of "Jews" you had written "East Germans" [i.e., Germans of the eastern territories], then the same holds true for one of the allies, with the difference that everything that has occurred since 1945 has become public knowledge, while the bloody terror of the Nazis in point of fact had been kept a secret from the German people.' ('An Exchange of Letters: Herbert Marcuse and Martin Heidegger', in HC 163). Heidegger's seemingly continual need to suggest comparable crimes on the part of others – here the Allies' treatment of Eastern Germans, in the key passage discussed from Das Ge-stell, the hydrogen bombs of the superpowers, the blockade by the Russians, in the lecture Die Gefahr, the famine in China (GA79, 56) – which Wolin likens to the common strategy of the Adenauer

years (HC 158–9) – betrays the fact that here, more than anywhere else, Heidegger engages in *criticism*: 'serious legitimate charges . . . bloody terror of the Nazis'. One can almost hear the strain to admit even this little. The other important part of this letter is Heidegger's admission of his own *guilt*: 'You are entirely correct that I failed to provide a public, readily comprehensible counter-declaration [to the Rectoral Address, after his resignation]; it would have been the end of both me and my family. On this point, Jaspers said: that we remain alive is our guilt' (p. 163). See Heidegger, *Correspondance avec Karl Jaspers*. As Rüdiger Safranski, *Martin Heidegger: between good and evil*, translated by Ewald Osers, Cambridge, MA: Harvard University Press, 1998, pp. 413–14, notes, Heidegger's understanding of technology and the holocaust bears comparison with that of Theodor Adorno in *Negative Dialectics*, translated by E. B. Ashton, London: Routledge, 1973. On these remarks, see Julian Young, *Heidegger, Philosophy, Nazism*, Cambridge: Cambridge University Press, 1997, Chapter 6.

44. The passage is cited and criticized by Lacoue-Labarthe, *La fiction du politique*, pp. 58ff; and his discussion has been the starting point for reflections by many others. See for example Krell, *Daimon Life*, pp. 138ff; Dominique Janicaud, *The Shadow of That Thought: Heidegger and the question of politics*, translated by Michael Gendre, Evanston IL: Northwestern University Press, 1996, Chapter Six; de Beistegui, *Heidegger and the Political*, pp. 153–7. See also, for a fascinating discussion, William V. Spanos, *Heidegger and Criticism: Retrieving the cultural politics of destruction*, Minneapolis: University of Minnesota Press, 1993, Chapter Six.

45. De Beistegui, *Heidegger and the Political*, p. 154.

46. On this see Harries, Heidegger as Political Thinker, especially p. 323: 'Heidegger's retreat from politics is inseparable from his characterisation of the essence of technology'.

47. On this particular point, and for a useful outline of Heidegger's views on technology, see Michael E. Zimmerman, Beyond 'Humanism': Heidegger's Understanding of Technology, in Sheehan (ed.) *Martin Heidegger: The man and the thinker*. The reference is of course implicitly to Descartes. Karsten Harries, Heidegger as Political Thinker, in Michael Murray (ed.), *Heidegger and Modern Philosophy*, New Haven: Yale University Press, 1978, p. 323, puts this succinctly: 'Cartesian metaphysics triumphs over the earth in technology. This triumph and the forgetting of earth belong together.' On the relationship between Nietzsche and Heidegger on this issue, see Hans Siegfried, Autonomy and Quantum Physics: Nietzsche, Heidegger, and Heisenberg, in *Philosophy of Science*, Vol. 57, No. 4, December 1990; and on Heidegger and science generally, Carl Friedrich von Weizsäcker, Heidegger and Natural Science, in Werner Marx (ed.), *Heidegger Memorial Lectures*, Pittsburgh: Duquesne University Press, 1982.

48. See Jan Popma, *The Worker: On nihilism and technology in Ernst Jünger*, Brussels: Economische Hogeschool Sint-Aloysius, 1991. Popma even goes so far as to argue that Jünger is suggesting a plunge into totalitarianism in order to save us from it. See also Roger Woods, *Ernst Jünger and the Nature of Political Commitment*, Stuttgart: Akademischer Verlag Hans-Dieter Heinz, 1982; and Daniel Johnson, Portrait: Ernst Jünger, *Prospect*, No. 17, March 1997. Woods

claims that the later Jünger, after about 1936, takes issue both with the Nazis and with his own earlier work. For instructive discussions, see Javier A. Ibáñez-Noé, 'Heidegger, Nietzsche, Jünger, and the Interpretation of the Contemporary Age', *The Southern Journal of Philosophy*, Vol. XXXIII, 1995; Michael E. Zimmermann, *Heidegger's Confrontation with Modernity: Technology, politics, art*, Bloomington: Indiana University Press, 1990; and Palmier, *Les Écrits politiques de Heidegger*.

49. Jünger, *Der Arbeiter*, in *Werke*, Vol. 6, p. 234.
50. Jünger, *Der Arbeiter*, in *Werke*, Vol. 6, p. 176.
51. On this see also Krell, Analysis, N IV, 286ff.
52. Jünger, *Über die Linie*, in *Werke*, Vol. 5, p. 280, cited in GA9, 220. For an interview with Ernst Jünger that touches upon many points, including Heidegger's critique, see Le Travailleur Planétaire: Entretien avec Ernst Jünger, in Michel Haar (ed.), *Cahier de L'Herne: Martin Heidegger*, Paris: Editions de L'Herne, 1983.
53. See Simon Critchley, *Very Little . . . Almost Nothing: Death, philosophy, literature*, London: Routledge, 1997, especially pp. 13–18.
54. VA 32; BW 333; GA79, 72; QCT 42; Hölderlin, Patmos, in *Selected Verse*, p. 203.
55. See Marjorie Grene, Landscape, in Ronald Bruzina and Bruce Wilshire (eds), *Phenomenology: Dialogues and bridges*, Albany: State University of New York Press, 1982, where she notes the lack of discussion of spatiality in *Being and Time*, but suggests that as the work on the fourfold is concerned with being rather than Dasein it is unable to fill the lacuna.
56. The source for the alternative translation is Jonathan Barnes, *Early Greek Philosophy*, Harmondsworth: Penguin, 1987, p. 124.
57. On this matter generally, see Edward S. Casey, *Getting Back into Place: Towards a renewed understanding of the place-world*, Bloomington: Indiana University Press, 1993; and Vincent Vycinas, *Earth and Gods: An introduction to the philosophy of Martin Heidegger*, The Hague: Martinus Nijhoff, 1969.
58. Hölderlin, In lovely blueness . . ., *Selected Verse*, pp. 245–6.
59. Krell, *Intimations of Mortality*, p. 141.
60. On this see David Kolb, *The Critique of Pure Modernity: Hegel, Heidegger and After*, Chicago: University of Chicago Press, 1986, pp. 189ff. Kolb concludes that though the romantic reading is appealing, it would be a mistake. He suggests that Heidegger is offering a different way of dealing with the modern world.
61. A useful discussion of this – though as I have noted in Chapter Two, marred by a lack of realization of the shifting attitude to space – is found in Chapter Nine of Miller, *Topographies*.
62. Both Hofstadter's English translation, and the French version translated by André Préau in *Essais et Conférences*, Paris: Gallimard, 1958, are slightly confusing. I have revised the translation carefully, consistently rendering *Raum* as 'space', *Stätte* as 'site', and *Ort* as 'place'. This is in accordance with my practice in this book as a whole.
63. Several of these themes are picked up in Hebel – Der Hausfreund, in GA13.
64. As noted in the French translation, this line did not feature in the original version, published in *L'Endurance de la pensée: Pour saluer Jean Beaufret*, Paris:

Plon, 1968. It is unclear as to whether it was present when the lecture was delivered in 1962. See Q IV, p. 224n. Robert J. Dostal, Time and Phenomenology in Husserl and Heidegger, in Charles Guignon (ed.), *The Cambridge Companion to Heidegger*, Cambridge: Cambridge University Press, 1993, p. 165, suggests that 'what Heidegger means by this largely unexplained comment is not entirely clear'. Dostal recognizes the radical implications of this comment, and how it would entail 'substantial revision' of the earlier Heidegger's project. He closes: 'it is hard to envision what shape an ontology based as much on spatiality as temporality would take. Perhaps the later Heidegger is attempting this in some way or another'.

Chapter Four: Towards a Spatial History

1. See David Macey, *The Lives of Michel Foucault*, London: Hutchinson, 1993, p. 450, for an encounter between Jana Sawicki and Foucault over precisely this point. Undaunted, Sawicki went on to produce *Disciplining Foucault: Feminism, power, and the body*, London: Routledge, 1991.
2. There are some excellent spatial analyses using Foucauldian concepts, though none of these undertake the detailed analysis this book purports to. See Peter Brown, *The Body and Society: Men, women and sexual renunciation in early Christianity*, London: Faber & Faber, 1989; Paul Carter, *The Road to Botany Bay: An essay in spatial history*, London: Faber & Faber, 1987; Paul Rabinow, *French Modern: Norms and forms of the social environment*, Cambridge, MA: The MIT Press, 1989; Felix Driver, *Power and Pauperism: The workhouse system 1834–1884*, Cambridge: Cambridge University Press, 1993; Kevin Hetherington, *The Badlands of Modernity: Heterotopia and social ordering*, London: Routledge, 1997; David Theo Goldberg, *Racist Culture: Philosophy and the politics of meaning*, Cambridge, MA: Oxford, 1993; Timothy Mitchell, *Colonizing Egypt*, Berkeley: University of California Press, 1991; Edward W. Said, *Orientalism: Western conceptions of the Orient*, reprinted with a new afterword, Harmondsworth: Penguin, 1995; and his *Culture and Imperialism*, London: Chatto & Windus, 1993.
3. The original text is *Folie et déraison: Histoire de la folie à l'âge classique*, Paris: Plon, 1961; later abridged as *Histoire de la folie*, Paris: Plon 10/18, 1964; and reissued as *Histoire de la folie à l'âge classique suivi de mon corps, ce papier, ce feu et la folie, l'absence d'œuvre*, Paris: Gallimard, 1972; and *Histoire de la folie à l'âge classique*, Paris: Gallimard, 1976. The English translation, *Madness and Civilisation*, translated by Richard Howard, London: Routledge, 1989, is largely only of the abridged version. Chapter Four has since been translated by Anthony Pugh as Experiences of Madness, *History of the Human Sciences*, Vol. 4 No. 1, 1991. I have used the 1976 *Tel* version, which is – bar the new preface and the absence of one footnote – the same as the 1961 original. The original preface and the 1972 appendices are found in *Dits et écrits*.
4. For some interesting comments on the notion of the limit, and its role in Foucault's thought, see Clare O'Farrell, *Foucault: Historian or philosopher?* Houndmills: Macmillan, 1989. O'Farrell also recognizes the influence of

Heidegger in this idea, and the importance for Foucault of Heidegger's *Nietzsche*.

5. In the original preface, Foucault suggested that his intent was to write a history, 'not of psychiatry, but of madness itself', but then he swiftly suggests that this is a 'doubly impossible task' (DE I, 164). Whilst he has been criticized by Jacques Derrida, Cogito and the History of Madness, in *Writing and Difference*, translated by Alan Bass, London: Routledge & Kegan Paul, 1978, for attempting this impossible task, Foucault is clear that he is really writing the history of 'that other form of madness', by which humans confine their neighbours (DE I, 159; MC xi). He undertakes this by making a study of the 'economic, political, ideological, and institutional conditions according to which the segregation of the insane was effected during the Classical period' (DE II, 223). This study of the links between discourse and practice prefigures its explicit formulation and the later dyad of power/knowledge.

6. On this see Pamela Major-Poetzl, *Michel Foucault's Archaeology of Western Culture: Toward a new science of history*, Brighton: Harvester Press, 1983. On transgression, see Peter Stallybrass and Allon White, *The Politics and Poetics of Transgression*, London: Methuen, 1986.

7. On Bataille, Blanchot, Hölderlin, and Flaubert see, respectively, A Preface to Transgression (DE I, 233–50; LCP 29–52); The Thought from Outside (DE I, 518–39); The Father's 'No' (DE I, 189–203; LCP 68–86); and Fantasia of the Library (DE I, 293–325; LCP 87–109). See also RR; Theatrum Philosophicum (DE II, 75–99; LCP 165–96); Le language de l'espace (DE I, 407–12) and Language to Infinity (DE I, 250–61; LCP 53–67). It has been suggested by Pierre Macherey, Présentation (RR xiii), that if Bataille brought Foucault to Nietzsche, 'it was certainly Blanchot who led Foucault to Heidegger, by means of his rumination on poetry and language' (see DE IV, 437; PPC 24). See Georges Bataille, *On Nietzsche*, translated by Bruce Boone, New York: Paragon House, 1992; and Maurice Blanchot, *The Space of Literature*, Lincoln: University of Nebraska Press, 1982.

8. James Miller, *The Passion of Michel Foucault*, London: HarperCollins, 1993, p. 130, suggests it was on the same day; Macey, *The Lives of Michel Foucault*, p. 129, the same month; the Chronology in *Dits et écrits* a month apart (DE I, 25).

9. Miller, *The Passion of Michel Foucault*, p. 130; Didier Eribon, *Michel Foucault*, translated by Betsy Wing, London: Faber & Faber, 1993, p. 152.

10. 'Transgression is an action which involves the limit, that narrow zone of a line where it displays the flash [*l'éclair* – lightning] of its passage, but perhaps also its entire trajectory, even its origin; it is likely that transgression has its entire space in the line it crosses' (DE I, 236; LCP 33–4). See Jon Simons, *Foucault and the Political*, London: Routledge, 1995.

11. See, for example, Didier Julia, *Dictionnaire de la philosophie*, Paris: Larousse, 1992, p. 97; Mark Poster, *Foucault, Marxism and History: Mode of production versus mode of information*, Cambridge: Polity Press, 1994, p. 74; Thomas R. Flynn, Foucault and the Spaces of History, *The Monist*, Vol. 74 No. 2, April 1991, p. 178.

12. Alan Sheridan, *Michel Foucault: The Will to Truth*, London: Tavistock, 1980, p. 14.

13. As Colin Gordon, Foucault in Britain, in Andrew Barry, Thomas Osborne and

Nikolas Rose (eds), *Foucault and Political Reason*, London: UCL Press, 1996, p. 261, suggests, this phrase arouses the 'double suspicion of historicism and irrationality' – especially within the empirically bound British culture. See also Thomas Flynn, Foucault's Mapping of History, in Gary Gutting (ed.), *The Cambridge Companion to Foucault*, Cambridge: Cambridge University Press, 1994, p. 30; and Beverley Brown and Mark Cousins, The Linguistic Fault: The Case of Foucault's Genealogy, in Mike Gane (ed.), *Towards a Critique of Foucault*, London: Routledge & Kegan Paul, 1986.
14. On this period of Foucault's thought, see Gilles Deleuze, A New Archivist, in *Foucault*, translated by Séan Hand, London: Athlone Press, 1988.
15. For a useful discussion of this work, and the role of Bachelard and Canguilhem in it, see François Delaporte, The History of Medicine According to Foucault, in Jan Goldstein (ed.), *Foucault and the Writing of History*, Oxford: Blackwell, 1994. See also Jeannette Colombel, Contrepoints poétiques, *Critique*, No. 471–2, August–September 1986.
16. 'It is understandable in these conditions that we should distinguish carefully between *scientific domains* and *archaeological territories* . . . Archaeological territories may extend to "literary" or "philosophical" texts, as well as scientific ones. Knowledge [*savoir*] *is to be found not only in demonstrations, it can also be found in fiction, reflection, narratives, institutional regulations, and political decisions*' *(AS 239; AK 183–4)*.
17. *'By truth I do not mean the ensemble of truths which are to be discovered and accepted, but rather the ensemble of rules according to which one can separate the true from the false, and attach to the true the specific effects of power' (DE III, 159; FR 74)*.
18. *We should note here that Foucault explicitly distances himself from what he calls the 'phenomenological approach', which 'gives absolute priority to the observing subject' (OT xiv). This is clearly not* a critique that pertains to Heidegger, as the previous chapters have shown. Rather, Foucault's targets are Sartre, Merleau-Ponty and Husserl.
19. See Robert D'Amico, Text and Context: Derrida and Foucault on Descartes, in John Fekete (ed.) *The Structural Allegory: Reconstructive encounters with the new French thought*, Minneapolis: University of Minnesota Press, 1984, p. 166, where he describes *Histoire de la folie* as 'a strong application of the structuralist method to historical research'; and Lois McNay, *Foucault: A critical introduction*, Cambridge: Polity Press, 1994, p. 1, who describes Foucault's work as a 'structural analysis of the development of Western thought since the Renaissance'. Useful discussions are found in Sheridan, *The Will to Truth*, pp. 198ff; Allan Megill, Foucault, Structuralism, and the Ends of History, *Journal of Modern History*, Vol. 51, No. 3, September 1979; and John Sturrock, *Structuralism*, London: Fontana, 1993.
20. Mark Neocleous, *Administering Civil Society*, London: Macmillan, 1996, pp. 62–3, 182 n30.
21. Miller, *The Passion of Michel Foucault*, p. 417 n37; also Macey, *The Lives of Michel Foucault*, p. 171; and Sheridan, *The Will to Truth*, p. 37. A detailed analysis of the revisions is made by James Bernauer, *Michel Foucault's Force of Flight: Towards an ethics of thought*, Atlantic Highlands, NJ: Humanities Press, 1990, pp. 188–92.

22. See Foucault's comment that structuralism 'does not entail a denial of time; but it is a certain manner of dealing with what we call time and what we call history' (DE IV, 752), and his admission that he is trying to introduce structural analysis into the history of ideas (DE I, 583).
23. On structuralism's relationship to space, see J. G. Merquior, *From Prague to Paris: A critique of structuralist and post-structuralist thought*, London: Verso, 1986, pp. 54–5. For an example, see Louis Althusser and Étienne Balibar, *Reading Capital*, translated by Ben Brewster, London: NLB, 1970, especially pp. 26–8. Neil Smith and Cindy Katz, Grounding Metaphor: Towards a Spatialised Politics, in Michael Keith and Steve Pile (eds), *Place and the Politics of Identity*, London: Routledge, 1993, pp. 71–4, suggest that Foucault is like Althusser in his use of metaphors without analysis. This and the following chapter aim to demonstrate the erroneousness of this judgement. On the use of spatial metaphors generally, see Ilana Friedrich Silber, Space, Fields, Boundaries: The Rise of Spatial Metaphors in Contemporary Social Theory, *Social Research*, Vol. 62, No. 2, Summer 1995.
24. Ian Hacking, The Archaeology of Foucault, in David Couzens Hoy (ed.), *Foucault: A critical reader*, Oxford: Basil Blackwell, 1986, p. 33.
25. It should be noted that whilst most commentators see this as a crucial essay for understanding Foucault, Mitchell Dean, *Critical and Effective Histories: Foucault's methods and historical sociology*, London: Routledge, 1994, p. 14, suggests that we should remember that it is about Nietzsche, and that we should not necessarily equate it with Foucault. It is, however, I suggest, clear from Foucault's genealogical studies – as he calls them – that the essay is part of a program of future work.
26. For a useful discussion of how these understandings distance Foucault from traditional history, see Michèle Barrett, *The Politics of Truth: From Marx to Foucault*, Cambridge: Polity Press, 1991, pp. 132–3.
27. Jürgen Habermas, *The Philosophical Discourse of Modernity*, Cambridge: Polity Press, 1987, p. 249, sees this rejection of *Ursprungphilosophie* as a point of difference between Foucault, and Heidegger and Derrida.
28. A different conception is provided by Philip Barker, *Michel Foucault: Subversions of the subject*, New York and London: Harvester Wheatsheaf, 1993, p. 71; and David Owen, *Maturity and Modernity: Nietzsche, Weber, Foucault and the ambivalence of reason*, London: Routledge, 1994, p. 151, who see archaeology as concentrating on the synchronic, genealogy on the diachronic.
29. In the interview, Critical Theory/Intellectual History (DE IV, 454–5; PPC 43), Foucault points out that if knowledge simply equalled power (as some critics would have him saying), then he would not have spent so much time examining their relation.
30. A particularly clear formulation is found in VS 123–7; WK 94–6. For discussions, see Randall McGowen, Power and Humanity, Or Foucault among the Historians, in Colin Jones and Roy Porter (eds), *Reassessing Foucault: Power, medicine and the body*, London: Routledge, 1994, p. 95; Sawicki, *Disciplining Foucault*, pp. 20–1; David M. Halperin, *Saint Foucault: Toward a gay hagiography*, New York: Oxford University Press, pp. 16–18; Deleuze, *Foucault*, p. 71; Barker, *Michel Foucault*, pp. 77–8. On the debt to Nietzsche, see many of those sources cited above, and notably Keith Ansell-Pearson, The

Significance of Michel Foucault's Reading of Nietzsche: Power, the Subject, and Political Theory, in Peter R. Sedgwick (ed.), *Nietzsche: A critical reader*, Oxford: Blackwell, 1996.
31. Niccolò Machiavelli, *The Prince*, in *Selected Political Writings*, edited and translated by David Wootton, Indianapolis: Hackett, 1994.
32. It would seem that the target here is particularly Louis Althusser, as shown in his *Lenin and Philosophy and Other Essays*, translated by Ben Brewster, London: NLB, 1971.
33. Michael Walzer, The Politics of Michel Foucault, in Hoy (ed.), *A Critical Reader*, p. 54.
34. Especially damaging for the overall purpose here is Henri Lefebvre's criticism in *The Survival of Capitalism: Reproduction of the relations of production*, translated by Frank Bryant, London: Allison & Busby, 1976, p. 116, that the concentration on marginal/peripheral groups in some studies (the allusion is clearly to Foucault) 'neglects the centres and centrality; it neglects the global'. Derek Gregory, *Geographical Imaginations*, Oxford: Blackwell, 1994, p. 365, suggests that this 'comprehensively missed Foucault's point', but Foucault's response shows this is not entirely accurate. A balance is needed, and when setting out the project of a history of spaces, Foucault indeed talked of extension 'from the grand strategies of geopolitics to the little tactics of the habitat' (DE III, 192; FL 228). Sensitive to questions of space, Edward Said provides some of the best work on extending the scope of Foucault's work from the micro to the macro level. See his *Orientalism* and *Culture and Imperialism*; and Michael Sprinker (ed.), *Edward Said: A critical reader*, Oxford: Blackwell, 1992.
35. Though see the work of Gilles Deleuze and Félix Guattari, particularly *Mille plateaux: capitalisme et schizophrénie 2*, Paris: Les Editions de Minuit, 1980; translated by Brian Massumi as *A Thousand Plateaus: Capitalism and schizophrenia*, London: Athlone Press, 1988. In the Notes on the Translation, Massumi points out that Deleuze and Guattari use *puissance* to signify potential, capacity – a translation of Nietzsche's *Macht* – and *pouvoir* 'in a sense very close to Foucault's, as a selective concretisation of potential'.
36. Alan Hunt, Governing the City: Liberalism and Early Modern Modes of Government, in Barry et al. (eds), *Foucault and Political Reason*, p. 184. Similar points are made by McNay, *Foucault*, pp. 164–5; and Russell Keat, The Human Body in Social Theory: Reich, Foucault and the Repressive Hypothesis, *Radical Philosophy*, No. 42, Winter/Spring 1986. See also Jean Baudrillard, *Forget Foucault*, translated by Nicole Dufresne, New York: Semiotext(e), 1987.
37. See also Michel Foucault, About the Beginning of the Hermeneutics of the Self: Two Lectures at Dartmouth, *Political Theory*, Vol. 21, No. 2, May 1993, p. 204, where Foucault admits his earlier emphasis on domination as a problem.
38. On the spatial side, Gregory, *Geographical Imaginations*, p. 276, sees this as a particular problem: 'Foucault's analysis does not lead as directly as Lefebvre's to a "politics of space", however, and one of the most controversial areas of his work is the limited support it seems to afford for any kind of resistance.'
39. Nancy Fraser, 'Foucault on Modern Power: Empirical Insights and Normative Confusions', *Praxis International*, No. 1, 1981, p. 283. Habermas, *The Philosophical Discourse of Modernity*, pp. 276ff, suggests that Foucault realizes this,

and other, problems, but 'does not draw any consequences from them'. On some of the issues around this, see Paul Patton, Taylor and Foucault on Power and Freedom, and Charles Taylor, Taylor and Foucault on Power and Freedom: A Reply, *Political Studies*, Vol. XXXVII, 1989; Leslie Paul Thiele, The Agony of Politics: The Nietzschean Roots of Foucault's Thought, *American Political Science Review*, Vol. 84, No. 3, September 1990; and Niko Kolodny, The Ethics of Cryptonormativism: A Defence of Foucault's Evasions, *Philosophy and Social Criticism*, Vol. 22, No. 5, September 1996.

40. For a more detailed discussion of this see the final pages of Stuart Elden, The Constitution of the Normal: Monsters and Masturbation at the Collège de France, *boundary 2*, Vol. 28, No. 1, Spring 2001.

41. See Carl von Clausewitz, *On War*, translated by J. J. Graham, revised by F. N. Maude, London: Wordsworth, 1997, p. 25. On this see Pasquale Pasquino, Political Theory of War and Peace: Foucault and the History of Modern Political Theory, *Economy and Society*, Vol. 22, No. 1, February 1993; and Thiele, 'The Agony of Politics', p. 921.

42. Though as Barry Smart, *Michel Foucault*, London: Routledge, 1988, p. 134, points out, his own definitions are often vague.

43. See, however, Mark Neocleous, Perpetual War, or, 'War and War Again': Schmitt, Foucault, Fascism, *Philosophy and Social Criticism*, Vol. 22, No. 2, March 1996, for the dangers in this militaristic conception of society, a point that is also made by some feminists. See Joseph Rouse, Power/Knowledge, in Gutting (ed.), *The Cambridge Companion*, p. 113, and, on Foucault and feminism more generally, Terry K. Aladjem, The Philosopher's Prism: Foucault, Feminism, and Critique, *Political Theory*, Vol. 19, No. 2, May 1991; and Caroline Ramazanoglu (ed.), *Up Against Foucault: Explorations of some tensions between Foucault and Feminism*, London: Routledge, 1993.

44. For a discussion of Heidegger and Foucault on technology, and specifically on the differences in their understandings, see Jana Sawicki, Heidegger and Foucault: Escaping Technological Nihilism, in Barry Smart (ed.), *Michel Foucault (1) Critical Assessments*, London: Routledge, 1994, Vol. III; Mitchell Dean, Putting the Technological into Government, *History of the Human Sciences*, Vol. 9, No. 3, 1996; and André Glucksmann, Michel Foucault's Nihilism, in Timothy J. Armstrong (ed.), *Michel Foucault Philosopher*, Hemel Hempstead, Harvester Wheatsheaf, 1992.

45. This point is developed out of a conversation with Morris Kaplan. See also Barry Hindess, *Discourses of Power: From Hobbes to Foucault*, London: Routledge, 1996, pp. 114–15, where he links Heidegger and Foucault on the essence of technology – constituting a human individual endowed with 'soul, consciousness, guilt, remorse' and so forth.

46. The first two terms are used in *The Will to Knowledge*, the central chapter of which is called 'The *Dispositif* of Sexuality'; 'apparatus' is used in *Power/Knowledge*; 'grid of intelligibility' is the suggestion of Hubert Dreyfus and Paul Rabinow, *Michel Foucault: Beyond structuralism and hermeneutics*, Brighton: Harvester, 1982. For a brief comment, see Halperin, *Saint Foucault*, pp. 189–90, n6.

47. For the former, see Martin Heidegger, *Essais et Conférences*, translated by André Preau, Paris: Gallimard, 1958; for the latter see *Approche de Hölderlin*,

translated by Henry Corbin, Michel Deguy, François Dédier and Jean Launay, Paris: Gallimard, 1973.
48. Mitchell Dean, Foucault, Government and the Enfolding of Authority, in Barry et al. (eds), *Foucault and Political Reason*, p. 226. See also Hindess, *Discourses of Power*, pp. 114–15; Alan Milchman and Alan Rosenberg, Michel Foucault, Auschwitz and Modernity, *Philosophy and Social Criticism*, Vol. 22, No. 1, January 1996, p. 113 n22; and Macey, *The Lives of Michel Foucault*, p. 355, all of whom conceive of *dispositif* in a way that corresponds closely to Heidegger's *Gestell*. For a discussion, see Gilles Deleuze, 'What is a *dispositif*?' in Armstrong (ed.), *Michel Foucault Philosopher*, and his Desire and Pleasure, in Arnold I. Davidson (ed.), *Foucault and his Interlocutors*, Chicago: University of Chicago Press, 1997. None of these thinkers, however, make the explicit link I am suggesting.
49. See also the unpaginated insert found in *L'usage des plaisirs* and *Le souci de soi*.
50. See also Michel Foucault, *Les Anormaux: Cours au Collège de France (1974–1975)*, Paris: Seuil/Gallimard, 1999. For a more detailed discussion of the Barbin case, see Stuart Elden and Sharon Cowan, Words, Ideas and Desires: Freud, Foucault and the Hermaphroditic Roots of Bisexuality, forthcoming.
51. Useful sources on Foucault's later work include Karlis Racevskis, *Postmodernism and the Search for Enlightenment*, Charlottesville: The University Press of Virginia, 1993; Barker, *Michel Foucault: Subversions of the Subject*; John Rajchman, *Truth and Eros: Foucault, Lacan and the question of ethics*, New York and London: Routledge, 1991; and Peter Dews, The Return of the Subject in Late Foucault, *Radical Philosophy*, No. 51, Spring 1989.
52. David Couzens Hoy, Introduction, in Hoy (ed.) *A Critical Reader*, p. 6, makes the connection between Nietzsche and Foucault, but, like others, does not see Heidegger as the crucial link in the chain.
53. As Deleuze, *Foucault*, p. 50, states, 'archaeology does not necessarily refer back to the past. There is an archaeology of the present'. See also John Rajchman, *Michel Foucault: The freedom of philosophy*, New York: Columbia University Press, 1985, p. 58; and the posthumously published interview What our Present Is (FL 407–15).
54. Deleuze, *Foucault*, p. 115.
55. Immanuel Kant, *Beantwortung der Frage: Was ist Aufklärung?* in *Werke: Gesamtausgabe in zehn Bänden*, Leipzig: Modes und Baumann, 1843, Vol. I, p. 111; An Answer to the Question: What is Enlightenment? translated by Ted Humphrey in *Perpetual Peace and Other Essays on Politics, History and Moral Practice*, Indianapolis: Hackett, 1983, p. 41.
56. In this, and other works of the time (dating back at least as far as 1978), Foucault increasingly identifies himself with a lineage of thought he traces back to the Enlightenment. Making use of Canguilhem's expression, he sees Enlightenment as 'our most "present past" [*actuel passé*]' (DE IV, 37).
57. On the question of ontology in Foucault, with some of the links to Heidegger, see Béatrice Han, *L'ontologie manquée de Michel Foucault*, Grenoble: Jérôme Millon, 1998.
58. Some have characterized Foucault as making a radical break with his previous ideas (especially centred around the relation to Kant); others find a more

nuanced shift as I am trying to do. For the former view, see Ian Hacking, Self-Improvement, in Hoy (ed.) *A Critical Reader*, p. 238; Jürgen Habermas, Taking Aim at the Heart of the Present: On Foucault's Lecture on Kant's *What is Enlightenment?*, in Michael Kelly (ed.) *Critique and Power: Recasting the Foucault/Habermas Debate*, Cambridge: MIT Press, 1994, p. 150; Christopher Norris, 'What is Enlightenment?': Kant According to Foucault, in Gutting (ed.), *Cambridge Companion*, pp. 170, 186. For the latter view, see James W. Bernauer and Michael Mahon, The Ethics of Michel Foucault, in Gutting (ed.), *Cambridge Companion*, p. 152; Barbara Becker-Cantarino, Foucault on Kant: Deconstructing the Enlightenment? in Sara Friedrichsmeyer and Barbara Becker-Cantarino (eds), *The Enlightenment and its Legacy*, Bonn: Bouvier, 1990; and Colin Gordon, Question, Ethos, Event: Foucault on Kant and Enlightenment, *Economy and Society*, Vol. 15, No. 1, February 1986. The shift is often situated around the critical engagement between Foucault and Habermas. On this see, particularly, Kelly (ed.) *Critique and Power*.

59. David Couzens Hoy, Foucault: Modern or Postmodern? in Jonathan Arac (ed.) *After Foucault: Humanistic knowledge, postmodern challenges*, New Brunswick: Rutgers University Press, 1988, p. 13. Progress was, for Nietzsche, merely a 'modern idea' (A 4).

60. As Dean, *Critical and Effective Histories*, p. 20, suggests, 'the general context for a consideration of genealogy and archaeology is, then, a third term which they both serve, that of a history of the present'. In this context, see also Patrick Baert, Foucault's History of the Present as Self-Referential Knowledge Acquisition, *Philosophy and Social Criticism*, Vol. 24, No. 6, November 1998.

61. Flynn, Foucault's Mapping of History, pp. 40–2. A similar statement is made by Edward W. Soja, *Postmodern Geographies: The reassertion of space in critical social theory*, London: Verso, 1989, p. 18.

62. David Harvey, *Justice, Nature and the Geography of Difference*, Oxford: Blackwell, 1996, p. 4. See, for example, Slavoj Žižek (ed.) *Mapping Ideology*, London: Verso, 1994, which seems to use the 'mapping' as a label and nothing more. On the defence of 'map' as a metaphor and more than a metaphor, see Gregory, *Geographical Imaginations*, p. 217.

63. Foucault's use of spatial metaphors occasionally leads others to make remarks of this nature. For example, George Steiner, The Order of Things, in Peter Burke (ed.) *Critical Essays on Michel Foucault*, Aldershot: Scolar Press, 1992, p. 85: 'one wonders whether "topology" would not have been more apt than "archaeology"'.

64. Jorge Luis Borges, Of Exactitude in Science, in *A Universal History of Infamy*, Harmondsworth: Penguin, 1984, p. 131.

65. See Soja, *Postmodern Geographies*, p. 16, where he suggests that Foucault's 'most explicit and revealing observations on the relative significance of space and time, however, appear not in his major published works but almost innocuously in his lectures and, after some coaxing interrogation, in two revealing interviews'. In his later *Thirdspace: Journeys to Los Angeles and other real-and-imagined places*, Oxford: Blackwell, 1996, p. 154, Soja again treats 'Of Other Spaces' as Foucault's central spatial contribution, though he recognizes the dangers in this.

66. Soja, *Postmodern Geographies*, p. 19, rightly suggests that 'Foucault's spatialisa-

tion took on a more demonstrative rather than declarative stance', a statement which makes Soja's attempts to synthesize Foucault's declarations rather than showcase his demonstrations all the more frustrating. As Gregory, *Geographical Imaginations*, p. 297, notes, Soja's approach also snaps the links between Foucault's pronouncements on space and his genealogy of the subject, a problem I attempt to avoid through the contextual readings of Foucault's spatial histories.
67. All translations from this piece are my own, in order to clarify Foucault's point. The piece is available as Of Other Spaces, translated by Jay Miskowiec, *Diacritics*, Vol. 16, No. 1, Spring 1986. But this translation is especially confusing when it translates *localization* as 'emplacement' and *emplacement* as 'site'; a problem that seems to haunt many critical expositions of this piece. See, for example, Soja, *Thirdspace*, p. 156.
68. James Harkess, Translator's Introduction, TNP 2.
69. See the translator's notes TNP 61 n5, 62 n14. On Magritte in general, see Marcel Paquet, *Magritte*, Cologne: Taschen, 1994. Foucault's comments on art generally show a strong spatial awareness. See, for example, the commentary on Velasquez (M&C 19–31; OT 3–16) and Le Force de fuir (DE II, 401–5). There is not the space here to discuss this further.
70. For a discussion and elaboration, see Soja, *Postmodern Geographies*, especially pp. 16–21; *Thirdspace*, pp. 154–63; John Marks, A New Image of Thought, *New Formations*, No. 25, Summer 1995; Hetherington, *The Badlands of Modernity*, Chapter Three; Edward S. Casey, *The Fate of Place: A philosophical history*, Berkeley: University Presses of California, 1997, pp. 297–301; Georges Teyssot, Heterotopias and the History of Spaces, in Barry Smart (ed.), *Michel Foucault (2) Critical Assessments*, London: Routledge, Vol. VII, 1995; Thomas L. Dumm, *Michel Foucault and the Politics of Freedom*, California: Sage, 1996, pp. 36ff. As Marks, pp. 68–9, and Hetherington, pp. 46ff note, in a corrective to Soja, Foucault's understanding of heterotopia is both for thought and social space.
71. This is at least part of the reason why 'mapping the present' is a useful term for describing Foucault's work. Gregory, *Geographical Imaginations*, p. 359, reads Lefebvre's history of space as a history of the present – indeed in many ways it is – but only rarely does Lefebvre do what Foucault does and undertake a spatial history, a *mapping* of the present.
72. Chris Philo, Foucault's Geographies, *Environment and Planning D: Society and Space*, Vol. 10, 1992. The critique of Soja is drawn from Gregory, *Chinatown*, Part Three? Uncovering postmodern geographies [1990], in *Geographical Imaginations*.

Chapter Five: The Spaces of Power

1. Colin Gordon, *Histoire de la folie*: an Unknown Book by Michel Foucault, *History of the Human Sciences*, Vol. 3, No. 1, 1990. Several responses to this article appeared in this journal issue, several more, and a reply by Gordon, History, Madness and Other Errors: A Response, appeared in Vol. 3, No. 3,

1990. Some of these papers, together with two additional, were collected in Arthur Still and Irving Velody (eds), *Rewriting the History of Madness: Studies in Foucault's Histoire de la Folie*, London, Routledge, 1992.
2. Though Gordon is guilty of simplifying the case in suggesting that the French reception of *Histoire de la folie* is more positive than the English, French commentators – whether critical or not – have tended to represent Foucault's arguments more accurately. See, for example, Roland Barthes, Taking Sides, in *Critical Essays*, translated by Richard Howard, Evanston: Northwestern University Press, 1972; Jacqueline Russ, *Profil d'une œuvre: Histoire de la folie: Foucault*, Paris: Hatier, 1979; and Georges Canguilhem's three pieces and Michel Serres, The Geometry of the Incommunicable, in Arnold I. Davidson (ed.), *Foucault and his Interlocutors*, Chicago: University of Chicago Press, 1997.
3. Reading the full text truly gives the lie to Peter Sedgwick's suggestion that 'the full text has many important passages but these are not crucial to Foucault's argument'. *Psycho Politics*, London: Pluto, 1982, p. 272, n16.
4. This sets up a distance from Pamela Major-Poetzl, *Michel Foucault's Archaeology of Western Culture: Toward a new science of history*, Brighton: Harvester Press, 1983, p. 134, where she suggests that *Histoire de la folie* has 'only a limited sense of spatial relationships', suggesting that a more radical break is only found in *The Birth of the Clinic* and later works. Far more in tune with my attempt here is Serres' valuable 'The Geometry of the Incommunicable: Madness', only recently translated into English, which emphasizes Foucault's language and the concomitant spatial analyses in this work.
5. Colin Gordon, History, madness and other errors: a response, p. 391.
6. See Clare O'Farrell, *Foucault: Historian or Philosopher?* Basingstoke: Macmillan, 1989, p. 71.
7. H. C. Erik Midelfort, Madness and Civilisation in Early Modern Europe: A Reappraisal of Michel Foucault, in Barbara C. Malament (ed.), *After the Reformation: Essays in Honor of J. H. Hexter*, Manchester: Manchester University Press, 1980, pp. 253, 256, 261, n13. The monastery critique is picked up by Lawrence Stone, *The Past and the Present Revisited*, London and New York: Routledge & Kegan Paul, 1987, p. 271; J. G. Merquior, *Foucault*, Berkeley: University of California Press, 1985, p. 28; and Sedgwick, *Psycho Politics*, p. 134. For a defence see Dominick LaCapra, Foucault, history and madness, *History of the Human Sciences*, Vol. 3, No. 1, 1990, p. 33.
8. The 'myth' of the ship of fools is discussed by Winifred Barbara Maher and Brendan Maher, The Ship of Fools: *Stultifera Navis* or *Ignis Fatuus? American Psychologist*, Vol. 37, No. 7, July 1982.
9. On Gheel, see William Ll. Parry-Jones, The Model of the Geel Lunatic Colony and Its Influence on the Nineteenth-century Asylum System in Britain, in Andrew Scull (ed.) *Madhouses, Mad-Doctors and Madmen: The social history of psychiatry in the Victorian era*, Philadelphia: University of Pennsylvania Press, 1981.
10. The lack of overall plan is supported by Andrew T. Scull, *Museums of Madness: The social organisation of insanity in 19th century England*, London: Allen Lane, 1979, pp. 18–19.
11. The English translation has 'the mad then led an easy wandering existence', a

translation Gordon suggests is simply wrong, *facilement* being an adverb rather than an adjective: easily, not easy. For Gordon, the sentence should read 'the existence of the mad at that time could easily be a wandering one' (*Histoire de la folie*, p. 17). A useful discussion of this is found in Allan Megill, Foucault, Ambiguity, and the Rhetoric of Historiography, *History of the Human Sciences*, Vol. 3, No. 3, pp. 344–7. Anthony Pugh, the putative translator of the (forthcoming) full English version, suggests 'the mad may well have led a wandering life at that time'. Pugh, 'Foucault, Rhetoric and Translation', in Still and Velody (eds), *Rewriting the History of Madness*, p. 139.

12. The real and imaginary role of water within madness is further discussed in L'eau et la folie (DE I, 268–72).
13. René Descartes, *Meditationes de Prima Philosophia* in *Œuvres Philosophiques: Tome II (1638–1642)*, Paris: Garnier Frères, 1967, pp. 178–82; *Meditations on First Philosophy*, in *Discourse on Method and Meditations on First Philosophy*, translated by Donald A. Cress, Indianapolis: Hackett, 1980, pp. 58–60. As Philip Barker, *Michel Foucault: Subversions of the subject*, New York and London: Harvester Wheatsheaf, 1993, p. 107, notes, St Augustine's foundation of thought – *credo ut intelligam* – takes into account the point of dreams and illusion, making him similar to Descartes (p. 209, n92). However, St Augustine crucially does not mention the possibility of madness, a point neglected by Barker. It would seem then that Descartes' introduction of madness as a source of doubt is as important as its subsequent dismissal.
14. Descartes, *Meditationes*, p. 183; *Meditations*, p. 61.
15. Descartes, *Meditationes*, p. 178; *Meditations*, p. 58. Emphasis added.
16. Descartes, *Meditationes*, p. 179; *Meditations*, p. 58.
17. This reading of Descartes is critiqued by Jacques Derrida in Cogito and the History of Madness, in *Writing and Difference*, translated by Alan Bass, London: Routledge & Kegan Paul, 1978. Derrida suggests that 'the sense of Foucault's entire project can be pinpointed in this reading of Descartes', but argues that it is a 'naive' reading (pp. 32, 61). Derrida does not read Descartes' 'but they are all demented' as dismissive and divisive, but argues that it can be read in the same way that Foucault claims Descartes deals with the other two misleading possibilities. Just as the possibility of dreaming or deceit did not preclude the possibility of thinking, and, indeed, actually helped to prove it, Derrida argues that the possibility of madness too proves the validity of thought. As he puts it, 'even if my thoughts are completely mad' I am still thinking: 'the Cogito is valid even for the maddest madman' (pp. 55, 58). Having claimed this, Derrida is in a position to criticize the inference that Foucault draws from Descartes: it requires 'neither the exclusion nor the circumventing of madness. Descartes never interns madness . . .' (p. 55). Foucault responded to parts of Derrida's critique in Mon corps, ce papier, ce feu (DE II, 245–68), and implicitly in other works, notably *The Archaeology of Knowledge*. On this debate see Roy Boyne, *Foucault and Derrida: The other side of reason*, London: Unwin Hyman, 1988; Robert D'Amico, Text and Context: Derrida and Foucault on Descartes, in John Fekete (ed.), *The Structural Allegory: Reconstructive encounters with the new French thought*, Minneapolis: University of Minnesota Press, 1984; Peter Flaherty, (Con)textual Contest: Derrida and Foucault on Madness and the Cartesian Subject, *Philosophy of the*

Social Sciences, Vol. 16, No. 1, March 1986 and, more generally, Christopher Norris, *Derrida*, London: Fontana, 1987; Edward W. Said, *The World, The Text, The Critic*, London: Faber & Faber, 1984. Derrida replies to some of Foucault's points in *Être juste avec Freud*, in Michel Delorme (ed.), *Penser la folie: Essais sur Michel Foucault*, Paris: Galilée, 1992.

18. The importance of vision only really becomes clear when the original French is returned to. The word translated as 'observation' in *Madness and Civilisation* is *regard*, usually rendered as 'gaze' in Foucault's books. Whilst both translations are accurate, noting the French shows how this notion develops in Foucault's work. The idea of the medical gaze is greatly developed in *The Birth of the Clinic*, and its wider social implications – already there in *Histoire de la folie* – are of course evident in *Discipline and Punish*. The notions of power [*pouvoir*] and knowledge [*savoir*] make use of a third dimension, that of the ability to see [*voir*], to survey and control space. On Foucault and vision see Martin Jay, *Downcast Eyes: The denigration of vision in twentieth-century French thought*, Berkeley: University of California Press, 1993; Thomas R. Flynn, Foucault and the Eclipse of Vision, in David Michael Levin (ed.), *Modernity and the Hegemony of Vision*, London: University of California Press, 1993; John Rajchman, Foucault's Art of Seeing, *October*, No. 44, Spring 1988.
19. See also Scull, *Museums of Madness*, pp. 159–60.
20. Louis-Sébastian Mercier, *Tableau de Paris*, Amsterdam, 1783, Vol. VIII, p. 1, quoted in HF 375; MC 202.
21. Samuel Tuke, *Practical Hints on the Construction and Economy of Pauper Lunatic Asylums*, York: William Alexander, 1815, p. 9.
22. Samuel Tuke, *Review of the Early History of the Retreat*, quoted in Anne Digby, *Madness, Morality and Medicine: A study of the York Retreat 1796–1914*, Cambridge: Cambridge University Press, 1985, p. 14. On the Tukes and the Retreat, see also Samuel Tuke, *Description of the Retreat*, York: W. Alexander, 1813; D. Hack Tuke, *Reform in the History of the Insane*, London: J. & A. Churchill, 1892; William K. and E. Margaret Sessions, *The Tukes of York*, York: William Sessions Limited, 1971; Mary R. Glover, *The Retreat York: An early experiment in the treatment of mental illness*, York: William Sessions Limited, 1984; and Kathleen Anne Stewart, *The York Retreat in the Light of the Quaker Way*, York: William Sessions Limited, 1992.
23. Samuel Tuke, *Practical Hints*, p. 11.
24. Digby, *Madness, Morality and Medicine*, pp. 54, 66, 71.
25. Erving Goffman, *Asylums*, New York: Anchor Books, 1961. See also Scull, *Museums of Madness*, p. 104. On several of these points, with a noticeably large debt to Foucault, see Michael Donnelly, *Managing the Mind: A study of mental psychology in early nineteenth century Britain*, London: Tavistock, 1983.
26. Digby, *Madness, Morality and Medicine*, pp. 158–9, 188. See also Scull, *Museums of Madness*, p. 104; Samuel Tuke, *Description of the Retreat*, p. 105.
27. Glover, *The Retreat York*, p. 31.
28. Gordon, *Histoire de la folie*, p. 16. On Pinel, see Walther Riese, *The Legacy of Philippe Pinel: An inquiry into thought on mental alienation*, New York: Springer Publishing Company, 1969.
29. Riese, *The Legacy of Philippe Pinel*, p. 154.
30. Riese, *The Legacy of Philippe Pinel*, p. 172.

31. Donnelly, *Managing the Mind*, p. 40. It should be noted that this was not always the case. See Samuel Tuke, *Practical Hints*, pp. 11, 17: 'It will be found necessary to separate them, rather according to the degree, than the species or the duration of the disease.'
32. Quoted in Riese, *The Legacy of Philippe Pinel*, p. 154.
33. Foucault explicitly states that he is only looking at the birth of the prison in the French penal system (SP 40n; DP 309n3), although the implicit suggestion is that some of his ideas would serve as a model for other countries. Foucault has been criticized for suggesting that the shift from torture to imprisonment is a European model, but it is clear from his 1972–3 course at the *Collège de France* that he only sees this as appropriate for French history. At the beginning of the course outline, a distinction is made between 'four grand forms of punitive strategies'; banishment, compensation, branding or other corporal punishment, and imprisonment. Having suggested these four strategies, he goes on to talk about how France shifted from the third to the fourth, a process he elaborates in more detail in *Discipline and Punish*. It is clear from this outline, if it were not already evident in his better known work, that on this point Foucault was making no claims for universality. See *La société punitive* (RC 29–51).
34. The French word *supplice* is usually translated as 'torture', but so too is *torture*. What is important about Foucault's use of *supplice* and related words is that it refers to the public spectacle of torture – such as that of Damiens. Alan Sheridan remarks that 'no single English word will cover the full range of the French', and therefore translates as 'torture', 'public execution' or 'scaffold' (Translator's Note in DP). To avoid confusion I have usually retained the French word.
35. Gordon, History, madness and other errors: a response, p. 391.
36. Foucault suggests that the French *police* and the German *Polizei* have this meaning, but that the English police 'is something very different' (DE IV, 820). I think that it has been convincingly demonstrated that the English were, albeit somewhat later, using the same understanding. See Leon Radzinowicz, *A History of English Criminal Law and its Administration from 1750*, London: Stevens & Sons, five volumes, 1948–86, particularly Volume III; Mark Neocleous, Policing and Pin-making: Adam Smith, Police and the State of Prosperity, *Policing and Society*, Vol. 8, 1998; and his *The Fabrication of Social Order: A critical theory of police power*, London: Pluto, 2000.
37. There are interesting parallels to be drawn between Foucault's understanding of this term and that of Hegel. See G. W. F. Hegel, *Elements of the Philosophy of Right*, edited by Allen W. Wood, translated by H. B. Nisbet, Cambridge: Cambridge University Press, 1991, §§236, 239–48. In seeing governmentality as a virtual synonym of police I am setting myself up in opposition to Nikolas Rose's suggestion in Government, Authority and Expertise in Advanced Liberalism, *Economy and Society*, Vol. 22, No. 3, 1993, p. 289, that 'governmentality, for Foucault, is specified in opposition to a notion of police'. As Foucault himself says, 'I do not think that one can fail to relate this search for an art of government to mercantilism and Cameralism' (DE III, 648; FE 96). On Foucault and police within the context of power generally, see Barry Hindess, *Discourses of Power: From Hobbes to Foucault*, London: Routledge, 1996,

pp. 118ff. For discussions of governmentality, see, amongst others, the essays in FE and Barry Hindess, Politics and Governmentality, *Economy and Society*, Vol. 26, No. 2, May 1997.

38. Some writers allude to this but do not necessarily follow through the implications it has for reading the book. See Thomas L. Dumm, *Michel Foucault and the Politics of Freedom*, California: Sage, 1996, p. 71. Rudi Visker, *Michel Foucault: Genealogy as critique*, London: Verso, 1995, p. 47, suggests that 'in contrast to the expectation which the subtitle creates, Foucault's subject here is not simply the birth of the prison, but also the birth of the human sciences'. See also James Miller, *The Passion of Michel Foucault*, London: HarperCollins, 1993, pp. 210–11; Pasquale Pasquino, 'Michel Foucault (1926–84): *The Will to Knowledge*', *Economy and Society*, Vol. 15, No. 1, Feb. 1986, p. 97. A much more penetrating analysis is found in the work of Frank Lentricchia, *Ariel and the Police*, Brighton: The Harvester Press, 1988.

39. See for example, David Stewart, Why Foucault? in Barry Smart (ed.) *Michel Foucault (2) Critical Assessments*, London: Routledge, Vol. VII, 1995, p. 95, who suggests that Foucault uses two general schemes – panopticism and heterotopias – in his work on space. Felix Driver, Geography and Power: The Work of Michel Foucault, in Peter Burke (ed.), *Critical Essays on Michel Foucault*, Aldershot: Scolar Press, 1992, talks at length of the Panopticon, but suggests that we should also look at the passage on the Mettray colony.

40. The English translation of this paragraph is somewhat dubious, not in the choice of words, but in the slip made in the alteration of the punctuation, such that a less-than-wholly attentive reader may miss Foucault's point.

41. Mark Neocleous, *Administering Civil Society*, London: Macmillan, 1996, p. 61. See also pp. 83–6, and his Perpetual War, or, 'War and War Again': Schmitt, Foucault, Fascism, *Philosophy and Social Criticism*, Vol. 22, No. 2, March 1996.

42. Foucault suggests that the poles of right and wrong, and good and sin map onto those of the normal and the pathological (SP 232–3; DP 199). See Georges Canguilhem, *On the Normal and Pathological*, translated by Carolyn R. Fawcett, Dordrecht: D. Reidel, 1978, p. 149: 'the abnormal, whilst logically second, is existentially first'; and Michel Foucault, *Les Anormaux: Cours au Collège de France (1974–1975)*, Paris: Seuil/Gallimard, 1999. I have discussed this at length in The Constitution of the Normal: Monsters and Masturbation at the Collège de France, *boundary 2*, Vol. 28, No. 1, Spring 2001.

43. Robin Evans, *The Fabrication of Virtue*, Cambridge: Cambridge University Press, 1982, p. 119, points out that the 'term penitentiary referred to a monastic cell, set aside for sinful monks – a place of penitence and remorse'. On monasteries, factories and prisons, see Dario Melossi and Massimo Pavarini, *The Prison and the Factory: Origins of the Penitentiary System*, translated by Glynis Cousin, London: Macmillan, 1981.

44. Bentham suggests that the prison be 'located in the neighbourhood of a great metropolis, the place which contains assembled the greatest number of men, including those who most need to have displayed before their eyes the punishment of crime', *Théorie des Peines et des Récompenses*, p. 203, quoted in Pasquale Pasquino, Criminology: the Birth of a Special Knowledge (FE 240). See also Jeremy Bentham, *The Rationale of Punishment*, London: Robert Heward, 1830, p. 353.

45. Details of the English translation perhaps help to explain the imbalance. In the French text 30 plates are included, showing a range of disciplinary diagrams and scenes – hospitals, schools, colleges, a menagerie, a number on the army, and several of penitentiaries. The English text cuts these down to merely ten, of which only one is of a military scene; none are of hospitals or schools, and the majority are of the prison.
46. Michel Foucault, Blandine Barrett Kriegel, Anne Thalamy, François Beguin and Bruno Fortier, *Généalogie des équipements de normalisation*, Fontenay sous-Bois: CERFI, 1976; *Les Machines à guérir (aux origines de l'hôpital moderne)*, Brussels: Pierre Mardaga, 1979. On the history of this research see David Macey, *The Lives of Michel Foucault*, London: Hutchinson, 1993, pp. 324–6.
47. In a 1977 interview, published as the preface to the French edition of Jeremy Bentham's *Panopticon*, Foucault suggests that the themes that struck him in the literature on prisons had previously seemed important in his study of hospital architecture (DE III, 190; FL 226).
48. On Foucault and diagrams generally see Gilles Deleuze, *Foucault*, translated by Séan Hand, London: Athlone Press, 1988, especially the chapter entitled A New Cartographer, and his What is a *dispositif?* in Timothy J. Armstrong (ed.), *Michel Foucault Philosopher*, Hemel Hempstead, Harvester Wheatsheaf, 1992. Foucault describes himself as a cartographer in *Sur la sellette* (DE II, 725).
49. The model is used by Paul Rabinow, *French Modern: Norms and forms of the social environment*, Cambridge, MA: The MIT Press, 1989, pp. 34ff, to relate to the 1832 cholera epidemic in Paris. See also Thomas Osborne, Security and Vitality: Drains, Liberalism and Power in the Nineteenth Century, in Andrew Barry, Thomas Osborne and Nikolas Rose (eds), *Foucault and Political Reason*, London: UCL Press, 1996. For two fictional accounts of the plague, but with a clear picture of the grid that Foucault uses as a model, see Daniel Defoe, *Journal of the Plague Year*, Harmondsworth: Penguin, 1966, especially pp. 57ff, with a commentary in John Bender, *Imagining the Penitentiary: Fiction and the architecture of mind in eighteenth-century England*, Chicago: University of Chicago Press, 1987, pp. 63–84; and Albert Camus, *The Plague*, translated by Stuart Gilbert, Harmondsworth, Penguin, 1960.
50. Notable exceptions are found in Sarah Nettleton, *Power, Pain and Dentistry*, Buckingham, Open University Press, 1992, and Inventing Mouths: Disciplinary Power and Dentistry, in Colin Jones and Roy Porter (eds), *Reassessing Foucault: Power, medicine and the body*, London: Routledge, 1994; and Alan Milchman and Alan Rosenberg, Michel Foucault, Auschwitz and Modernity, *Philosophy and Social Criticism*, Vol. 22, No. 1, January 1996.
51. Bender, *Imagining the Penitentiary*, p. 44.
52. Liz Eckermann, Foucault, Embodiment and Gendered Subjectivities. The Case of Voluntary Self-Starvation, in Alan Petersen and Robin Bunton (eds), *Foucault, Health and Medicine*, London: Routledge, 1997, p. 164. See Charles Taylor and Richard Rorty's contributions to David Couzens Hoy (ed.) *Foucault: A critical reader*, Oxford: Basil Blackwell, 1986. On the shift from bodies to population, and the concept of bio-power, see Martin Hewitt, Bio-politics and Social Policy: Foucault's Account of Welfare, in Mike Featherstone, Mike Hepworth and Bryan S. Turner (eds), *The Body: Social process and cultural*

theory, London: Sage, 1991; and Barry et al. (eds), *Foucault and Political Reason*.

53. For Foucault, the 'political significance of the problem of sex is due to the fact that sex is located at the point of intersection of the discipline of the body and the control of the population' (DE III, 153; FR 67). See also VS 191–2; WK 145.

54. For an introduction to Bentham's life and thought, see James Steintrager, *Bentham*, London: George Allen & Unwin Ltd, 1977; L. J. Hume, *Bentham and Bureaucracy*, Cambridge: Cambridge University Press, 1981; and Elie Halévy, *The Growth of Philosophical Radicalism*, London: Faber & Faber, 1972. On the Panopticon itself, see Gertrude Himmelfarb, The Haunted House of Jeremy Bentham, in *Victorian Minds: Essays on nineteenth century intellectuals*, Gloucester, MA: Peter Smith, 1975; Janet Semple, *Bentham's Prison: A study of the panopticon penitentiary*, Oxford: Clarendon Press, 1993, and her Foucault and Bentham: A Defence of Panopticism, *Utilitas*, Vol. 4, No. 1, May 1992. James Mill, Prisons and Prison Discipline, in *Political Writings*, Cambridge: Cambridge University Press, 1992, provides a exposition of Benthamite attitudes to punishment; his relationship to Foucault's reading of Bentham is discussed in Terence Ball's introduction, and Ball's *Reappraising Political Theory*, Oxford: Oxford University Press, 1995.

55. For the various uses envisaged, see Jeremy Bentham, *Panopticon; or The Inspection-House*, London: T. Payne, 1791, Vol. 1, pp. 107, 110, 113, 121, Vol. 2, pp. 184, 191n; *Pauper Management Improved: Particularly by Means of an Application of the Panopticon Principle of Construction*, London: Baldwin and Ridgway, 1812; and the pamphlet *Thoughts on the Plan of Construction on the Panopticon, or Universal Inspection Principle for a Proposed Lunatic Hospital Asylum for the Lodgement of Persons Labouring under Insanity in all its Various Forms*, London: C. H. Reynell, 1828.

56. Jeremy Bentham, *The Works of Jeremy Bentham*, edited by John Bowring, Edinburgh: William Tait, 1838–43, Vol. XI, p. 104. On this see Giovanna Procacci, Social Economy and the Government of Poverty, in FE; Felix Driver, *Power and Pauperism: The workhouse system 1834–1884*, Cambridge: Cambridge University Press, 1993; and Mitchell Dean, *The Constitution of Poverty: Towards a genealogy of liberal governance*, London: Routledge, 1991.

57. On panopticism see Michel Serres, Panoptic Theory, in Thomas M. Kavanagh (ed.), *The Limits of Theory*, Stanford: Stanford University Press, 1989; Miran Božovič's introduction to Jeremy Bentham, *The Panopticon Writings*, London: Verso, 1995; and Jacques-Alain Miller, Jeremy Bentham's Panoptic Device, *October*, No. 41, Summer 1987.

58. Foucault suggests that the Enlightenment, 'which discovered the liberties, also invented the disciplines' (SP 258; DP 222), something it drew from the Romans, in their Republicanism and their military schema (SP 171–2; DP 146).

59. On the correspondence between programmes and practice see Barry Smart, *Foucault, Marxism and Critique*, London: Routledge, 1989, p. 128, and Rabinow, *French Modern*, pp. 12, 212. On Foucault and the Panopticon see Paul Patton, On Power and Prisons, in Meaghan Morris and Paul Patton (eds), *Michel Foucault: Power, truth, strategy*, Sydney: Feral Publications, 1979; and

Barry Smart, On Discipline and Social Regulation: A Review of Foucault's Genealogical Analysis, in David Garland and Peter Young, *The Power To Punish*, London: Heinemann, 1983.

Many critics contend that as the Panopticon was 'never built', it was 'a failure', and cannot stand as a viable exemplar. See, for example, Semple, 'Foucault and Bentham', p. 111; Ball, *Reappraising Political Theory*, p. 160. Paul Q. Hirst, Power/Knowledge – Constructed Space and the Subject, in Richard Fardon (ed.) *Power & Knowledge: Anthropological and sociological Approaches*, Edinburgh: Scottish Academic Press, 1985, p. 188, similarly suggests that it was not built, but argues that this does not invalidate it as an example. It is necessary to set the matter straight. Simply regarding its potential as a prison, the Panopticon was characterized by two points – its architectural design, and the system of private contract that Bentham envisaged. The reason it was not built in its exact form in Britain was mainly because the control aspects of the design could not be separated from the financial ones. Prisons that existed before were usually privately run, and Bentham looked to continue this, but he was out of date in this area, as there was a crucial shift toward the state taking over the control of administration. John Howard, author of two important works on enclosed institutions in Europe, was one of the first to suggest that the county, rather than the prisoner, should pay the fees. See his *State of the Prisons in England and Wales*, Warrington, 1778, and *An Account of the Principal Lazarettos in Europe*, Warrington: William Eyres, 1789. See also Evans, *The Fabrication of Virtue*, p. 10. For an analysis of the rise of the prison that is more attentive to the shifts in state power see Michael Ignatieff, *A Just Measure of Pain: The penitentiary in the industrial revolution 1750–1850*, London: Macmillan, 1978. The neglect of the state seems to be a more serious charge than one which suggests that the shift in penal practice is determined by economic changes. The classic case for this is made by Georg Rusche and Otto Kirchheimer, *Punishment and Social Structure*, New York: Russell & Russell, 1968. See also Melossi and Pavarini, *The Prison and the Factory*; and Theodor W. Adorno and Max Horkheimer, *The Dialectic of Enlightenment*, translated by J. Cumming, London: Allen Lane, 1973. For a discussion of the problems in these analyses, see David Garland, *Punishment and Modern Society: A study in social theory*, Oxford: Clarendon Press, 1990, especially pp. 83–110; and Mark Poster, *Foucault, Marxism and History: Mode of production versus mode of information*, Cambridge: Polity Press, 1994.

However, the Millbank penitentiary and Pentonville were both heavily influenced by Bentham's work, for all the botched nature of these institutions, such as the many blind spots. Outside of Britain, Panopticons *were* built. Norman Johnston has provided a survey of some of the other penitentiaries based on Bentham's plan, citing one built in Spain in 1852, three in Holland in the 1880s, the Stateville penitentiary in Illinois, the notorious Cuban Isle of Pines in 1926, and as recently as 1952 the Badajoz Provincial Prison in Spain. Norman Johnston, *The Human Cage: A brief history of prison architecture*, New York: Walker & Company, 1973, p. 20. See also Norval Morris, 'The Contemporary Prison: 1965–Present', in Norval Morris and David J. Rothman (eds), *The Oxford History of the Prison*, New York: Oxford University Press, 1995. Indeed in *Discipline and Punish* Foucault suggests various variants of the basic design – its strict form, semi-circle, cross-plan, the star shape (SP 290; DP 250) – and in the French text refers the reader to nine of the plates for examples (SP 290n4; see SP plates 18–26; DP plates 4–6).

Conclusion

1. Henri Lefebvre, *Espace et politique*, in *Le droit à la ville* suivi de *Espace et politique*, Éditions Anthropos, Paris, 1972, p. 192.
2. Edward W. Soja, *Thirdspace: Journeys to Los Angeles and Other Real-and-Imagined Places*, Oxford: Blackwell, 1996, pp. 172–3(&n).

Bibliography

Adorno, Theodor W., *The Jargon of Authenticity*, translated by Knut Tarnowski and Frederic Will, London: Routledge & Kegan Paul, 1973.
Adorno, Theodor, *Negative Dialectics*, translated by E. B. Ashton, London: Routledge, 1973.
Adorno, Theodor W. and Horkheimer, Max, *The Dialectic of Enlightenment*, translated by J. Cumming, London: Allen Lane, 1973.
Aladjem, Terry K., The Philosopher's Prism: Foucault, Feminism, and Critique, *Political Theory*, Vol. 19, No. 2, May 1991.
Allemann, Beda, *Hölderlin und Heidegger*, Zürich: Atlantic Verlag, 1954.
Althusser, Louis, *For Marx*, translated by Ben Brewster, London: Verso, 1969.
Althusser, Louis, *Lenin and Philosophy and Other Essays*, translated by Ben Brewster, London: NLB, 1971.
Althusser, Louis and Balibar, Étienne, *Reading Capital*, translated by Ben Brewster, London: NLB, 1970.
Anonymous *Thoughts on the Plan of Construction on the Panopticon, or Universal Inspection Principle for a Proposed Lunatic Hospital Asylum for the Lodgement of Persons Labouring under Insanity in all its Various Forms*, London: C. H. Reynell, 1828.
Arac, Jonathan (ed.), *After Foucault: Humanistic knowledge, postmodern challenges*, New Brunswick: Rutgers University Press, 1988.
Arisaka, Yoko, Heidegger's Theory of Space: A Critique of Dreyfus, *Inquiry*, Vol. 38, No. 4, 1995.
Aristotle, *Physics*, Oxford: Clarendon Press, 1936.
Aristotle, *The Politics*, translated by T. A. Sinclair, revised and represented by Trevor S. Sanders, Harmondsworth: Penguin, 1981.
Aristotle, *Physics*, translated by Robin Waterfield, Oxford: Oxford University Press, 1996.
Armstrong, Timothy J. (ed.), *Michel Foucault Philosopher*, Hemel Hempstead, Harvester Wheatsheaf, 1992.
Bachelard, Gaston, *The Poetics of Space*, translated by Maria Jolas, New York: Orion Press, 1964.
Baert, Patrick, Foucault's History of the Present as Self-Referential Knowledge Acquisition, *Philosophy and Social Criticism*, Vol. 24, No. 6, November 1998.
Baeumler, Alfred, *Nietzsche: Der Philosoph und Politiker*, Leipzig: Reclam, 1931.
Balibar, Etienne, From Bachelard to Althusser: The Concept of the Epistemological Break, *Economy and Society*, Vol. 7, No. 3, August 1978.
Ball, Terence, *Reappraising Political Theory*, Oxford: Oxford University Press, 1995.

Ballard, Edward G. and Scott, Charles E. (eds), *Martin Heidegger in Europe and America*, The Hague: Martinus Nijhoff, 1973.
Bambach, Charles R., *Heidegger, Dilthey, and the Crisis of Historicism*, Ithaca: Cornell University Press, 1995.
Barker, Philip, *Michel Foucault: Subversions of the subject*, New York and London: Harvester Wheatsheaf, 1993.
Barnes, Jonathan, *Early Greek Philosophy*, Harmondsworth: Penguin, 1987.
Barnes, Trevor and Gregory, Derek (eds), *Reading Human Geography: The Poetics and politics of inquiry*, London: Edward Arnold, 1997.
Barrett, Michèle, *The Politics of Truth: From Marx to Foucault*, Cambridge: Polity Press, 1991.
Barry, A., Osborne, T. and Rose, N. (eds), *Foucault and Political Reason*, London: UCL Press, 1996.
Barthes, Roland, *Critical Essays*, translated by Richard Howard, Evanston: Northwestern University Press, 1972.
Bast, Rainer A. and Delfosse, Heinrich P., *Handbuch zum Textstudium von Martin Heideggers 'Sein und Zeit'*. Vol. 1: *Stellenindizes; Philologisch-Kritischer Apparat*, Stuttgart-Bad Cannstatt: frommann-holzboog, 1979.
Bataille, Georges, *On Nietzsche*, translated by Bruce Boone, New York: Paragon House, 1992.
Bataille, Georges, *Visions of Excess: Selected Writings 1927–39*, edited by Allan Stoekl, Minneapolis: University of Minnesota Press, 1993.
Baudrillard, Jean, *Forget Foucault*, translated by Nicole Dufresne, New York: Semiotext[e], 1987.
Bender, John, *Imagining the Penitentiary: Fiction and the Architecture of Mind in Eighteenth-Century England*, Chicago: University of Chicago Press, 1987.
Bentham, Jeremy, *Panopticon; or, The Inspection-House*, London: T. Payne, two volumes, 1791.
Bentham, Jeremy, *Pauper Management Improved: Particularly by means of an application of the Panopticon principle of construction*, London: Baldwin and Ridgway, 1812.
Bentham, Jeremy, *The Rationale of Punishment*, London: Robert Heward, 1830.
Bentham, Jeremy, *The Works of Jeremy Bentham*, edited by John Bowring, Edinburgh: William Tait, Eleven Volumes, 1838–43.
Bentham, Jeremy, *The Panopticon Writings*, London: Verso, 1995.
Berkowitz, Peter, Nietzsche's Ethics of History, *The Review of Politics*, Vol. 56, No. 1, Winter 1994.
Bernauer, James, *Michel Foucault's Force of Flight: Towards an ethics of thought*, Atlantic Highlands, NJ: Humanities Press, 1990.
Bernstein, J. M., *The Fate of Art: Aesthetic alienation from Kant to Derrida and Adorno*, Cambridge: Polity Press, 1992.
Biemel, Walter, *Martin Heidegger*, translated by J. L. Mehta, London: Routledge & Kegan Paul, 1977.
Blanchot, Maurice, *The Space of Literature*, Lincoln: University of Nebraska Press, 1982.
Borges, Jorge Luis, Of Exactitude in Science, in *A Universal History of Infamy*, Harmondsworth: Penguin, 1984.

Borges, Jorge Luis, Funes the Memorious, translated by Anthony Kerrigan, in *Fictions*, London: Calder Publications, 1991.
Bourdieu, Pierre, *The Political Ontology of Martin Heidegger*, translated by Peter Collier, Cambridge: Polity Press, 1988.
Boutot, Alain, *Heidegger*, Paris: Presses Universitaires de France, 1989.
Boyne, Roy, *Foucault and Derrida: The other side of reason*, London: Unwin Hyman, 1988.
Brown, Peter, *The Body and Society: Men, Women and Sexual Renunciation in Early Christianity*, London: Faber & Faber, 1989.
Bruzina, Ronald and Wilshire, Bruce (eds), *Phenomenology: Dialogues and Bridges*, Albany: State University of New York Press, 1982.
Burke, Peter (ed.), *Critical Essays on Michel Foucault*, Aldershot: Scolar Press, 1992.
Camus, Albert, *The Plague*, translated by Stuart Gilbert, Harmondsworth, Penguin, 1960.
Canguilhem, Georges, *The Normal and the Pathological*, translated by Carolyn R. Fawcett, Dordrecht: D. Reidel, 1978.
Carter, Paul, *The Road to Botany Bay: An essay in spatial history*, London: Faber & Faber, 1987.
Casey, Edward S., *Getting Back into Place: Toward a renewed understanding of the place-world*, Bloomington: Indiana University Press, 1993.
Casey, Edward S., *The Fate of Place: A philosophical history*, Berkeley: University Presses of California, 1997.
Cassirer, Ernst, *The Myth of the State*, New Haven: Yale University Press, 1946.
Clausewitz, Carl von, *On War*, translated by J. J. Graham, revised by F. N. Maude, London: Wordsworth, 1997.
Colombel, Jeannette, Contrepoints poétiques, *Critique*, No. 471–472, August–September 1986.
Constantine, David J., *The Significance of Locality in the Poetry of Friedrich Hölderlin*, London: The Modern Humanities Research Association, 1979.
Constantine, David, *Hölderlin*, Oxford: Clarendon Press, 1988.
Critchley, Simon, *The Ethics of Deconstruction: Derrida and Levinas*, Oxford: Blackwell, 1992.
Critchley, Simon, *Very Little . . . Almost Nothing: Death, philosophy, literature*, London: Routledge, 1997.
Dallmayr, Fred, *The Other Heidegger*, Ithaca: Cornell University Press, 1993.
Davidson, Arnold I. (ed.), Symposium on Heidegger and Nazism, *Critical Inquiry*, No. 15, Winter 1989.
Davidson, Arnold I. (ed.), *Foucault and his Interlocutors*, Chicago: University of Chicago Press, 1997.
de Beistegui, Miguel, *Heidegger and the Political: Dystopias*, London: Routledge, 1998.
Dean, Mitchell, *The Constitution of Poverty: Toward a Genealogy of Liberal Governance*, London: Routledge, 1991.
Dean, Mitchell, *Critical and Effective Histories: Foucault's methods and historical sociology*, London: Routledge, 1994.
Dean, Mitchell, Putting the Technological into Government, *History of the Human Sciences*, Vol. 9, No. 3, 1996.
Defoe, Daniel, *Journal of the Plague Year*, Harmondsworth: Penguin, 1966.

Delaporte, François, The History of Medicine According to Foucault, in Jan Goldstein (ed.), *Foucault and the Writing of History*, Oxford: Blackwell, 1994.
Deleuze, Gilles, *Foucault*, translated by Séan Hand, London: Athlone Press, 1988.
Deleuze, Gilles and Guattari, Félix, *Mille plateaux: capitalisme et schizophrenie 2*, Paris: Les Éditions de Minuit, 1980.
Deleuze, Gilles and Guattari, Félix, *A Thousand Plateaus: Capitalism and schizophrenia*, translated by Brian Massumi, London: Athlone Press, 1988.
Delorme, Michel (ed.), *Penser la folie: Essais sur Michel Foucault*, Paris: Galilée, 1992.
Derrida, Jacques, *Of Grammatology*, translated by Gayatri Chakravorty Spivak, Baltimore: Johns Hopkins University Press, 1976.
Derrida, Jacques, *Éperons/Spurs: Nietzsche's styles*, translated by Barbara Harlow, Chicago: University of Chicago Press, 1978.
Derrida, Jacques, *Writing and Difference*, translated by Alan Bass, London: Routledge & Kegan Paul, 1978.
Derrida, Jacques, *Margins of Philosophy*, translated by Alan Bass, Hemel Hempstead: Harvester Wheatsheaf, 1982.
Derrida, Jacques, *The Truth in Painting*, translated by Geoff Bennington and Ian McLeod, Chicago: University of Chicago Press, 1987.
Derrida, Jacques, *Of Spirit: Heidegger and the question*, translated by Geoff Bennington and Rachel Bowlby, Chicago: The University of Chicago Press, 1989.
Derrida, Jacques, *Khōra*, Paris: Éditions Galilée, 1993.
Derrida, Jacques, *Points . . . Interviews, 1974–1994*, edited by Elizabeth Weir, translated by Peggy Kamuf and others, Stanford: Stanford University Press, 1995.
Derrida, Jacques, *Politics of Friendship*, translated by George Collins, London: Verso, 1997.
Descartes, René, *Œuvres Philosophiques: Tome II (1638–1642)*, Paris: Garnier Frères, 1967.
Descartes, René, *Discourse on Method* and *Meditations on First Philosophy*, translated by Donald A. Cress, Indianapolis: Hackett, 1980.
Dews, Peter, The Return of the Subject in Late Foucault, *Radical Philosophy*, No. 51, Spring 1989.
Digby, Anne, *Madness, Morality and Medicine: A study of the York retreat 1796–1914*, Cambridge: Cambridge University Press, 1985.
Dillon, Michael, *Politics of Security: Towards a Political Philosophy of Continental Thought*, London: Routledge, 1996.
Doel, Marcus, *Poststructuralist Geographies: The Diabolical Art of Spatial Science*, Edinburgh: Edinburgh University Press, 1999.
Donnelly, Michael, *Managing the Mind: A study of mental psychology in early nineteenth century Britain*, London: Tavistock, 1983.
Dreyfus, Hubert L., *Being-in-the-World: A commentary on Heidegger's being and time, division I*, Cambridge, MASS: MIT Press, 1991.
Dreyfus, Hubert L. and Hall, Harrison (eds), *Heidegger: A critical reader*, Oxford: Basil Blackwell, 1992.
Dreyfus, Hubert and Rabinow, Paul, *Michel Foucault: Beyond structuralism and hermeneutics*, Brighton: Harvester, 1982.

Driver, Felix, *Power and Pauperism: The Workhouse System 1834–1884*, Cambridge: Cambridge University Press, 1993.
Dumm, Thomas L., *Michel Foucault and the Politics of Freedom*, California: Sage, 1996.
Elden, Stuart, Heidegger's Hölderlin and the Importance of Place, *Journal of the British Society for Phenomenology*, Vol. 30, No. 3, October 1999.
Elden, Stuart, Rethinking the *Polis*: Implications of Heidegger's Questioning the Political, *Political Geography*, Vol. 19, No. 4, May 2000.
Elden, Stuart, The Constitution of the Normal: Monsters and Masturbation at the Collège de France, *boundary 2*, Vol. 28, No. 1, Spring 2001.
Elden, Stuart, The Place of Geometry: Heidegger's Mathematical Excursus on Aristotle, *The Heythrop Journal*, Vol. XLII, No. 3, July 2001.
Elden, Stuart, Politics, Philosophy, Geography: Henri Lefebvre in Anglo-American Scholarship, *Antipode: A radical journal of geography*, Vol. 33, No. 5, Nov 2001.
Elden, Stuart, Reading Genealogy as Historical Ontology, in Alan Rosenberg and Alan Milchman (eds), *Foucault and Heidegger: Critical encounters*, Minneapolis: University of Minnesota Press, 2002.
Elden, Stuart and Cowan, Sharon, Words, Ideas and Desires: Freud, Foucault and the Hermaphroditic Roots of Bisexuality, forthcoming.
Eribon, Didier, *Michel Foucault*, translated by Betsy Wing, London: Faber & Faber, 1993.
Eribon, Didier, *Michel Foucault et ses contemporains*, Paris: Fayard, 1994.
Ermarth, Elizabeth Deeds, *Sequel to History: Postmodernism and the crisis of representational time*, Princeton: Princeton University Press, 1992.
Ettinger, Elżbieta, *Hannah Arendt Martin Heidegger*, New Haven: Yale University Press, 1995.
Evans, Robin, *The Fabrication of Virtue: English Prison Architecture 1750–1840*, Cambridge: Cambridge University Press, 1982.
Fardon, Richard (ed.), *Power and Knowledge: Anthropological and Sociological Approaches*, Edinburgh: Scottish Academic Press, 1985.
Farías, Victor, *Heidegger and Nazism*, translated by Paul Burrell and Gabriel R. Ricci, Philadelphia: Temple University Press, 1989.
Featherstone, Mike, Hepworth, Mike and Turner, Bryan S. (eds), *The Body: Social process and cultural theory*, London: Sage, 1991.
Fekete, John (ed.), *The Structural Allegory: Reconstructive encounters with the new French thought*, Minneapolis: University of Minnesota Press, 1984.
Fell, Joseph P., *Heidegger and Sartre: An essay on being and place*, New York: Columbia University Press, 1979.
Fink-Eitel, Hinrich, Zwischen Nietzsche und Heidegger: Michel Foucaults 'Sexualität und Wahrheit' im Spiegel neuerer Sekundärliteratur, *Philosophisches Jahrbuch*, Vol. 97, No. 2, 1990.
Flaherty, Peter, (Con)textual Contest: Derrida and Foucault on Madness and the Cartesian Subject, *Philosophy of the Social Sciences*, Vol. 16, No. 1, March 1986.
Flynn, Thomas R., Foucault and the Spaces of History, *The Monist*, Vol. 74, No. 2, April 1991.
Foltz, Bruce V., *Inhabiting the Earth: Heidegger, Environmental Ethics, and the Metaphysics of Nature*, New Jersey: Humanities Press, 1995.

Foucault, Michel, *Folie et déraison: Histoire de la folie à l'âge classique*, Paris: Plon, 1961.
Foucault, Michel, *Histoire de la folie*, Paris: Plon 10/18, 1964.
Foucault, Michel, *Histoire de la folie à l'âge classique suivi de mon corps, ce papier, ce feu et la folie, l'absence d'œuvre*, Paris: Gallimard, 1972.
Foucault, Michel, Of Other Spaces, translated by Jay Miskowiec, *Diacritics*, Vol. 16, No. 1, Spring 1986.
Foucault, Michel, Experiences of Madness, translated by Anthony Pugh, *History of the Human Sciences*, Vol. 4, No. 1, 1991.
Foucault, Michel, About the Beginning of the Hermeneutics of the Self: Two Lectures at Dartmouth, *Political Theory*, Vol. 21, No. 2, May 1993.
Foucault, Michel, *Les Anormaux: Cours au Collège de France (1974–1975)*, Paris: Seuil/Gallimard, 1999.
Foucault, Michel, Barrett Kriegel, B., Thalamy, A., Beguin, F. and Fortier, B., *Généalogie des équipements de normalisation*, Fontenay sous-Bois: CERFI, 1976.
Foucault, Michel, Barrett Kriegel, B., Thalamy, A., Beguin, F. and Fortier, B., *Les machines à guérir (aux origines de l'hôpital moderne)*, Brussels: Pierre Mardaga, 1979.
Franck, Didier, *Heidegger et le problème de l'espace*, Paris: Les Éditions de Minuit, 1986.
Fraser, Nancy, Foucault on Modern Power: Empirical Insights and Normative Confusions, *Praxis International*, No. 1, 1981.
Fraser, Nancy, *Unruly Practices: Power, discourse and gender in contemporary social theory*, Cambridge: Polity Press, 1989.
Friedrichsmeyer, Sara and Becker-Cantarino, Barbara (eds), *The Enlightenment and Its Legacy*, Bonn: Bouvier, 1990.
Frings, Manfred S., Parmenides: Heidegger's 1942–43 Lecture Course Held at Freiburg University, *Journal of the British Society for Phenomenology*, Vol. 19, No. 1, January 1988.
Frodeman, Robert, Being and Space: A Re-reading of Existential Spatiality in Being and Time, *Journal of the British Society for Phenomenology*, Vol. 23, No. 1, January 1992.
Froment-Meurice, Marc, *That is to Say: Heidegger's poetics*, translated by Jan Plug, Stanford: Stanford University Press, 1998.
Fynsk, Christopher, *Heidegger: Thought and historicity*, Ithaca: Cornell University Press, 1986.
Gadamer, Hans-Georg, *Philosophical Hermeneutics*, edited and translated by David E. Linge, Berkeley: University of California Press, 1976.
Gane, Mike (ed.), *Towards a Critique of Foucault*, London: Routledge & Kegan Paul, 1986.
Garland, David, *Punishment and Modern Society: A study in social theory*, Oxford: Clarendon Press, 1990.
Garland, David and Young, Peter, *The Power to Punish*, London: Heinemann, 1983.
Glover, Mary R., *The Retreat York: An early experiment in the treatment of mental illness*, York: William Sessions Limited, 1984.
Goffman, Erving, *Asylums*, New York: Anchor Books, 1961.

Goldberg, David Theo, *Racist Culture: Philosophy and the politics of meaning*, Cambridge, MA: Oxford, 1993.
Gordon, Colin, Question, Ethos, Event: Foucault on Kant and Enlightenment, *Economy and Society*, Vol. 15, No. 1, Feb. 1986.
Gordon, Colin, *Histoire de la folie*: an Unknown Book by Michel Foucault, *History of the Human Sciences*, Vol. 3, No. 1, 1990.
Gordon, Colin, History, Madness and Other Errors: A Response, *History of the Human Sciences*, Vol. 3, No. 3, 1990.
Graybeal, Jean, *Language and 'the Feminine' in Nietzsche and Heidegger*, Bloomington and Indianapolis: Indiana University Press, 1990.
Greene, Marjorie, *Martin Heidegger*, London: Bowes & Bowes, 1957.
Gregory, Derek, *Geographical Imaginations*, Oxford: Blackwell, 1994.
Grugan, Arthur, Heidegger on Hölderlin's *Der Rhein*: Some External Considerations, *Philosophy Today*, Vol. 39, No. 1, Spring 1995.
Guignon, Charles (ed.), *The Cambridge Companion to Heidegger*, Cambridge: Cambridge University Press, 1993.
Gutting, Gary, *Michel Foucault's Archaeology of Scientific Reason*, Cambridge: Cambridge University Press, 1989.
Gutting, Gary (ed.), *The Cambridge Companion to Foucault*, Cambridge: Cambridge University Press, 1994.
Haar, Michel (ed.), *Cahier de L'Herne: Martin Heidegger*, Paris: L'Herne, 1983.
Haar, Michel, *Heidegger et l'essence de l'homme*, Grenoble: Jérôme Millon, 1990.
Habermas, Jürgen, *The Philosophical Discourse of Modernity*, Cambridge: Polity Press, 1987.
Habermas, Jürgen, Jürgen Habermas on the Legacy of Jean-Paul Sartre: Conducted by Richard Wolin, *Political Theory*, Vol. 20, No. 3, August 1992.
Halévy, Elie, *The Growth of Philosophical Radicalism*, London: Faber & Faber, 1972.
Hall, R. L., Heidegger and the Space of Art, *Journal of Existentialism*, Vol. VIII, No. 29, Fall 1967.
Halperin, David M., *Saint Foucault: Towards a gay hagiography*, New York: Oxford University Press, 1995.
Han, Béatrice, Au-delà de la métaphysique et de la subjectivité: Musique et *Stimmung*, *Les Études philosophiques*, No. 4, 1997.
Han, Béatrice, *L'ontologie manquée de Michel Foucault*, Grenoble: Jérôme Millon, 1998.
Harvey, David, *The Condition of Postmodernity*, Oxford: Blackwell, 1989.
Harvey, David, *Justice, Nature and the Geography of Difference*, Oxford: Blackwell, 1996.
Hayes, Donna Gene, Nietzsche's Eternal Recurrence: A Prelude to Heidegger, *Journal of Existentialism*, Vol. VI, No. 22, Winter 1965/66.
Hegel, G. W. F., *Elements of the Philosophy of Right*, edited by Allen W. Wood, translated by H. B. Nisbet, Cambridge: Cambridge University Press, 1991.
Heidegger, Martin, *Essais et Conférences*, translated by André Preau, Paris: Gallimard, 1958.
Heidegger, Martin, *Approche de Hölderlin*, translated by Henry Corbin, Michel Deguy, François Dédier and Jean Launay, Paris: Gallimard, 1973.
Heidegger, Martin, Letter to Carl Schmitt, 22 August 1933, English/German version, *Telos*, No. 72, 1987.

Heidegger, Martin, *Zollikoner Seminar: Protokolle – Gespräche – Briefe*, edited by Medard Boss, Frankfurt am Main: Vittorio Klostermann, 1987.
Heidegger, Martin, *Correspondance avec Karl Jaspers*, texte établi par Walter Biemel et Hans Saner, traduite de l'allemand par Claude-Nicolas Grimbert, suivi de *Correspondance avec Elizabeth Blochmann*, traduite de l'allemand par Pascal David, Paris: Gallimard, 1996.
Heidegger, Martin and Kästner, Erhart, *Briefwechsel*, edited by Heinrich Wiegand Petzet, Frankfurt am Main: Insel, 1986.
Hemming, Laurence Paul, Speaking Out of Turn: Martin Heidegger and *die Kehre*, *International Journal of Philosophical Studies*, Vol. 6, No. 3, 1998.
Herf, Jeffrey, *Reactionary Modernism: Technology, culture and politics in Weimar and the Third Reich*, Cambridge: Cambridge University Press, 1984.
Hetherington, Kevin, *The Badlands of Modernity: Heterotopia and social ordering*, London: Routledge, 1997.
Himmelfarb, Gertrude, The Haunted House of Jeremy Bentham, in *Victorian Minds*, Gloucester, MA: Peter Smith, 1975.
Hindess, Barry, *Discourses of Power: From Hobbes to Foucault*, London: Routledge, 1996.
Hindess, Barry, Politics and Governmentality, *Economy and Society*, Vol. 26, No. 2, May 1997.
Hölderlin, Friedrich, *Selected Verse*, translated by Michael Hamburger, Harmondsworth: Penguin, 1961.
Howard, John, *State of the Prisons in England and Wales*, Warrington: 1778.
Howard, John, *An Account of the Principal Lazarettos in Europe*, Warrington, William Eyres, 1789.
Hoy, David Couzens (ed.), *Foucault: A Critical Reader*, Basil Blackwell: Oxford, 1986.
Hume, L. J., *Bentham and Bureaucracy*, Cambridge: Cambridge University Press, 1981.
Husserl, Edmund, *Husserliana: Gesammelte Werke*, The Hague: Martinus Nijhoff, 1950.
Ibáñez-Noé, Javier A., Heidegger, Nietzsche, Jünger, and the Interpretation of the Contemporary Age, *The Southern Journal of Philosophy*, Vol. XXXIII, 1995.
Ignatieff, Michael, *A Just Measure of Pain: The penitentiary in the Industrial Revolution 1750–1850*, London: Macmillan, 1978.
Inwood, Michael, *Heidegger*, Oxford: Oxford University Press, 1997.
Janicaud, Dominique, *The Shadow of that Thought: Heidegger and the question of politics*, translated by Michael Gendre, Evanston IL: Northwestern University Press, 1996.
Jay, Martin, *Downcast Eyes: The denigration of vision in twentieth-century French thought*, Berkeley: University of California Press, 1993.
Johnson, Daniel, Portrait: Ernst Jünger, *Prospect*, No. 17, March 1997.
Johnston, Norman, *The Human Cage: A brief history of prison architecture*, New York: Walker & Company, 1973.
Jones, Colin and Porter, Roy (eds), *Reassessing Foucault: Power, Medicine and the Body*, London: Routledge, 1994.
Julia, Didier, *Dictionnaire de la philosophie*, Paris: Larousse, 1992.
Jünger, Ernst, *Werke*, Stuttgart: Ernst Klett, Ten Volumes, 1960.

Kant, Immanuel, *Werke: Gesamtausgabe in zehn Bänden*, Leipzig: Modes und Baumann, 1843.
Kant, Immanuel, *Werke*, edited by Ernst Cassirer, Berlin: Bruno Cassirer, Eleven Volumes, 1912–22.
Kant, Immanuel, *Kritik der reinen Vernunft*, Hamburg: Felix Meiner, 1956.
Kant, Immanuel, *Perpetual Peace and Other Essays on Politics, History and Moral Practice*, translated by Ted Humphrey, Indianapolis: Hackett, 1983.
Kant, Immanuel, *Groundwork for the Metaphysic of Morals* and *Prolegomena to Any Future Metaphysics*, translated by Paul Carus and James W. Ellington, in Stephen M. Cahn (ed.), *Classics of Western Philosophy*, Indianapolis: Hackett, third edition, 1990.
Kant, Immanuel, *Critique of Pure Reason*, edited by Vasilis Politis, London: J. M. Dent, 1993.
Keat, Russell, The Human Body in Social Theory: Reich, Foucault and the repressive hypothesis, *Radical Philosophy*, No. 42, Winter/Spring 1986.
Keith, Michael and Pile, Steve (eds), *Place and the Politics of Identity*, London: Routledge, 1993.
Kelly, Michael (ed.), *Critique and Power: Recasting the Foucault/Habermas Debate*, Cambridge: MIT Press, 1994.
Kern, Stephen, *The Culture of Time and Space 1880–1918*, Cambridge, MA: Harvard University Press, 1983.
Kisiel, Theodore, *The Genesis of Heidegger's Being and Time*, Berkeley: University of California Press, 1993.
Kisiel, Theodore, Situating Rhetorical Politics in Heidegger's Protopractical Ontology (1923–1925: The French Occupy the Ruhr), *Existentia*, Vol. IX, 1999.
Kisiel, Theodore and Van Buren, John (eds), *Reading Heidegger From the Start: Essays in his earliest thought*, Albany: State University of New York Press, 1994.
Kockelmans, Joseph J. (ed.), *Phenomenology: The philosophy of Edmund Husserl and its interpretation*, New York: Anchor Books, 1967.
Kolb, David, *The Critique of Pure Modernity: Hegel, Heidegger, and after*, Chicago: The University of Chicago Press, 1986.
Kolodny, Niko, The Ethics of Cryptonormativism: A Defence of Foucault's Evasions, *Philosophy and Social Criticism*, Vol. 22, No. 5, September 1996.
Kovacs, George, *The Question of God in Heidegger's Phenomenology*, Evanston, Northwestern University Press, 1990.
Kovacs, George, An Invitation to Think through and with Heidegger's *Beiträge zur Philosophie*, *Heidegger Studies*, Vol. 12, 1996.
Krell, David Farrell, *Intimations of Mortality: Time, truth, and finitude in Heidegger's thinking of being*, Philadelphia: Pennsylvania State University Press, 1986.
Krell, David Farrell, *Daimon Life: Heidegger and life philosophy*, Bloomington: Indiana University Press, 1992.
Krell, David Farrell and Wood, David (eds), *Exceedingly Nietzsche – Aspects of Contemporary Nietzsche Interpretation*, London: Routledge, 1988.
Kuhn, Thomas S., *The Structure of Scientific Revolutions*, Chicago: University of Chicago Press, third edition, 1996.
LaCapra, Dominick, Foucault, history and madness, *History of the Human Sciences*, Vol. 3, No. 1, 1990.

Lacoue-Labarthe, Philippe, *La fiction du politique: Heidegger, l'art et la politique*, Paris: Christian Bourgois, 1987.
Lacoue-Labarthe, Philippe, *Typography: Mimesis, philosophy, politics*, edited by Christopher Fynsk, Cambridge, MA: Harvard University Press, 1989.
Lacoue-Labarthe, Philippe and Nancy, Jean-Luc, *Retreating the Political*, edited by Simon Sparks, London: Routledge, 1997.
Lash, Scott and Urry, John, *Economies of Signs and Space*, London: Sage, 1994.
Lecourt, Dominique, *Marxism and Epistemology: Bachelard, Canguilhem, Foucault*, translated by Ben Brewster, London: NLB, 1975.
Lefebvre, Henri, *Nietzsche*, Paris: Éditions Sociales Internationales, 1939.
Lefebvre, Henri, *Le droit à la ville* suivi de *Espace et politique*, Éditions Anthropos: Paris, 1972.
Lefebvre, Henri, *La production de l'espace*, Paris: Anthropos, 1974.
Lefebvre, Henri, *Hegel, Marx, Nietzsche ou le royaume des ombres*, Paris-Tournoi: Casterman, 1975.
Lefebvre, Henri, *The Survival of Capitalism: Reproduction of the relations of production*, translated by Frank Bryant, London: Allison & Busby, 1976.
Lefebvre, Henri, *The Production of Space*, translated by Donald Nicolson-Smith, Oxford: Blackwell, 1991.
Lefebvre, Henri, *Writings on Cities*, translated and edited by Eleonore Kofman and Elizabeth Lebas, Oxford: Blackwell, 1996.
Lentricchia, Frank, *Ariel and the Police*, Brighton: The Harvester Press, 1988.
Levin, David Michael (ed.), *Modernity and the Hegemony of Vision*, London: University of California Press, 1993.
Levy, Neil, The Prehistory of Archaeology: Heidegger and the Early Foucault, *Journal of the British Society for Phenomenology*, Vol. 27, No. 2, May 1996.
Liggett, Helen and Perry, David C. (eds), *Spatial Practices*, Thousand Oaks: Sage, 1995.
Löwith, Karl, *Nietzsche's Philosophy of the Eternal Recurrence of the Same*, translated by J. Harvey Lomax, Berkeley: University of California Press, 1997.
Macann, Christopher (ed.), *Martin Heidegger: Critical assessments*, London: Routledge, four volumes, 1992.
Macey, David, *The Lives of Michel Foucault*, London: Hutchinson, 1993.
Machiavelli, Niccolò, *Selected Political Writings*, edited and translated by David Wootton, Indianapolis: Hackett, 1994.
Magee, Bryan, *Aspects of Wagner*, London: Alan Ross, 1968.
Magee, Bryan, *The Great Philosophers*, London: BBC Books, 1987.
Maher, Winifred Barbara and Maher, Brendan, The Ship of Fools: *Stultifera Navis* or *Ignis Fatuus*? *American Psychologist*, Vol. 37, No. 7, July 1982.
Major-Poetzl, Pamela, *Michel Foucault's Archaeology of Western Culture: Toward a new science of history*, Brighton: Harvester Press, 1983.
Malament, Barbara C. (ed.), *After the Reformation: Essays in Honor of J. H. Hexter*, Manchester: Manchester University Press, 1980.
Malpas, Jeff, *Place and Experience: A philosophical topography*, Cambridge: Cambridge University Press, 1999.
Marks, John, A New Image of Thought, *New Formations*, No. 25, Summer 1995.

Marx, Werner, *Heidegger and the Tradition*, translated by Theodore Kisiel and Murray Greene, Evanston, Northwestern University Press, 1971.
Marx, Werner (ed.), *Heidegger Memorial Lectures*, Pittsburgh: Duquesne University Press, 1982.
Marx, Werner, *Is There a Measure on Earth? Foundations for a nonmetaphysical ethics*, translated by Thomas J. Nenon and Reginald Lilly, Chicago: University of Chicago Press, 1987.
Massey, Doreen, Politics and Space/Time, *New Left Review*, No. 192, Nov./Dec. 1992.
McNay, Lois, *Foucault: A Critical Introduction*, Cambridge: Polity Press, 1994.
McNeill, Will, Care for the Self: Originary Ethics in Heidegger and Foucault, *Philosophy Today*, Vol. 42, No. 1, Spring 1998.
McNeill, William, *The Glance of the Eye: Heidegger, Aristotle and the ends of theory*, Albany: State University of New York Press, 1999.
Megill, Allan, Foucault, Structuralism and the Ends of History, *Journal of Modern History*, Vol. 51, No. 3, September 1979.
Megill, Allan, *Prophets of Extremity: Nietzsche, Heidegger, Foucault, Derrida*, Berkeley: University of California Press, 1985.
Megill, Allan, Foucault, Ambiguity, and the Rhetoric of Historiography, *History of the Human Sciences*, Vol. 3, No. 3, 1990.
Melossi, Dario and Pavarini, Massimo, *The Prison and the Factory: Origins of the penitentiary system*, translated by Glynis Cousin, London: Macmillan, 1981.
Merleau-Ponty, Maurice, *La phénoménologie de perception*, Paris: Gallimard, 1945.
Merquior, J. G., *Foucault*, Berkeley: University of California Press, 1985.
Merquior, J. G., *From Prague to Paris: A critique of structuralist and post-structuralist thought*, London: Verso, 1986.
Milchman, Alan and Rosenberg, Alan, Michel Foucault, Auschwitz and Modernity, *Philosophy and Social Criticism*, Vol. 22, No. 1, January 1996.
Miller, J. Hillis, *Topographies*, Stanford: Stanford University Press, 1995.
Miller, Jacques-Alain, Jeremy Bentham's Panoptic Device, *October*, No. 41, Summer 1987.
Miller, James, *The Passion of Michel Foucault*, London: Harper Collins, 1993.
Minson, Jeffrey, *Genealogies of Morals: Nietzsche, Foucault, Donzelot and the eccentricity of ethics*, Basingstoke: Macmillan, 1985.
Mitchell, Timothy, *Colonizing Egypt*, Berkeley: University of California Press, 1991.
Morris, Meaghan and Patton, Paul (eds), *Michel Foucault: Power, truth, strategy*, Sydney: Feral Publications, 1979.
Morris, Norval and Rothman, David J. (eds), *The Oxford History of the Prison*, New York: Oxford University Press, 1995.
Mosse, George (ed.), *Nazi Culture*, London: W. H. Allen, 1966.
Mouffe, Chantal, *The Return of the Political*, London: Verso, 1993.
Mulhall, Stephen, *Heidegger and Being and Time*, London: Routledge, 1996.
Murray, Michael (ed.), *Heidegger and Modern Philosophy*, New Haven: Yale University Press, 1978.
Murray, Michael, Heidegger's Hermeneutic Reading of Hölderlin: The Signs of Time, *The Eighteenth Century*, Vol. 21, No. 1, 1980.
Nehamas, Alexander, *Nietzsche: Life as literature*, Cambridge MA: Harvard University Press, 1985.

Neocleous, Mark, *Administering Civil Society: Towards a theory of state power*, London: Macmillan, 1996.
Neocleous, Mark, Perpetual War, or, 'War and War Again': Schmitt, Foucault, Fascism, *Philosophy and Social Criticism*, Vol. 22, No. 2, March 1996.
Neocleous, Mark, Policing and Pin-Making: Adam Smith, Police and the State of Prosperity, *Policing and Society*, Vol. 8, 1998.
Neocleous, Mark, *The Fabrication of Social Order: A critical theory of police power*, London: Pluto, 2000.
Nettleton, Sarah, *Power, Pain and Dentistry*, Buckingham, Open University Press, 1992.
Nietzsche, Friedrich, *Ainsi parlait Zarathustra*, traduction révisée de Geneviève Bianquis, Paris: Flammarion, 1969.
Norris, Christopher, *Derrida*, London: Fontana, 1987.
O'Farrell, Clare, *Foucault: Historian or Philosopher?* Houndmills: Macmillan, 1989.
O'Neill, John, The Disciplinary Society: From Weber to Foucault, *The British Journal of Sociology*, Vol. XXXVII, No. 1, March 1986.
Olafson, Frederick A., Being, Truth and Presence in Heidegger's Thought, *Inquiry*, Vol. 41, No. 1, 1998.
Osborne, Peter, Tactics, Ethics, or Temporality? Heidegger's Politics Reviewed, *Radical Philosophy*, No. 70, March/April 1995.
Ott, Hugo, *Martin Heidegger: A Political Life*, translated by Allan Blunden, London: HarperCollins, 1993.
Owen, David, *Maturity and Modernity: Nietzsche, Weber, Foucault and the Ambivalence of Reason*, London: Routledge, 1994.
Palmier, Jean-Michel, *Les Écrits politiques de Heidegger*, Paris: L'Herne, 1968.
Paquet, Marcel, *Magritte*, Cologne: Taschen, 1994.
Pasquino, Pasquale, 'Michel Foucault (1926-84): *The Will to Knowledge*', *Economy and Society*, Vol. 15, No. 1, Feb. 1986.
Pasquino, Pasquale, Political Theory of War and Peace: Foucault and the History of Modern Political Theory, *Economy and Society*, Vol. 22, No. 1, February 1993.
Patton, Paul, Taylor and Foucault on Power and Freedom, *Political Studies*, Vol. XXXVII, 1989.
Patton, Paul (ed.), *Nietzsche, Feminism and Political Theory*, London: Routledge, 1993.
Peacock, Ronald, *Hölderlin*, London: Methuen & Co, 1973.
Petersen, Alan and Bunton, Robin (eds), *Foucault, Health and Medicine*, London: Routledge, 1997.
Philo, Chris, Foucault's Geographies, *Environment and Planning D: Society and space*, Vol. 10, 1992.
Plato, *The Collected Dialogues of Plato Including the Letters*, edited by Edith Hamilton and Huntingdon Cairns, Princeton University Press, 1961.
Plato, *Timaeus and Critias*, translated by Desmond Lee, Harmondsworth: Penguin, 1971.
Plato, *Republic*, translated by Robin Waterfield, Oxford: Oxford University Press, 1993.
Platon, *Der Staat*, translated and edited by Karl Vretske, Stuttgart: Reclam, 1958.

Pöggeler, Otto, Den Führer führen? Heidegger und kein Ende, *Philosophische Rundschau*, Vol. 32, 1985.
Popma, Jan, *The Worker: On nihilism and technology in Ernst Jünger*, Brussels: Economische Hogeschool Sint-Aloysius, 1991.
Poster, Mark, *Foucault, Marxism and History: Mode of production versus mode of information*, Cambridge: Polity Press, 1984.
Rabinow, Paul, *French Modern: Norms and forms of the social environment*, Cambridge, MA: The MIT Press, 1989.
Racevskis, Karlis, *Postmodernism and the Search for Enlightenment*, Charlottesville: The University Press of Virginia, 1993.
Radzinowicz, Leon, *A History of English Criminal Law and its Administration from 1750*, London: Stevens & Sons, five volumes, 1948–86.
Rajchman, John, *Michel Foucault: The freedom of philosophy*, New York: Columbia University Press, 1985.
Rajchman, John, Foucault's Art of Seeing, *October*, No. 44, Spring 1988.
Rajchman, John, *Truth and Eros: Foucault, Lacan and the question of ethics*, New York & London: Routledge, 1991.
Ramazanoglu, Caroline (ed.), *Up Against Foucault: Explorations of some tensions between Foucault and feminism*, London: Routledge, 1993.
Richardson, William J., *Heidegger: Through Phenomenology to Thought*, The Hague: Martinus Nijhoff, 1963.
Riese, Walther, *The Legacy of Philippe Pinel: An inquiry into thought on mental alienation*, New York: Springer Publishing Company, 1969.
Rockmore, Tom, *On Heidegger's Nazism and Philosophy*, London: Harvester Wheatsheaf, 1992.
Rockmore, Tom, *Heidegger and French Philosophy: Humanism, antihumanism and being*, London: Routledge, 1995.
Rose, Nikolas, Government, Authority and Expertise in Advanced Liberalism, *Economy and Society*, Vol. 22, No. 3, August 1993.
Rusche, Georg and Kirchheimer, Otto, *Punishment and Social Structure*, New York: Russell & Russell, 1968.
Russ, Jacqueline, *Profil d'une œuvre: Histoire de la folie: Foucault*, Paris: Hatier, 1979.
Safranski, Rüdiger, *Martin Heidegger: Between good and evil*, translated by Ewald Osers, Cambridge, MA: Harvard University Press, 1998.
Said, Edward W., *The World, The Text, The Critic*, London: Faber & Faber, 1984.
Said, Edward W., *Culture and Imperialism*, London: Chatto & Windus, 1993.
Said, Edward W., *Orientalism: Western Conceptions of the Orient*, reprinted with a new afterword, Harmondsworth: Penguin, 1995.
Sallis, John (ed.) *Heidegger and the Path of Thinking*, Pittsburgh: Duquesne University Press, 1970.
Sallis, John (ed.) *Radical Phenomenology: Essays in honor of Martin Heidegger*, Atlantic Highlands: Humanities Press, 1978.
Sallis, John (ed.) *Deconstruction and Philosophy*, Chicago: The University of Chicago Press, 1987.
Sallis, John, *Echoes: after Heidegger*, Bloomington: Indiana University Press, 1990.
Sallis, John, *Crossings: Nietzsche and the space of tragedy*, Chicago: The University of Chicago Press, 1991.

Sallis, John (ed.), *Reading Heidegger: Commemorations*, Bloomington: Indiana University Press, 1993.
Sallis, John and Maly, Kenneth (eds), *Heraclitean Fragments: A companion volume to the Heidegger/Fink seminar on Heraclitus*, Alabama: University of Alabama Press, 1980.
Sartre, Jean-Paul, *L'être et le néant: Essai d'ontologie phénoménologique*, Paris: Gallimard, 1943.
Sartre, Jean-Paul, *Being and Nothingness: An essay on phenomenological ontology*, translated by Hazel E. Barnes, London: Routledge, 1958.
Sawicki, Jana, *Disciplining Foucault: Feminism, power, and the body*, London: Routledge, 1991.
Schalow, Frank, *The Renewal of the Heidegger-Kant Dialogue: Action, thought and responsibility*, Albany: State University of New York Press, 1992.
Schmitt, Carl, *The Concept of the Political*, translated by George Schwab, Chicago: University of Chicago Press, 1996.
Schwartz, Michael, Critical Reproblemization: Foucault and the Task of Modern Philosophy, *Radical Philosophy*, No. 91, Sept./Oct. 1998.
Scott, Charles E., Heidegger and Psychoanalysis: The Seminars in Zollikon, *Heidegger Studies*, Vol. 6, 1990.
Scott, Charles E., *The Question of Ethics: Nietzsche, Foucault, Heidegger*, Bloomington: Indiana University Press, 1990.
Scull, Andrew T. *Museums of Madness: The social organisation of insanity in 19th century England*, London: Allen Lane, 1979.
Scull, Andrew (ed.), *Madhouses, Mad-Doctors and Madmen: The Social History of Psychiatry in the Victorian Era*, Philadelphia: University of Pennsylvania Press, 1981.
Sedgwick, Peter, *Psycho Politics*, London: Pluto Press, 1982.
Sedgwick, Peter R. (ed.), *Nietzsche: A critical reader*, Oxford: Blackwell, 1996.
Semple, Janet, Foucault and Bentham: A Defence of Panopticism, *Utilitas*, Vol. 4, No. 1, May 1992.
Semple, Janet, *Bentham's Prison: A study of the Panopticon penitentiary*, Oxford: Clarendon Press, 1993.
Serres, Michel, Panoptic Theory, in Thomas M. Kavanagh (ed.), *The Limits of Theory*, Stanford: Stanford University Press, 1989.
Sessions, William K. and Sessions, E. Margaret, *The Tukes of York*, York: William Sessions Limited, 1971.
Shapiro, Gary and Sica, Alan (eds), *Hermeneutics: Questions and proposals*, Amherst: University of Massachusetts Press, 1984.
Sheehan, Thomas (ed.), *Martin Heidegger: The man and the thinker*, Chicago: Precedent Publishing, 1981.
Sheridan, Alan, *Michel Foucault – The Will to Truth*, London: Tavistock, 1980.
Sherover, Charles M., *Heidegger, Kant and Time*, Lanham: University Press of America, 1988.
Shields, Rob, *Places on the Margin*, London: Routledge, 1991.
Siegfried, Hans, Autonomy and Quantum Physics: Nietzsche, Heidegger and Heisenberg, *Philosophy of Science*, Vol. 57, No. 4, December 1990.
Silber, Ilana Friedrich, Space, Fields, Boundaries: The Rise of Spatial Metaphors in Contemporary Social Theory, *Social Research*, Vol. 62, No. 2, Summer 1995.

Simmel, Marianne L. (ed.), *The Reach of Mind: Essays in memory of Kurt Goldstein*, New York: Springer Publishing Company, 1968.
Simons, Jon, *Foucault and the Political*, London: Routledge, 1995.
Skelton, Geoffrey, *Wagner at Bayreuth*, London: White Lion, 1976.
Sluga, Hans, *Heidegger's Crisis: Philosophy and politics in Nazi Germany*, Cambridge MA: Harvard University Press, 1993.
Smart, Barry, *Foucault, Marxism, Critique*, London: Routledge & Kegan Paul, 1983.
Smart, Barry, *Michel Foucault*, London: Routledge, 1988.
Smart, Barry (ed.), *Michel Foucault (1) Critical Assessments*, London: Routledge, three volumes, 1994.
Smart, Barry (ed.), *Michel Foucault (2) Critical Assessments*, London: Routledge, four volumes, 1995.
Soja, Edward W., *Postmodern Geographies: The reassertion of space in critical social theory*, London: Verso, 1989.
Soja, Edward W., *Thirdspace: Journeys to Los Angeles and other real-and-imagined places*, Oxford: Blackwell, 1996.
Sophocles, *The Three Theban Plays: Antigone, Oedipus the King, Oedipus at Colonus*, translated by Robert Fagles, New York: Quality Paperback Book Club, 1994.
Spanos, William V., *Heidegger and Criticism: Retrieving the cultural politics of destruction*, Minneapolis: University of Minnesota Press, 1993.
Sprinker, Michael (ed.), *Edward Said: A critical reader*, Oxford: Blackwell, 1992.
Stallybrass, Peter and White, Allon, *The Politics and Poetics of Transgression*, London: Methuen, 1986.
Stambaugh, Joan, *The Problem of Time in Nietzsche*, London: Associated University Presses, 1987.
Steiner, George, *Heidegger*, third edition, London: Fontana, 1992.
Steintrager, James, *Bentham*, London: George Allen & Unwin Ltd, 1977.
Stern, J. P., *Ernst Jünger: A writer of our time*, Cambridge: Bowes & Bowes, 1953.
Stewart, Kathleen Anne, *The York Retreat in the Light of the Quaker Way*, York: William Sessions Limited, 1992.
Stewart, Lynn, Bodies, Visions and Spatial Politics: a Review Essay of Henri Lefebvre's *The Production of Space*, Environment and Planning D: Society and Space, Vol. 13, 1995.
Still, Arthur and Velody, Irving (eds), *Rewriting the History of Madness: Studies in Foucault's Histoire de la folie*, London: Routledge, 1992.
Stone, Lawrence, *The Past and the Present Revisited*, London and New York: Routledge & Kegan Paul, 1987.
Sturrock, John, *Structuralism*, London: Fontana, 1993.
Taminiaux, Jacques, *Heidegger and the Project of Fundamental Ontology*, translated by Michael Gendre, Albany: State University of New York Press, 1991.
Taylor, Charles, Taylor and Foucault on Power and Freedom: A Reply, *Political Studies*, Vol. XXXVII, 1989.
The Holy Bible, New International Version, London: Hodder & Stoughton, 1984.
Thiele, Leslie Paul, The Agony of Politics: The Nietzschean Roots of Foucault's Thought, *American Political Science Review*, Vol. 84, No. 3, Sept. 1990.
Thrift, Nigel, *Spatial Formations*, London: Sage, 1996.

Tuke, D. Hack, *Reform in the History of the Insane*, London: J. & A. Churchill, 1892.
Tuke, Samuel, *Description of the Retreat*, York: W. Alexander, 1813.
Tuke, Samuel, *Practical Hints on the Construction and Economy of Pauper Lunatic Asylums*, York: William Alexander, 1815.
Vernant, Jean Pierre, *Mythe et pensée chez les Grecs*, Paris: François Maspero, second edition, 1969.
van Buren, John, *The Young Heidegger: Rumor of the hidden king*, Bloomington: Indiana University Press, 1995.
Villa, Dana R., *Arendt and Heidegger: The fate of the political*, Princeton: Princeton University Press, 1996.
Visker, Rudi, *Michel Foucault: Genealogy as critique*, London: Verso, 1995.
Vollrath, Ernst, The 'Rational' and the 'Political': An Essay in the Semantics of Politics, *Philosophy and Social Criticism*, Vol. 13, No. 1, 1987.
Vycinas, Vincent, *Earth and Gods: An introduction to the philosophy of Martin Heidegger*, The Hague: Martinus Nijhoff, 1969.
Wagner, Richard, *The Art-Work of the Future and Other Works*, translated by W. Ashton Ellis, Lincoln and London: University of Nebraska Press, 1993.
Ward, James F., *Heidegger's Political Thinking*, Amherst: University of Massachusetts Press, 1995.
Warminski, Andrej, *Readings in Interpretation: Hölderlin, Hegel, Heidegger*, Minneapolis: University of Minnesota Press, 1987.
Werkmeister, W. H., *Martin Heidegger on the Way*, edited by Richard T. Hull, Amsterdam: Rodopi, 1996.
Windshuttle, Keith, *The Killing of History*, Paddington NSW: Macleay Press, 1996.
Wolin, Richard, *The Politics of Being: The political thought of Martin Heidegger*, New York: Columbia University Press, 1990.
Woods, Roger, *Ernst Jünger and the Nature of Political Commitment*, Stuttgart: Akademischer Verlag Hans-Dieter Heinz, 1982.
Young, Julian, *Heidegger, Philosophy, Nazism*, Cambridge: Cambridge University Press, 1997.
Ziarek, Krysztof, Semiosis of Listening: The Other in Heidegger's Writings on Hölderlin and Celan's 'The Meridian', *Research in Phenomenology*, Vol. XXIV, 1994.
Zimmermann, Michael E., *Heidegger's Confrontation with Modernity: Technology, politics, art*, Bloomington: Indiana University Press, 1990.
Žižek, Slavoj (ed.), *Mapping Ideology*, London: Verso, 1994.

Index

agency, 101
agriculture, 76, 77–8
Althusser, Louis, 101, 152, 155 n. 2
Antigone, 33, 70–1
archaeology, 5, 13, 95–102, 104, 111, 153
Architecture, 49–51, 64, 87, 119, 129–31, 134, 135, 140–1, 144, 147
archive, 95, 103
Arendt, Hannah, 61
Aristotle, 27, 60; on time, 13–14, 160 n. 22; and scholasticism, 27; *Nicomachean Ethics*, 19; *Physics*, 20; *The Politics*, 69, 72; *see* Heidegger, reading Aristotle.
army, 6, 108, 115, 135, 136, 139–41, 146, 148
Arnauld, Antoine, 101
art, 42, 63–7, 87, 89–90, 109–10, 118
Augenblick, 12, 14, 44–9, 56–7, 62, 75, 115, 159 n. 18
Augustine, 27, 189 n. 13
Auseinandersetzung, 39, 61, 164 n. 64
authority, 105

Bachelard, Gaston, 2, 101, 155 n. 2
Bambach, Charles, 12
Barbin, Herculine, 111
Barnes, Jonathan, 82
Bataille, Georges, 94
Bayle, Pierre, 94, 96
Bayreuth theatre, 50
Beaufret, Jean, 157 n. 8
Beccaria, Cesare, 137, 147
Becker, Oskar, 117
Bender, John, 146

Bentham, Jeremy, 114, 135–7, 146–9, 195 n. 59
Berlin blockade, 77–8
Bernstein, J. M., 36, 66
Bichat, Xavier, 143
Binswanger, Ludwig, 115, 117, 157 n. 8
bio-power, 147
biology, biologism, 39, 44, 54, 55, 61, 97, 111, 127
Blanchot, Maurice, 94
Blitzkrieg, 52
body, 53–6, 103–4, 127–8, 136–8, 139, 141–3, 146, 149, 170 n. 59
Borges, Jorge Luis, 96, 118, 159 n. 10
Boss, Medard, 170 n. 59
boundary, 94–5
bridge, 86–7, 89, 90
Brissot, Jacques, 129, 132, 137
building, 85–7
Bultmann, Rudolf, 27–8

calculation, 18–19, 41, 56–7
Canguilhem, Georges, 2, 96, 101, 155 n. 2
Casey, Edward, 161 n. 31
class, 108
Clausewitz, Carl von, 108
Cohen, Hermann, 22
connaissance/savoir, 5, 6, 8, 97, 98–100, 152

De Beistegui, Miguel, 78, 174 n. 25
Dean, Mitchell, 111
Derrida, Jacques, 43, 44, 66, 87, 152,

Derrida, Jacques — *continued*
  155 n. 1, 161 n. 30, 165–6 n. 4, 172
  n. 5, 180 n. 5, 189 n. 17
Descartes, René, 17, 19, 20, 24–5, 27,
  36, 44, 51–2, 54, 56, 57, 58–9, 61,
  62, 78, 82, 85, 86, 90, 105, 114,
  117, 127, 189 n. 13, 189 n. 17;
  Meditations, 124–5, 126, 127
de-struction, 12–13, 28, 53, 57, 87,
  164 nn. 1 & 64
Dilthey, Wilhelm, 21, 27, 162 n. 37
discourse, 94
dispositif, 3, 5, 6, 79, 108, 110–11, 119,
  148–9, 153
Don Quixote, 96–7
Dostal, Robert, 179 n. 64
Dreyfus, Hubert, 2, 15, 61, 155–6 n. 3
Dumézil, Georges, 94

Eckermann, Liz, 146
education, 102
enlightenment, 113–14
énoncé, 95–6, 104, 110
episteme, 57, 94, 96–8, 110
epistemology, 22, 99, 100
equipment, 16, 17, 67, 87
ereignis, 49, 56
eternal return, 44–9, 56
extermination camps, 77–8

famine, 77–8
Flaubert, Gustave, 94
Flynn, Thomas, 114
Foucault, Michel; *The Archaeology of
  Knowledge*, 2, 94, 102, 114–15, 143;
  The Birth of the Clinic, 2, 3, 6, 93, 94,
  96, 98, 101, 102, 104, 105, 114,
  121, 134, 141–3; *Collège de France*
  lectures, 6, 144, 149, 191 n. 33;
  Discipline and Punish, 3, 6, 93, 104,
  108, 119, 120, 121, 126, 133–50;
  Dits et écrits, 100; *Histoire de la folie à
  l'âge classique*, 3, 6, 93, 94, 102, 105,
  116, 120–33, 134; *The History of
  Sexuality*, Volume One, 104, 109,
  110, 111, 112, 135, 150; later
  volumes, 106, 110; *'Il faut défendre la
  société'*; *Madness and Civilisation*, 6,
  119, 120–33; Nietzsche, Genealogy,
  History, 55, 103; Of Other Spaces,
  3, 116–18; *The Order of Discourse*,
  102; *The Order of Things*, 2, 57, 94,
  96, 97–8, 99, 100, 110, 112, 114,
  117–18, 119, 121, 127, 135; The
  Politics of Health in the Eighteenth
  Century, 144; *Raymond Roussel*, 94;
  reading Nietzsche, 1, 2, 4, 55, 94,
  102–3, 104, 105, 106, 107, 111–12;
  Rio lectures on Medicine, 3, 141,
  143–5; thesis on Kant's
  Anthropology, 2, 113; *This is Not a
  Pipe*, 118; What is Enlightenment?,
  113–14
fourfold, 63, 67, 82–4, 86–7, 88–9
Franck, Didier 161 n. 31
freedom, 2, 106–7
führung, 30, 69, 72
fundamental ontology, 8, 60

Galileo, Galilei, 60, 90, 116
gas chambers, 77–8
gaze, 96, 143, 190 n. 18
genealogy, 3, 5, 6, 23, 60, 102–13, 153
geography, 2–3, 43
geometry, 16, 17, 19
German language, 32, 38
ge-stell, 78–9, 110–11
Goethe, Johann Wolfgang von, 11
Goffman, Erving, 131
Goldstein, Kurt, 172 n. 5
Gordon, Colin, 6, 120–1, 131, 133,
  188 n. 2, 188–9 n. 11
grammar, general, 97, 100
Greek
  language, 32, 37, 68
  temple, 66
  theatre, 50
Gregory, Derek, 183 n. 34, 183 n. 38,
  187 n. 71

Habermas, Jürgen, 156 n. 6
Hacking, Ian, 102
hammer, 19, 89
Harkess, James, 118
Harvey, David, 114, 115

Hebel, Johann Peter, 34, 82
Hegel, Georg Wilhelm Friedrich, 58, 103, 147, 191 n. 37
Heidegger, Martin; Age of the World Picture, 60–1; Art and Space, 20, 85, 89–91; *The Basic Concepts of Metaphysics*, 14, 26, 60; *The Basic Problems of Phenomenology*, 13–14, 25; *Being and Time*, 2, 8–28, 29–30, 31, 32, 35, 38, 44, 56, 61, 63, 68, 82, 87, 88, 92, 112, 152, 164 n. 1; *Beiträge zur Philosophie (Vom Ereignis)*, 56–7, 91; Building Dwelling Thinking, 85–7, 90; *The Concept of Time*, 21; *Gesamtausgabe*, 5, 8, 33, 56, 70; Das Ge-stell, 75–8; *History of the Concept of Time*, 21, 24; *Holzwege*, 2, 33, 63, 70, 174 n. 22; *An Introduction to Metaphysics*, 29–33, 40, 65, 69–70, 73; the *Kehre*, 4, 28, 29, 152, 164–5 n. 1, 171–2 n. 2; *Letter on Humanism*, 2, 43–4, 101; and Nazism, 5, 29–60, 66–75, 77–81; *On the Way to Language*, 33, 91; *Ontology: The Hermeneutic of Facticity*, 17–19, 20–1; *The Origin of the Work of Art*, 63–7, 78; The Question of Technology, 75–9; reading Aristotle, 5, 8, 19–20, 28, 91; reading the early Greeks, 2, 28, 30, 31, 32, 33, 37, 62, 67, 82; reading Hölderlin, 2, 5, 28, 29, 33–43, 44, 53, 61–2, 63, 67, 70–4, 81, 82–4, 151; reading Kant, 2, 5, 8, 21–7, 28, 63, 88, 89, 160 n. 23; reading Nietzsche, 5, 10–13, 14, 28, 29, 30, 33, 37, 43–62, 63, 79–80, 82, 104, 112; reading Plato, 19, 32–3, 36, 68–9, 72, 73, 74; Rectorship, 4, 30, 38, 39, 66, 68–75, 79; The Thing, 75, 87–9; Time and Being, 27, 91–2; *Vorträge und Aufsätze*, 2, 33; *Wegmarken*, 70
Hellingrath, Norbert von, 38, 40
Herkunft, 14, 67, 103–4
hermaphrodites, 111
Hérodote, 108, 139
heterotopias, 3, 116–18, 152

historical *a priori*, 8, 96, 97, 102, 159 n. 8
historical ontology, 3, 4, 5, 6, 23, 28, 31, 60, 99, 100, 113, 152
historiography, 12, 13
history of being, 8, 31, 38, 57–8, 83–4, 158 n. 5
history of the present, 3, 5, 6, 49, 60, 104, 112, 115, 152
Hitler, Adolf, 39
Hitler Youth, 34
Hölderlin, Friedrich, 33–43, 94; *see* Heidegger, reading Hölderlin
holocaust, 78
Hôpital Général, 125, 126
hospitals, 124–7, 128–9, 135, 141–5, 148
Howard, John, 195 n. 59
humanism, 2, 61, 101
Hume, David, 23
Hunt, Alan, 106
Husserl, Edmund, 8, 21, 117, 162 n. 37
hydrogen bomb, 77–8, 87

Imperium, 73

Janicaud, Dominique, 29, 43, 62
Jaspers, Karl, 34
jug, 87–9, 90
Jünger, Ernst, 52, 69, 79–81, 84
Justi, J. H. von, 134

Kandinsky, Vassily, 118
Kant, Immanuel, 21–8, 96, 103, 147, 152; *Anthropology*, 2; Categories, 23–4; Categorical imperative, 23; *Critique of Pure Reason*, 21–4, 25; *Groundwork for the Metaphysic of Morals*, 24; Synthetic *a priori*, 22–3; Transcendental aesthetic, 23–4, 25; Transcendental logic, 23–4; *see* Heidegger, reading Kant.
Kierkegaard, Søren, 12, 13, 14, 27
Kisiel, Theodore, 8, 21, 28, 160 n. 20, 162 n. 37, 164 n. 64, 165 n. 1, 173 n. 13
Klee, Paul, 118

Kolbenheyer, E. G., 39
knowledge, 12, 58, 94, 96–102, 104–5, *see connaissance/savoir*
Krell, David Farrell, 8, 60, 84, 164–5 n. 1
Kuhn, Thomas, 61

Lacan, Jacques, 101, 152
Lacoue-Labarthe, Philippe, 77
Lask, Emil, 27
Latin language, 32, 37, 68
Lebensraum, 42, 73
Lefebvre, Henri, 119, 151, 152, 157 n. 13, 183 n. 34, 183 n. 38, 187 n. 71
legitimacy, 105
leprosy, 121–2, 128, 145–6, 147
Lévi-Strauss, Claude, 101
limit, 93–5, 98
limit-attitude, 114
Linnaeus, Carolus (Carl von Linné), 95, 101, 136
Los Angeles, 151
Löwith, Karl, 34
Luther, Martin, 27, 45

Mably de, G., 136
Machiavelli, Niccolò, 105
Magritte, René, 118
maps, mapping, 6, 7, 49, 114–15
Marburg, 8, 20, 22
Marcuse, Herbert, 176–7 n. 43
Marx, Karl, 103, 104, 105, 108
Marx, Werner, 160 n. 22
mathematics, 18–20, 51–2, 56–7
Mayenne, Louis Turquet de, 134
Midelfort, H. C. Erik, 122
medicine, 6, 141–5
Megill, Allan, 39, 43
Merleau-Ponty, Maurice, 55, 152
Miller, James, 2, 101
military, 6, 108, 115, 135, 136, 139–41, 146, 148
modernity, 113–14
Murray, Michael, 167–8 n. 22

Natorp, Paul, 22
natural history, 97, 100

Neocleous, Mark, 101, 139
New Order, 73
Newton, Isaac, 8, 58, 90
Nietzsche, Friedrich; *Beyond Good and Evil*, 23, 99; *The Birth of Tragedy*, 10, 50, 152; *The Gay Science*, 49, 59; and National Socialism, 30, 38, 44; *Thus Spoke Zarathustra*, 44–9, 51, 53, 115; *The Will to Power*, 49, 53, 55; *Untimely Meditations*, 10–12, 111–12, *see* Foucault, reading Nietzsche; Heidegger, reading Nietzsche
nihilism, 31, 45, 73, 79–81
nostalgia, 11, 67, 74, 103

ontic, 8, 22, 57, 88, 99, 104, 152
ontology, 6, 8, 22, 57, 88, 99, 100, 104, 107, 108, 113–14, 152, 158 n. 5
origins, 64, 67, 95, 103
overcoming metaphysics, 41, 42, 56, 58

Panopticon, 3, 6, 114, 115, 116, 120, 135–6, 141, 145–50, 152, 195 n. 59
Pasquino, Pasquale, 136
peasant shoes, 65–6
perspectivism, 57–61, 107
Petty, William, 101
phenomenology, 8, 21, 28, 57, 60, 158 n. 5, 164 n. 63
Philo, Chris, 119
philology, 10, 97
philosopher-kings, 68–9, 72
physiology, 53
Pinel, Philippe, 131–3, 142
plague, 145–6
platial, 36–7, 62, 70, 73, 76, 80, 84–9, 91
Plato, 19, 33, 68–9, 72, 73, 74
plural realism, 61
poetic dwelling, 40, 67, 76, 82–4, 86–7, 88–9, 90
poetry, 34, 39
police, 126, 134–5, 144, 147, 149, 191 nn. 36 & 37
Polis, 5, 33, 60, 62, 63, 67–75, 87, 151

political economy, 97, 151
politics/political, 74–5, 78
Pomme, Pierre, 94, 96
population, 135, 145, 146–7
poverty, 126, 129
power, 3, 6, 55, 57–61, 102, 104–11, 119, 120
power/knowledge, 3, 6, 58, 102, 104, 119, 153
present, presence, 14, 32, 49, 112–13, 115

Rabinow, Paul, 2, 155–6 n. 3
racism, 39, 44, 54, 61
real and imaginary, 93, 94, 119, 123, 124, 125, 140
Reich, Wilhelm, 106
repérage, 114–15
resistance, 106–7
Rickert, Heinrich, 22, 27
ring of the Nibelung, 50
Rivière, Pierre, 111
Rome, 73
Rorty, Richard, 146, 167 n. 22
Rosenberg, Alfred, 39

Sade, Marquis de, 97, 130
Said, Edward, 183 n. 34
Sartre, Jean-Paul, 16, 101, 152, 160 n. 28, 170 n. 59
Sauvages, François Boissier de, 142
Schapiro, Meyer, 66, 172 n. 5
Schmitt, Carl, 74, 78
sculpture, 64–5, 89–91
sexuality, 102, 111
Sheridan, Alan, 95
ship of fools, 122–4
site, 15, 33, 70, 76
soil, 15, 38
Soja, Edward, 119, 152, 160–1 n. 29, 186 n. 65, 186–7 n. 66

Sophocles, *Antigone*, 33, 70–1
spatial metaphors, 94–5, 101–2, 108, 114, 119, 139, 182 n. 33
Spengler, Oswald, 57
structuralism, 1, 98, 101–2, 103, 114, 182 nn. 22 & 23
struggle, 108
swastika, 34
Sydenham, Thomas, 128

table, 17–19
Taminiaux, Jacques, 175 n. 29
Taylor, Charles, 146
technology, 3, 5, 6, 30–1, 37, 39, 41, 63, 69, 73, 75–81, 84, 86, 87, 90, 108–11, 119, 153
threshold, 85, 94
total mobilisation, 52
Trakl, George, 85
Trotsky, Leon, 108
truth, 8, 58, 64, 84, 104
Tuke, Samuel, 130–3
Tuke, William, 130

Van Gogh, Vincent, 65–6, 87
Velázquez, Diego, 114
venereal disease, 122, 126
Villela-Petit, Maria, 27
vitalism, 44, 54
Volk, 38, 69

Wagner, Richard, 10, 50
Walzer, Michael, 105
war, 108, *see* military
wealth, analysis of, 97, 100
Weber, Max, 156–7 n. 6
Wolin, Richard, 69
worldview, 57, 59–61

Xenophon, 109

York retreat, 130–1